Meaningful Learning with Technology

D0520201

Meaningful Learning with Technology

FOURTH EDITION

Jane L. Howland

University of Missouri

David Jonassen

University of Missouri

Rose M. Marra

University of Missouri

Boston   Columbus   Indianapolis   New York   San Francisco   Upper Saddle River
Amsterdam   Cape Town   Dubai   London   Madrid   Milan   Munich   Paris   Montreal   Toronto
Delhi   Mexico City   Sao Paulo   Sydney   Hong Kong   Seoul   Singapore   Taipei   Tokyo

Senior Acquisitions Editor: Kelly Villella Canton
Editorial Assistant: Annalea Manalili
Senior Marketing Manager: Darcy Betts
Production Editor: Gregory Erb
Editorial Production Service: Element LLC
Manufacturing Buyer: Megan Cochran
Electronic Composition: Element LLC
Photo Researcher: Annie Pickert
Cover Designer: Jennifer Hart

Library of Congress Cataloging-in-Publication Data
Howland, Jane L.
  Meaningful learning with technology/Jane L. Howland, David Jonassen, Rose M. Marra. – 4th ed.
     p. cm.
  Prev. ed.: Learning with technology / Dave Jonassen, Kyle L. Peck, Brent G. Wilson. 3rd ed. c2008.
  Includes index.
  ISBN 978-0-13-256558-5
  1. Educational technology. 2. Teaching–Aids and devices. 3. Learning. 4. Constructivism
     (Education)
I. Jonassen, David H. II. Marra, Rose M. III. Jonassen, David H. Learning with technology.
IV. Title.
  LB1028.3.J685 2012
  371.33–dc22   2011002141

10 9 8 7 6 5 4 3 2 1 RRD-VA 15 14 13 12 11

www.pearsonhighered.com

ISBN-10: 0-13-256558-7
ISBN-13: 978-0-13-256558-5

About the Authors

Jane L. Howland, PhD, is an Associate Teaching Professor in the School of Information Science and Learning Technologies at the University of Missouri. After teaching kindergarten and multiage classrooms at the Stephens College Children's School, Dr. Howland earned her doctorate in Information Science and Learning Technologies from the University of Missouri. She has developed and teaches graduate courses related to the use of learning technologies, with an emphasis on K–12 learning environments. Dr. Howland's current work focuses on designing and evaluating online learning environments in K–12 and higher education. She has been the principal investigator on federally funded research projects related to faculty development and modeling technology use with preservice teachers, and with K–12 teachers' use of technology for assessing student learning.

David Jonassen, PhD, is Curators' Professor at the University of Missouri where he teaches in the areas of Learning Technologies and Educational Psychology. Since earning his doctorate in educational media and experimental educational psychology from Temple University, Dr. Jonassen has taught at the University of Missouri, Pennsylvania State University, University of Colorado, the University of Twente in the Netherlands, the University of North Carolina at Greensboro, and Syracuse University. He has published 35 books and hundreds of articles, papers, and reports on text design, task analysis, instructional design, computer-based learning, hypermedia, constructivism, cognitive tools, and problem solving. His current research focuses on the cognitive processes engaged by problem solving and models and methods for supporting those processes during learning, culminating in the book, *Learning to Solve Problems: A Handbook for Designing Problem-Solving Learning Environments*.

Rose M. Marra, PhD, is an Associate Professor at the University of Missouri in the School of Information Science and Learning Technologies. Dr. Marra teaches courses on assessment, evaluation, and the design and implementation of effective online learning experiences. She holds a master's degree in Computer Science and worked as a software engineer for AT&T Bell Laboratories before completing her PhD and beginning her career in academia at Penn State University in their College of Engineering. At Penn State, she began her advocacy for and research into women and girls in STEM careers. Specific research interests include factors that influence persistence of women in STEM, women's self-efficacy in studying and completing STEM degrees, gender differences in perceptions of STEM classroom climates, and the epistemological development of college students. Dr. Marra has been the principal investigator or co-principal investigator on numerous funded research projects including the Assessing Women and Men in Engineering (www.engr.psu.edu/awe) and the National Girls Collaborative Project (www.ngcproject.org).

Brief Contents

Contents

Preface

Implications of Learning with Technology

Welcome to the fourth edition of this book. Each edition, including this one, is based on the assumption that meaningful learning requires active engagement in authentic learning tasks, articulation, and reflection on personally and socially constructed meaning, collaboration in those tasks whenever possible and, most important, an intention to learn. This assumption is grounded in a constructivist epistemology. Constructivism is a philosophy for describing processes of meaning making. Although it is a philosophy that is relatively new to educational practice, it has always existed. Since the beginning, humans have interacted with the world and struggled to make sense out of what they have experienced. This is as natural to humans as breathing and explains why we have a relatively large cerebral cortex. People naturally construct their own meaning for experiences. Unfortunately, that is where the rub occurs with our industrial model of education, where learners are evaluated by high-stakes tests for reproducing what "experts" deem important. Regardless of what we teach students or the experiences they have, they will naturally construct their own interpretations of those experiences. They may learn what we teach them, but what they will remember and use in the future are their own personal and socially relevant interpretations.

Like the previous three editions, the purpose of this edition is to demonstrate ways that technology can be used to engage and support meaningful learning. As in the third edition, the structure and treatment of learning in this edition is organized around learning processes, such as inquiring, experimenting, writing, modeling, community building, communicating, designing, visualizing, and assessing. That is, in each chapter, we describe how different technologies can be used to engage and support the learning processes stated above. The chapters describe the learning-with-technology processes conceptually. In most examples, we discuss specific software applications, many of which are web-based or available to download from the Internet. We focus on how to use technologies to engage meaningful learning, not on cookbook lessons that you can apply tomorrow morning. If we took that approach (providing specific lesson plans), they probably would not work the way that we intended in your classrooms, because students naturally construct their own meaning from experiences. So, our purpose is not to demonstrate how to use these technologies, but rather to demonstrate how *learners* can use these technologies. The process may be more difficult, but the meaning that you and your students derive from it will be deeper. We believe this approach is worth the effort.

What's New in This Edition

The Fourth Edition of *Meaningful Learning with Technology* includes the following significant revisions and additions:

- Review/discussion of ISTE NETS, 21st Century Skills, and Technological Pedagogical Content Knowledge (TPACK)

- NET Standards for Students and 21st Century Skills that may be met through the learning activities described

- Chapter Objectives at the beginning of each chapter

- Addition of *Rubrics for Assessing Characteristics of Meaningful Learning* in the Appendix

- Focus on social educational networking and Web 2.0 tools for learning and collaboration

- Expanded section on information literacy skills (e.g., evaluating Web resources, online privacy, and safety issues)

- Updated and expanded use of examples to support the described learning technologies with additional examples of primary grade elementary students

- Emphasis on practical application with technologies that many teachers currently use (e.g., interactive whiteboards, PowerPoint)

Evolution of Technology's Potential

As stated in Chapter 1, we believe that although technologies can be used to provide additional testing practice, when they are used to engage students in active, constructive, intentional, authentic, and cooperative learning, then students will derive more meaning. Throughout this book, we contend that learning takes place in environments where students truly understand and engage in the nature of the tasks they are undertaking. Only then, when individuals understand and freely invest the effort needed to complete a task or activity, does meaningful, authentic learning occur. When learning tasks are relevant and embedded in a meaningful context, students see them as more than simply busywork.

Using technologies to engage meaningful learning assumes that our conceptions of education will change, that schools or classrooms (at least those that use technologies in the ways that we describe) will rethink the educational process. Although few people would ever publicly state that schools should not emphasize meaningful learning, meaningful learning is not engaged or assessed using standardized tests. Meaningful learning presupposes that parents, students, and teachers will realize the implications and demand change, so that meaningful learning is valued more than memorization and simple recall of information. Technologies may not be the cause of the social change that is required for a renaissance in learning, but they can catalyze that change and support it if it comes.

Implications for Teachers

In order for students to learn *with* technology, teachers must accept and learn a new model of learning. Traditionally, teachers' primary responsibility and activity have been directly instructing students, where teachers were the purveyors of knowledge and students the recipients. That is, the teacher told the students what they knew and how they interpreted the world according to the curriculum, textbooks, and other resources they have studied. Teachers are hired and rewarded for their content expertise. This assumes that the ways that teachers know the world are correct and should be emulated by the students. Students take notes on what teachers tell them and try to comprehend the world as their teachers do. Successful students develop concepts similar to those of their teachers. In this kind of learning context, students will not be able to learn *with* technology because they will not be able to construct their own meaning and manage their own learning if the teacher does it for them.

So, first and foremost, teachers must relinquish at least some of their authority, especially intellectual. If teachers determine what is important for students to know, how they should know it, and how they should learn it, then students cannot become intentional, constructive learners. They aren't allowed. In those classroom contexts, there is no reason for students to make sense of the world–only to comprehend the teacher's understanding of it. We believe that the students' task should not be to understand the world as the teacher does. Rather, students should construct their own meaning for the world. If they do, then the teachers' roles shift from dispensing knowledge to helping learners construct more viable conceptions of the world. We said earlier that we believe that not all meaning is created equally. So the teacher needs to help students to discover what the larger community of scholars regards as meaningful concepts and to evaluate their own beliefs and understandings in terms of those standards. Science teachers should help students comprehend the beliefs of the scientific community. Social studies teachers should examine with their students the values and beliefs that societies have constructed. In this role, the teacher is not the arbiter of knowledge but rather is a coach who helps students to engage in a larger community of scholars.

Teachers must also relinquish some of their authority in their management of learning. They cannot control all of the learning activities in the classroom. If teachers determine not only what is important for students to know, but how they should learn it, then students cannot be self-regulated learners. They aren't allowed.

Finally, teachers must gain some familiarity with the technology. They must gain skills and fluency with the technology. However, they will be unsuccessful in helping students to learn *with* technology if they learn about the technologies in order to function as the expert. Rather, they should learn to coach the learning of technology skills. In many instances, teachers will be learning with the students. This may be a bit uncomfortable for some teachers, but we posit that it may be necessary! We have worked in many school situations where the students were constantly pushing our understanding of the technology. Often, we were barely keeping ahead of the students. They can and will learn *with* technologies, with or without the help of the teacher. That does not mean that as a teacher, you can abdicate any responsibility for learning the technologies. Rather, teachers should recognize that it isn't necessary for them to be the expert all of the time.

These implications can be problematic for teachers. They require that teachers assume new roles, sometimes with different beliefs than they have traditionally pursued. Although these implications may be challenging, we believe that the results will justify the efforts. And just as teachers must assume new roles, learning *with* technology requires that students also assume new roles.

Implications for Students

If teachers relinquish authority, learners must assume it. Learners must develop skills in articulating, reflecting on, and evaluating what they know; setting goals for themselves (determining what is important to know) and regulating their activities and effort in order to achieve those goals; and collaborating and conversing with others so that the understanding of all students is enriched. Many students are not ready to assume that much responsibility. They do not want the power to determine their own destiny. It is much easier to allow others to regulate their lives for them. How skilled are students at setting their own agendas and pursuing them? Many students believe in their roles as passive students; they are used to that role! However, our experience and the experiences of virtually every researcher and educator involved with every technology project described in this book show that most students readily accept responsibilities for learning when those learning opportunities are meaningful. When given the opportunity, students of all ages readily experiment with technologies, articulate their own beliefs, and construct, co-construct, and criticize each others' ideas. When learners are allowed to assume ownership of the product, they are diligent and persevering builders of knowledge.

Constructivist approaches to learning, with or without technology, are fraught with risks for students, parents, teachers, and administrators. Change always assumes risks. Many of the activities described in this book entail risks. We encourage you to take those risks. The excitement and enthusiasm generated by students while they construct their own understanding using technology-based tools is more than sufficient reward for taking those risks.

Standards and Frameworks for Learning

Teachers are challenged to ensure that students meet a myriad of required national, state, and local standards. It was impossible to tie each of our recommended activities to these myriad standards so we chose the most relevant national standards, National Educational Technology Standards (NETS), provided by the International Society for Technology in Education (ISTE), as our focus. We also address 21st Century Skills that are embodied in the Framework for 21st Century Learning. NETS and 21st Century Skills are designed to provide educators with frameworks and standards that guide them in creating rich, technology-supported learning environments. Teachers often become overwhelmed by the numerous indicators students are required to demonstrate in meeting state standards, see each of these indicators as discrete, and subsequently design disconnected instruction that isolates individual objectives. Instead, teachers should think broadly, recognizing that rich project-based learning that incorporates problem-solving and authentic tasks can meet many standards simultaneously. Rather than structure this book around specific grade level lesson plans, we focus each chapter on a type of learning (e.g., writing) and offer ways that several types of technologies can be used to enhance that category of learning outcomes.

With thoughtful planning, it is also just as feasible to simultaneously meet a number of content standards. This results in efficient use of students' time, but most important, it helps pull teachers away from an isolated standards model of teaching, where instruction is more likely to be prescriptive and disconnected from authentic learning activities. With a deeper focus, not only will teachers be helping students meet a multitude of standards, they will also be offering rich, interesting learning opportunities that engage students and compel them to think beyond the superficial. Challenging students' cognitive skills by providing motivating instruction that fulfills multiple standards is a worthy accomplishment—one that all teachers should strive for.

We encourage you to consider the complex learning outcomes described in this book as you design instruction for your students. Although authentic, complex, technology-supported activities may seem to be the antithesis of what is needed to prepare students for high achievement on tests, they are not. On the contrary, the meaningful learning that results from this work can not only encompass the knowledge needed for successful test taking, but will also develop individuals who are capable of real thinking—the kind of thinking that is perhaps even more essential than ever for success in the 21st century.

New! CourseSmart eTextbook Available

CourseSmart is an exciting new choice for students looking to save money. As an alternative to purchasing the printed textbook, students can purchase an electronic version of the same content. With a CourseSmart eTextbook, students can search the text, make notes online, print out reading assignments that incorporate lecture notes, and bookmark important passages for later review. For more information, or to purchase access to the CourseSmart eTextbook, visit www.coursesmart.com.

Supplements

An **Instructor's Resource Manual and Test Bank**, downloadable from our password-protected Instructor Resource Center, is available to adopters of this text. If you are already registered, log in at www.pearsonhighered.com/irc or visit this URL to request access, which will be granted after Pearson verifies instructor status.

The manual contains chapter overviews and outlines, additional class activities, discussion questions, and resources for each chapter, as well as a test bank of multiple choice, true/false, short answer, and constructed response questions.

Acknowledgments

We would like to thank the reviewers for their insightful comments and suggestions. They are Sherry Baker, Rich Mountain Community College; Judy Donovan, Indiana University Northwest; Paige Jaeger, University at Albany, State University of New York; Lyda Jo Martinelli, Fordham University; and Bruce A. Montes, Loyola University Chicago.

Goal of Technology Integrations: Meaningful Learning

CHAPTER 1

Shutterstock

Chapter Objectives

1. Identify the characteristics of meaningful learning

2. Contrast learning from technology and learning with technology

3. Compare National Educational Technology Standards (NETS) for students with teacher activities that foster them

4. Describe how technology can foster 21st Century Skills

5. Describe the components of technological pedagogical content knowledge

This edition of *Meaningful Learning with Technology* is one of many books describing how technologies can and should be used in schools. What distinguishes this book from the others is our focus on learning, especially meaningful learning. Most of the other books are organized by technology. They provide advice on how to use technologies, but often the purpose for using those technologies is not explicated.

Meaningful Learning with Technology, on the other hand, is organized by kinds of learning. What drives learning, more than anything else, is understanding and persisting on some task or activity. The nature of the tasks best determines the nature of the students' learning. Unfortunately, the nature of the tasks that so many students most commonly experience in schools is completing standardized tests or memorizing information for teacher-constructed tests. Schools in the United States have become testing factories. Federal legislation (No Child Left Behind) has mandated continuous testing of K–12 students in order to make schools and students more accountable for their learning. In order to avoid censure and loss of funding, many K–12 schools have adopted test preparation as their primary curriculum. Perhaps the most unfortunate phenomenon of this process is the current generation of students who will complete their K–12 education knowing only how to take tests. Because the purpose of those tests is administrative, students are seldom fully invested in the process so they make little attempt to understand the knowledge being tested. The students do not ask to take the tests. The tests assess skills and knowledge that are detached from their everyday experience, so they have little meaning. The testing process is individual, so students are prevented from cooperating with others. The tests represent only a single form of knowledge representation, so students are not able to develop conceptual understanding, which requires representing what you know in multiple ways. Simply stated, learning to take tests does not result in meaningful learning.

In order for students to learn meaningfully, they must be willfully engaged in a meaningful task. In order for meaningful learning to occur, the task that students pursue should engage active, constructive, intentional, authentic, and cooperative activities. Rather than testing inert knowledge, schools should help students to learn how to recognize and solve problems, comprehend new phenomena, construct mental models of those phenomena, and, given a new situation, set goals and regulate their own learning (learn how to learn). In order to help students accomplish those goals, we have organized the book around meaningful learning activities, not technologies.

- Inquiring with Technologies—Information gathering and literacy
- Experimenting with Technologies—Predicting outcomes
- Designing with Technologies—Creative knowledge construction
- Communicating with Technologies—Meaningful discourse
- Community Building and Collaborating with Technologies—Social interactions and identity building
- Writing with Technologies—Constructing meaningful prose
- Modeling with Technologies—Building models for conceptual change
- Visualizing with Technologies—Constructing visual representations

■ Assessing Meaningful Learning and Teaching with Technologies—Resources for assessment, for both teachers and students

Those tasks are meaningful when they require intentional, active, constructive, cooperative, and authentic learning (see Figure 1.1). These attributes of meaningful learning are emphasized throughout the book as the goals for using technologies as well as the criteria for evaluating the uses of technology. Let's examine these attributes a little more closely.

■ **Active (Manipulative/Observant)** Learning is a natural, adaptive human process. Humans have survived and therefore evolved because they were able to learn about and adapt to their environment. Humans of all ages, without the intervention of formal instruction, have developed sophisticated skills and advanced knowledge about the world around them when they need to or want to. When learning about things in natural contexts, humans interact with their environment and manipulate the objects in that environment, observing the effects of their interventions and constructing their own interpretations of the phenomena and the results of their manipulations. For instance, before playing sandlot baseball, do kids subject themselves to lectures and multiple-choice examinations about the theory of games, the aerodynamics of orbs, and vector forces applied to them? No! They start swinging the bat and chasing fly balls, and they negotiate the rules as they play the game. Through formal and informal apprenticeships in communities of play and work, learners develop skills and knowledge that they then share with other members of those communities with whom they learned and practiced those skills. In all of these situations, learners are actively manipulating the objects and tools of the trade and observing the effects of what they have done. The batter who consistently hits foul balls will adjust his or her stance and grip on the bat in order to manipulate the ball's path of flight and observe the effects of each manipulation. Meaningful learning requires learners who are active—actively engaged by a meaningful task in which they manipulate objects and parameters of the environment they are working in and observing the results of their manipulations.

■ **Constructive (Articulative/ Reflective)** Activity is necessary but not sufficient for meaningful learning. It is essential that learners articulate what they have accomplished and reflect on their activity and observations—to learn the lessons that their activity has to teach. New experiences often provide a discrepancy between what learners observe

Figure 1.1

Characteristics of Meaningful Learning

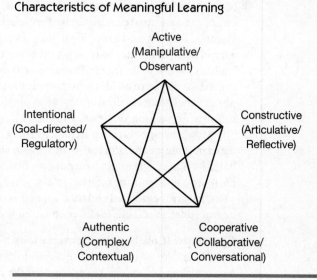

and what they understand. That is when meaningful learning begins. They are curious about or puzzled by what they see. That puzzlement is the catalyst for meaning making. By reflecting on the puzzling experience, learners integrate their new experiences with their prior knowledge about the world, or they establish goals for what they need to learn in order to make sense out of what they observe. Learners begin constructing their own simple mental models that explain what they observe, and with experience, support, and more reflection, their mental models become increasingly complex. Ever more complex models require that learners mentally represent their understanding in different ways using different thought processes. The active and constructive parts of the meaning-making process are symbiotic.

- **Intentional (Goal-Directed/Regulatory)** All human behavior is goal directed (Schank, 1994). That is, everything that we do is to fulfill some goal. That goal may be simple, like satiating hunger or getting more comfortable, or it may be more complex, like developing new career skills or studying for a master's degree. When learners are actively and willfully trying to achieve a cognitive goal (Scardamalia & Bereiter, 1993/1994), they think and learn more because they are fulfilling an intention. Technologies have traditionally been used to support teachers' goals, but not those of learners. Technologies need to engage learners in articulating and representing their understanding, not the teachers'. When learners use technologies to represent their actions and construction, they understand more and are better able to use the knowledge that they have constructed in new situations. When learners use computers to do skillful planning for doing everyday tasks or constructing and executing a way to research a problem they want to solve, they are intentional and are learning meaningfully.

- **Authentic (Complex/Contextual)** Most lessons taught in schools focus on general principles or theories that may be used to explain phenomena that we experience. However, teachers and professors remove those ideas from their natural contexts in order to be able to cover the curriculum more efficiently. When they do, they strip those principles of the contextual cues that make them meaningful. Physics courses are a prime example. Teachers read a simplified problem and immediately represent the problem in a formula. Students may learn to get the correct answer, but what are they learning? The students learned to understand the ideas only as algorithmic procedures outside of any context, so they have no idea how to apply the ideas to real-world contexts. Everything physical that occurs in the world involves physics. Why not learn physics through baseball, driving, walking, or virtually any other physical process on earth?

    Most contemporary research on learning has shown that learning tasks that are situated in some meaningful real-world task or simulated in some case-based or problem-based learning environment are not only better understood and remembered, but also are more consistently transferred to new situations. Rather than abstracting ideas in rules that are memorized and then applied to other canned problems, learning should be embedded in real life, useful contexts for learners to practice using those ideas.

- **Cooperative (Collaborative/Conversational)** Humans naturally work together in learning and knowledge-building communities, exploiting each others' skills and appropriating each others' knowledge in order to solve problems and perform tasks. So, why do educators insist that learners work independently so much of the time? Schools generally function based on the belief that learning is an independent process, so learners seldom have the opportunity to "do anything that counts" in collaborative teams despite their natural inclinations. When students collaborate without permission, educators may even accuse them of cheating despite the fact that such cross-fertilization is encouraged in any self-respecting design studio. However, we believe that relying solely on independent methods of instruction cheats learners out of more natural and productive modes of thinking. Often, educators will promote collaborative methods of learning, only to resort to independent assessment of learning. Learners, they believe, must be accountable for their own knowledge, so even if you agree, at least in principle, with collaborative learning principles, the hardest part of applying your beliefs will be assessing learners in teams. Most of the technology-based activities described throughout this book are more effectively performed collaboratively in groups, so we must assess the performance of the groups, as well as individuals. Learners are strategic enough to know "what counts" in classrooms, so if they are evaluated individually, collaborative learning activities will fail because students realize that their outcomes are not important.

Collaboration most often requires conversation among participants. Learners working in groups must socially negotiate a common understanding of the task and the methods they will use to accomplish it. That is, given a problem or task, people naturally seek out opinions and ideas from others. Technologies can support this conversational process by connecting learners in the same classroom, across town, or around the world (see Chapters 6 and 7). When learners become part of knowledge-building communities both in class and outside of school, they learn that there is more than one way to view the world and there are multiple solutions to most of life's problems. Conversation should be encouraged because it is the most natural way of making meaning.

As is depicted in Figure 1.1, these characteristics of meaningful learning are interrelated, interactive, and interdependent. That is, learning and instructional activities should engage and support combinations of active, constructive, intentional, authentic, and cooperative learning. Why? Because we believe that these characteristics are synergetic. That is, learning activities that represent a combination of these characteristics result in even more meaningful learning than the individual characteristics would in isolation.

There are many kinds of learning activities that engage meaningful learning, just as there are teachers who for years have engaged students in meaningful learning. We argue throughout this book that technologies can and should become the tools of meaningful learning. Technologies afford students the opportunities to engage in meaningful learning when they learn *with* the technology, not *from* it.

How Does Technology Facilitate Meaningful Learning?

Learning *from* Technology

Some of the first educational technologies were illustrations in 17th-century books and slate chalkboards in 18th-century classrooms. Educational technologies in the 20th century included lantern-slide and opaque projectors, later radio, and then motion pictures.

During the 1950s, programmed instruction emerged as the first true educational technology, that is, the first technology developed specifically to meet educational needs. With every other technology, including computers, educators recognized its importance and debated how to apply each nascent commercial technology for educational purposes. Unfortunately, educators have almost always tried to use technologies to teach students in the same ways that teachers had always taught. So information was recorded in the technology (e.g., the content presented by films and television programs), and the technology presented that information to the students. The effectiveness of each technology has been determined by how effectively it communicates ideas to students. The students' role was to learn the information presented by the technology, just as they learned information presented by the teacher. The role of the technology was to deliver lessons to students, just as trucks deliver groceries to supermarkets (Clark, 1983). If you deliver groceries, people will eat. If you deliver instruction, students will learn, right? Not necessarily! We will tell you why later.

The introduction of modern computer technologies in classrooms has followed the same pattern of use. Before the advent of microcomputers in the 1980s, mainframe computers were used to deliver drill and practice and simple tutorials for teaching students lessons. When microcomputers began populating classrooms, the natural inclination was to use them in the same way. A 1983 national survey of computer use showed that drill and practice was the most common use of microcomputers (Becker, 1985).

Later in the 1980s, educators began to perceive the importance of computers as productivity *tools*. The growing popularity of word processing, databases, spreadsheets, graphics programs, and desktop publishing was enabling businesses to become more productive. So students in the classroom began word processing and using graphics packages and desktop publishing programs to write with (see Chapter 4). This tool conception pervaded computer use according to a 1993 study by Hadley and Sheingold that showed that well-informed teachers were extensively using text-processing tools (word processors), analytic and information tools (especially databases and some spreadsheet use), and graphics tools (paint programs and desktop publishing) along with instructional software (including problem-solving programs along with drill and practice and tutorials).

The development of inexpensive multimedia computers and the eruption of the Internet in the mid-1990s quickly changed the nature of educational computing. Communications tools (e-mail and computer conferences) and multimedia, little used according to Hadley and Sheingold, have dominated the role of technologies in the classroom ever since. Now, Web 2.0 is more rapidly changing the landscape of educational computing. According to Schrum and Levin (2009), Web 2.0 is more distributed, collaborative, open source, and free, with more shared content produced by multiple users than Web 1.0. But what are the students producing? Too often, they are using the technology to reproduce what the teacher or textbook told them or what they copy from the Internet.

Our conception of educational computing and technology use, described next, is that technologies are not just repositories and distributors of information but rather tools. We believe that students should use the technology to represent what they know rather than reproducing what teachers and textbooks tell them. Technologies provide rich and flexible media that students can use to communicate their ideas with other students in collaborative groups. A great deal of research on computers and other technologies has shown that technologies are no more effective at teaching students than teachers, but if we begin to think about technologies as learning tools that students learn *with*, not *from*, then the nature of student learning will change.

Learning *with* Technology?

If schools are to foster meaningful learning, then the ways that technologies are used in schools must change from technology-as-teacher to technology-as-partner in the learning process. Before, the authors argued that students do not learn from technology but that technologies can support productive thinking and meaning making by students. That will happen when students learn *with* the technology. But, how is that done? How can technologies become intellectual partners with students? Throughout this book, the authors assume that:

- Technology is more than hardware. Technology consists also of the designs and the environments that engage learners. Technology can also consist of any reliable technique or method for engaging learning, such as cognitive-learning strategies and critical-thinking skills.

- Learning technologies can be any environment or definable set of activities that engage learners in active, constructive, intentional, authentic, and cooperative learning.

- Technologies are not conveyors or communicators of meaning. Nor should they prescribe and control all of the learner interactions.

- Technologies support meaningful learning when they fulfill a learning need—when interactions with technologies are learner initiated and learner controlled, and when interactions with the technologies are conceptually and intellectually engaging.

- Technologies should function as intellectual tool kits that enable learners to build more meaningful personal interpretations and representations of the world. These tool kits must support the intellectual functions that are required by a course of study.

- Learners and technologies should be intellectual partners, where the cognitive responsibility for performance is distributed to the partner that performs it better.

How Technologies Foster Learning

If technologies are used to foster meaningful learning, then they will not be used as delivery vehicles. Rather, technologies should be used as engagers and facilitators of thinking. Based on our conception of meaningful learning (Figure 1.1), we suggest the following roles for technologies in supporting meaningful learning:

- Technology as tools to support knowledge construction:
  - for representing learners' ideas, understandings, and beliefs
  - for producing organized, multimedia knowledge bases by learners
- Technology as information vehicle for exploring knowledge to support learning by constructing:
  - for accessing needed information
  - for comparing perspectives, beliefs, and worldviews

- Technology as authentic context to support learning by doing:
  - for representing and simulating meaningful real-world problems, situations, and contexts
  - for representing beliefs, perspectives, arguments, and stories of others
  - for defining a safe, controllable problem space for student thinking

- Technology as social medium to support learning by conversing:
  - for collaborating with others
  - for discussing, arguing, and building consensus among members of a community
  - for supporting discourse among knowledge-building communities

- Technology as intellectual partner (Jonassen, 2000a) to support learning by reflecting:
  - for helping learners to articulate and represent what they know
  - for reflecting on what they have learned and how they came to know it
  - for supporting learners' internal negotiations and meaning making
  - for constructing personal representations of meaning
  - for supporting mindful thinking

Alternative Conceptions of Meaningful Technology Use

Several organizations have worked to develop conceptions and standards for meaningful learning with technology. Here, the International Society for Technology in Education (ISTE) standards, Partnership for 21st Century Skills, and Technological Pedagogical Content Knowledge (TPACK) are presented and discussed.

ISTE NET Standards

The ISTE (www.iste.org) published a new set of National Educational Technology Standards (NETS) in 2007. Table 1.1 lists the standards for students and for teachers. They also published standards for administrators, but those are beyond the scope of this book.

The NETS provide a challenging set of expectations for students and teachers that, if fulfilled, could change the nature of education in our schools. They emphasize knowledge construction, collaboration, and critical thinking that are congruent with the 21st Century Skills that are described next. Although they can be interpreted in many ways, students and teachers who choose to achieve those standards should certainly find useful suggestions from this book, as well as the professional development materials and activities provided by ISTE.

21st Century Skills

The Partnership for 21st Century Skills is a national organization that advocates for 21st-century readiness for every student. As the United States continues to compete in a global economy that demands innovation, P21 and its members provide tools and resources to help the U.S. education system keep up by fusing the three Rs and four Cs (critical thinking and problem solving, communication, collaboration, and creativity and innovation). The

Table 1.1 ISTE's National Educational Technology Standards (NETS)

NETS—Students	NETS—Teachers

1. Creativity and Innovation
  a. apply existing knowledge to generate new ideas, products, or processes
  b. create original works as a means of personal or group expression
  c. use models and simulations to explore complex systems and issues
  d. identify trends and forecast possibilities
	1. Facilitate and Inspire Student Learning and Creativity
	  a. promote, support, and model creative and innovative thinking and inventiveness
	  b. engage students in exploring real-world issues and solving authentic problems using digital tools and resources
	  c. promote student reflection using collaborative tools to reveal and clarify students' conceptual understanding and thinking, planning, and creative processes
	  d. model collaborative knowledge construction by engaging in learning with students, colleagues, and others in face-to-face and virtual environments

2. Communication and Collaboration
  a. interact, collaborate, and publish with peers, experts, or others employing a variety of digital environments and media
  b. communicate information and ideas effectively to multiple audiences using a variety of media and formats
  c. develop cultural understanding and global awareness by engaging with learners of other cultures
  d. contribute to project teams to produce original works or solve problems
	2. Design and Develop Digital-Age Learning Experiences and Assessments
	  a. design or adapt relevant learning experiences that incorporate digital tools and resources to promote student learning and creativity
	  b. develop technology-enriched learning environments that enable all students to pursue their individual curiosities and become active participants in setting their own educational goals, managing their own learning, and assessing their own progress
	  c. customize and personalize learning activities to address students' diverse learning styles, working strategies, and abilities using digital tools and resources
	  d. provide students with multiple and varied formative and summative assessments aligned with content and technology standards and use resulting data to inform learning and teaching

3. Research and Information Fluency
  a. plan strategies to guide inquiry
  b. locate, organize, analyze, evaluate, synthesize, and ethically use information from a variety of sources and media
  c. evaluate and select information sources and digital tools based on the appropriateness to specific tasks
  d. process data and report results
	3. Model Digital-Age Work and Learning
	  a. demonstrate fluency in technology systems and the transfer of current knowledge to new technologies and situations
	  b. collaborate with students, peers, parents, and community members using digital tools and resources to support student success and innovation
	  c. communicate relevant information and ideas effectively to students, parents, and peers using a variety of digital-age media and formats
	  d. model and facilitate effective use of current and emerging digital tools to locate, analyze, evaluate, and use information resources to support research and learning

(continued)

Table 1.1   ISTE's National Educational Technology Standards (NETS) (*continued*)

NETS—Students	NETS—Teachers
4. Critical Thinking, Problem Solving, and Decision Making a. identify and define authentic problems and significant questions for investigation b. plan and manage activities to develop a solution or complete a project c. collect and analyze data to identify solutions and/or make informed decisions d. use multiple processes and diverse perspectives to explore alternative solutions	**4. Promote and Model Digital Citizenship and Responsibility** a. advocate, model, and teach safe, legal, and ethical use of digital information and technology, including respect for copyright, intellectual property, and the appropriate documentation of sources b. address the diverse needs of all learners by using learner-centered strategies and providing equitable access to appropriate digital tools and resources c. promote and model digital etiquette and responsible social interactions related to the use of technology and information d. develop and model cultural understanding and global awareness by engaging with colleagues and students of other cultures using digital-age communication and collaboration tools
5. Digital Citizenship a. advocate and practice safe, legal, and responsible use of information and technology b. exhibit a positive attitude toward using technology that supports collaboration, learning, and productivity c. demonstrate personal responsibility for lifelong learning d. exhibit leadership for digital citizenship	**5. Engage in Professional Growth and Leadership** a. participate in local and global learning communities to explore creative applications of technology to improve student learning b. exhibit leadership by demonstrating a vision of technology infusion, participating in shared decision making and community building, and developing the leadership and technology skills of others c. evaluate and reflect on current research and professional practice on a regular basis to make effective use of existing and emerging digital tools and resources in support of student learning d. contribute to the effectiveness, vitality, and self-renewal of the teaching profession and of their school and community
6. Technology Operations and Concepts a. understand and use technology systems b. select and use applications effectively and productively c. troubleshoot systems and applications d. transfer current knowledge to learning of new technologies	

Partnership for 21st Century Skills (www.p21.org) has articulated a set of skills needed by 21st-century graduates (Figure 1.2). The key elements of 21st-century learning are represented in the graphic and descriptions that follow. The 21st Century Skills student outcomes are illustrated in the arches of the rainbow. Those skills include life and career skills (beyond the scope of this book) and learning and innovation skills and information literacy skills, which are the focus of this book. The core subject skills are discipline specific. They may be enhanced by students' learning and innovation skills and information literacy skills. Table 1.2 lists elements of the framework and shows the classes of Learning and Innovation Skills.

Although open to interpretation, this set of skills describes the abilities possessed by ideal students who are able to function independently and collaboratively in schools. The degree to which technologies can support development of these skills in students may determine whether we are able to change the culture of education in this country.

Technological Pedagogical Learning Content Knowledge

Koehler and Mishra (2009) and Mishra and Koehler (2006) articulated a model of Technological Pedagogical Content Knowledge (TPACK) that focused on what teachers ought to know about integrating technology in their instruction. We, however, believe that it does not go far enough. But first, what is the source of this issue? Prior to their work, educational researchers have been concerned with what teachers ought to know about teaching. This movement began with Lee Shulman's (1986, 1987) conception of pedagogical content knowledge (PCK). Shulman assumed that, in order to be effective, teachers should possess pedagogical content knowledge. Pedagogical content knowledge includes the conceptual union of content knowledge and pedagogical knowledge.

Content knowledge describes a teacher's knowledge of the subject matter content that he or she teaches. Most educators assume that the more you know about the discipline that you teach, the better teacher you will be. Well-developed content knowledge seems essential to the ability to convey accepted information to students in order to avoid the acquisition of misconceptions by students.

Shulman rightly believed that content knowledge alone is not sufficient for being a good teacher. He argued that teachers also need pedagogical knowledge. Pedagogical knowledge describes a teacher's knowledge of the activities of instructing or teaching, including those teaching behaviors that impart knowledge or skill. Although some conceptions of pedagogy include

Figure 1.2

Framework for 21st Century Learning

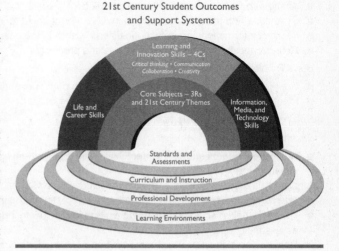

Source: Courtesy of the Partnership for 21st Century Skills.

Table 1.2   Elements of the 21st Century Skills Framework

Learning and Innovation Skills

Creativity and Innovation Skills

Think Creatively

- Use a wide range of idea-creation techniques (such as brainstorming)
- Create new and worthwhile ideas (both incremental and radical concepts)
- Elaborate, refine, analyze, and evaluate their own ideas in order to improve and maximize creative efforts

Work Creatively with Others

- Develop, implement, and communicate new ideas to others effectively
- Be open and responsive to new and diverse perspectives; incorporate group input and feedback into the work
- Demonstrate originality and inventiveness in work and understand the real-world limits to adopting new ideas
- View failure as an opportunity to learn; understand that creativity and innovation is a long-term, cyclical process of small successes and frequent mistakes

Implement Innovations

- Act on creative ideas to make a tangible and useful contribution to the field in which the innovation will occur

Critical Thinking and Problem Solving

Reason Effectively

- Use various types of reasoning (inductive, deductive, etc.) as appropriate to the situation

Use Systems Thinking

- Analyze how parts of a whole interact with each other to produce overall outcomes in complex systems

Make Judgments and Decisions

- Effectively analyze and evaluate evidence, arguments, claims, and beliefs
- Analyze and evaluate major alternative points of view
- Synthesize and make connections between information and arguments
- Interpret information and draw conclusions based on the best analysis
- Reflect critically on learning experiences and processes

Solve Problems

- Solve different kinds of nonfamiliar problems in both conventional and innovative ways
- Identify and ask significant questions that clarify various points of view and lead to better solutions

Communication and Collaboration Skills

Communicate Clearly

- Articulate thoughts and ideas effectively using oral, written, and nonverbal communication skills in a variety of forms and contexts
- Listen effectively to decipher meaning, including knowledge, values, attitudes, and intentions
- Use communication for a range of purposes (e.g., to inform, instruct, motivate, and persuade)
- Utilize multiple media and technologies, and know how to judge their effectiveness a priori as well as assess their impact
- Communicate effectively in diverse environments (including multilingual)

Collaborate with Others

- Demonstrate ability to work effectively and respectfully with diverse teams
- Exercise flexibility and willingness to be helpful in making necessary compromises to accomplish a common goal
- Assume shared responsibility for collaborative work, and value the individual contributions made by each team member

Information, Media, and Technology Skills

Information Literacy

Access and Evaluate Information

- Access information efficiently (time) and effectively (sources)
- Evaluate information critically and competently

Use and Manage Information

- Use information accurately and creatively for the issue or problem at hand
- Manage the flow of information from a wide variety of sources
- Apply a fundamental understanding of the ethical/legal issues surrounding the access and use of information

Media Literacy

Analyze Media

- Understand both how and why media messages are constructed, and for what purposes
- Examine how individuals interpret messages differently, how values and points of view are included or excluded, and how media can influence beliefs and behaviors
- Apply a fundamental understanding of the ethical/legal issues surrounding the access and use of media

Create Media Products

- Understand and utilize the most appropriate media creation tools, characteristics, and conventions
- Understand and effectively utilize the most appropriate expressions and interpretations in diverse, multicultural environments

ICT Literacy

Apply Technology Effectively

- Use technology as a tool to research, organize, evaluate, and communicate information
- Use digital technologies (computers, PDAs, media players, GPS, etc.), communication/networking tools and social networks appropriately to access, manage, integrate, evaluate, and create information to successfully function in a knowledge economy
- Apply a fundamental understanding of the ethical/legal issues surrounding the access and use of information technologies

Courtesy of the Partnership for 21st Century Skills.

understanding how students learn and how to assess student understanding, pedagogy is more commonly associated with acts of teaching, not learning.

While Shulman's conceptions of teacher knowledge make a great deal of sense, we believe that there are some fundamental problems with the concepts of content knowledge and pedagogical knowledge: the epistemological assumptions, the nature of knowledge, and the importance of learning.

First, we consider the epistemology of content knowledge. Epistemology is the philosophy of knowledge: what it means to know, how we develop knowledge, and what is truth.

When educators speak of content, it is assumed that the content exists in objective reality. Content is the stuff that we should learn. Content is the stuff that teachers deliver to students. If content can be delivered, then it must exist in some objective form. From a constructivist epistemological framework, knowledge is constructed individually and socially based on students' interactions with the world and each other. Knowledge cannot be delivered. Information can. When a teacher tells students what she or he knows, too often the teacher assumes that students will know it just like the teachers, that is, that the teacher has transferred knowledge to the students. That is impossible for a book full of reasons.

We also argue that content knowledge is a somewhat impoverished concept, because it does not articulate *how* teachers should know, only *what* they should know. Teachers and professors often experience difficulties in teaching because the knowledge of content that they have constructed is fragile and underdeveloped. Teachers and professors whose knowledge is exclusively based on textbooks and lectures cannot know content as well as an experienced practitioner who has constructed knowledge by using it. Also, content knowledge does not distinguish among the many kinds of knowledge, that is, how teachers should know. There are many kinds of knowledge that are constructed based on different kinds of activities and interactions. Jonassen (2009) identified numerous kinds of knowledge that can be constructed, including:

- *Declarative knowledge:* The most common kind when "knowledge" is delivered
- *Structural knowledge:* The knowledge of the propositional relationships among concepts
- *Conceptual knowledge:* The knowledge of frameworks that support conceptual change
- *Procedural knowledge:* The knowledge of how to perform some process
- *Situational knowledge:* The knowledge of contextual situations
- *Strategic knowledge:* The knowledge of when and why to perform some process
- *Tacit knowledge:* The knowledge that we know but cannot express
- *Sociocultural knowledge:* The knowledge of one's worldview, belief systems, attitudes, and socially shared knowledge among a culture of people
- *Experiential (episodic) knowledge:* The knowledge of the stories about our experiences

There are numerous other kinds of knowledge that have been conceived. Which kinds of knowledge should students learn? Clearly, the nature of the instruction will determine to a large degree the kinds of knowledge that students construct. It should also be obvious that pedagogical knowledge is not monolithic. Rather, it must articulate the numerous kinds of knowledge required to effectively teach students. Because the goal of pedagogy is, or at least should be, learning, a deeper understanding of learning is essential for developing any understanding of teaching. Therefore, we would like content knowledge to be conceived as disciplinary knowledge, where the different kinds of knowledge common to various disciplines could be articulated. That would provide a much clearer goal for constructing pedagogical knowledge (how to teach those different kinds of disciplinary knowledge).

Articulating the kinds of knowledge that students can construct about the discipline (content) they are studying brings up perhaps the most important issue related to pedagogical content knowledge: learning. Although some conceptions of pedagogical knowledge include the teacher's understanding of how students learn, pedagogy mostly refers to how teachers teach. We argue that pedagogical content knowledge needs another dimension: learning knowledge. There are many more alternative conceptions of learning than there are concepts of knowledge. Learning theory courses are replete with alternative conceptions of how people learn, each of which is based on different philosophies and relies on different pedagogies. For each theory, there are numerous ways of thinking (far too many to review here). Suffice it to say that the most common kind of thinking required of students is recall. In order to engage students in deeper-level, more meaningful learning, students must learn how to perform analogical reasoning (comparing ideas structurally), causal reasoning (predictions, inferences, and implications), conceptual model building, argumentation (rhetorical and dialectic), and metacognitive reasoning (Jonassen, 2011). Understanding how students learn meaningfully is essential to teaching. The challenge of that assumption is tough: If you as a teacher are unable to articulate how your students need to think in order to learn what you want them to learn, how can you know what or how or why to teach?

Koehler and Mishra (2009) and Mishra and Koehler (2006) have added to PCK what teachers ought to know about integrating technology in their instruction. This newer component argues that good teaching requires knowledge of content, pedagogy, and technology. Ergo, they argue for the importance of TPACK, the union of those three kinds of knowledge (see Figure 1.3). Technological pedagogical content knowledge (TPACK) is the knowledge of how technologies can best be employed in different pedagogies for facilitating the acquisition of content knowledge. To their credit, Koehler and Mishra have focused on the affordances of each technology for teaching content. What kinds of activities do technologies afford (support or enable)? For example, e-mail affords the asynchronous exchange and storage of interpersonal messages. Unfortunately, e-mail does not afford synchronous exchanges or nonverbal aspects of communication, such as tone, mood, or expressiveness. Focusing on affordances is a very useful framework for examining educational technologies. Perhaps the most important ideas from the model in Figure 1.3 are the interactions among these kinds of knowledge, including pedagogical content knowledge, technological content knowledge, and technological pedagogical knowledge.

Notwithstanding our previously expressed concerns about pedagogical and content knowledge, one can also argue that teaching with technology is merely another kind of pedagogy and therefore an unnecessary dimension. For purposes of this book, however, we must accept the importance of learning with technologies (the primary topic and title of this book). However, if we accept technology knowledge as an essential kind of knowledge for teachers, then we also argue that we should also include a learning knowledge dimension, which would expand TPACK into TPLACK. We believe that it is impossible to make meaningful recommendations about technology use without a clear conception of how students are supposed to learn. Too often, technologies are implemented for their own sake. If you use technologies, they will learn (maybe). TPLACK decisions would then focus on which technology engages the particular kinds of thinking and learning about aspects of different disciplines employing a particular pedagogy. For example, if I want my biology students to construct structural knowledge of different phyla, then I might recommend having students use a constructive pedagogy by building concept maps. An obvious complaint about TPLACK will be that it is too complicated. Perhaps, but design is complex. It is not nearly as

Figure 1.3

Technological Pedagogical Content Knowledge (TPACK)

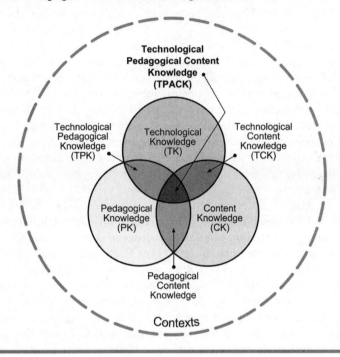

Source: http://tpack.org. Reprinted with permission.

formulaic as many texts describe. Design is the most complex and ill-structured kind of problem that teachers must solve (Jonassen, 2000b). PCK, TPACK, and TPLACK are all about design decision making. That is an essential part of the job of teaching. The assumption underlying this book is that the most important factor in deciding what and how you should teach is what and how your students should learn. That is the major difference between this book and so many other teaching with technology textbooks.

Conclusion

An underlying assumption of this book is that the most productive and meaningful uses of technology will not occur if technologies are used in traditional ways: as delivery vehicles for instructional lessons. Technology cannot teach students. Rather, students learn as they use technology. Meaningful learning will result when technologies engage learners in:

- knowledge construction, not reproduction;
- conversation, not reception;
- articulation, not repetition;

- collaboration, not competition; and
- reflection, not prescription.

We argue that technologies can support meaningful learning when students learn through the use of the technology, not from it. When students use technologies to inquire (Chapter 2), experiment (Chapter 3), design (Chapter 4), communicate with others (Chapter 5), build communities (Chapter 6), write (Chapter 7), build models (Chapter 8), and visualize (Chapter 9), then they are engaged in deeper levels of thinking and reasoning, including causal, analogical, expressive, experiential, and problem solving. Technologies are lousy teachers, but they can be powerful tools to think with. That is the theme that we describe in the remainder of this book.

A caveat. Implementation of the values and beliefs underlying this book and all of the standards described in this chapter will represent a significant paradigm shift in education. Fostering that paradigm shift in education is a gigantic diffusion-and-adoption-of-change problem. Changing the beliefs of educators, students, parents, and communities will require enormous collaborations. Whether these beliefs are able to change the culture of testing and memorization in our schools remains to be seen. For the sake of our children and the next generation of leaders in our society, we truly hope so.

Things to Think About

If you would like to reflect on the ideas that we presented in this chapter, consider your responses to the following questions.

1. If learners cannot know what the teacher knows because they do not share a common knowledge and experience base, how can we be certain that students learn important things? For instance, if you want to teach students about the dangers of certain chemical reactions in the lab, how do we ensure that learners know and understand those important lessons?

2. What is your theory of learning? From your perspective, how do people learn? What are the important processes?

3. Which of the skills described in this chapter are most important to you as an educator? Which are most important to comprehending and being able to apply ideas in your discipline?

4. Is it possible to learn (construct personal meaning) without engaging in some activity; that is, is it possible to learn simply by thinking about something? Which technology-based activities will result in the most thinking and learning? Can you think of an example?

5. When learners construct knowledge, what are they building? How is it possible to observe the fruits of their labor, that is, the knowledge they construct? How can technologies help? Which technologies are most effective at representing what students know?

6. Think about a recent controversial topic that you have heard or read about. What are different sides arguing about? What do they believe? What assumptions do they make about what is causing the controversy? Where did those beliefs come from?

7. Radical constructivists argue that reality exists only in the mind of the knower. If that is true, is there a physical world that we live in? Prove it.

8. Some educators argue that we learn much more from our failures than from our successes. Why? They believe that we should put students in situations where their hypotheses or predictions fail. Can you think of a situation in which you learned a lot from a mistake?

9. Recall the last difficult problem that you had to solve. Did you solve it alone, or did you solicit the help of others? What did you learn from solving that problem? Can that learning be used again?

10. Can you learn to cook merely from watching cooking shows on television? What meaning do you make from the experiences that you observe? Will the experience that you have when you prepare a dish be the same as that of the television chef? How will it be different?

11. Technology is the application of scientific knowledge, according to many definitions. Can you think of a teaching technology (replicable, proven teaching process) that does not involve machines?

12. Can you calculate the exact square root of 2,570 without a calculator? Does the calculator make you smarter? Is the calculator intelligent?

13. Describe the difference in thinking processes engaged by a short answer versus a multiple-choice test question. Are they different? Are they assessing knowledge? Is that knowledge meaningful? Why or why not?

14. Can you think of an activity that makes you dumber, not smarter? Do you not learn anything from that activity?

15. Have you ever produced your own video, movie, slide show, or computer program? How did it make you think? How did it make you feel?

References

Becker, H. J. (1985). *How schools use microcomputers: Summary of a 1983 national survey.* (ERIC Document Reproduction Service, ED 257448).

Clark, R. (1983). Mere vehicles. *Review of Educational Research, 53*(4), 445–459.

Hadley, M., & Sheingold, K. (1993). Commonalities and distinctive patterns in teacher interaction of computers. *American Journal of Education, 101*(3), 261–315.

Jonassen, D. H. (2000a). *Computers as mindtools in schools: Engaging critical thinking.* Columbus, OH: Merrill/Prentice Hall.

Jonassen, D. H. (2000b). Toward a design theory of problem solving. *Educational Technology: Research & Development, 48*(4), 63–85.

Jonassen, D. H. (2009). Reconciling a human cognitive architecture. In S. Tobias & T. M. Duffy (Eds.), *Constructivist theory applied to instruction: Success or failure?* New York: Routledge.

Jonassen, D. H. (2011). *Learning to solve problems: A handbook for designing problem-solving learning environments.* New York: Routledge.

Koehler, M. J., & Mishra, P. (2009). What is technological pedagogical content knowledge? *Contemporary Issues in Technology and Teacher Education, 9*(1). Retrieved from www.citejournal.org/vol9/iss1/general/article1.cfm

Mishra, P., & Koehler, M. J. (2006). Technological pedagogical content knowledge: A framework for integrating technology in teacher knowledge. *Teachers College Record, 108*(6), 1017–1054.

Polkinghorne, D. (1988). *Narrative knowing and the human sciences.* Albany: State University of New York Press.

Schank, R. C. (1994). Goal-based scenarios. In R. C. Schank & E. Langer (Eds.), *Beliefs, reasoning, and decision making: Psycho-logic in honor of Bob Abelson.* Hillsdale, NJ: Lawrence Erlbaum.

Schrum, L., & Levin, B. B. (2009). *Leading 21st century schools: Harnessing technology for engagement and achievement.* Thousand Oaks, CA: Corwin Press.

Shulman, L. (1986). Those who understand: Knowledge growth in teaching. *Educational Researcher, 15*(2), 4–14.

Shulman, L. S. (1987). Knowledge and teaching: Foundations of the new reform. *Harvard Educational Review, 57*(1), 1–22.

Chapter Objectives

1. Introduce readers to technology tools that support student inquiry

2. Describe processes of information gathering: searching, managing, evaluating

3. List the differences between different types of search tools

4. List questions that help students evaluate information

5. Describe ways to help students avoid plagiarism

6. Detail ways to help students learn skills in online safety and privacy

7. Provide examples of using information to build knowledge through open-ended, student-directed research projects

8. Describe how mobile devices can assist in inquiry-based learning

9. Describe how the development of NETS and 21st Century Skills can be advanced by the technology-based activities in this chapter

Technology Trends Supporting Inquiry

When teachers offer students opportunities for inquiry, they create the potential for rich, meaningful learning experiences. Technology can provide the means for active, authentic learning through investigation both in the classroom and in the field.

More than a decade ago, the Web-based Education Committee (2000) made several predictions in a national report, all of which have come to pass. Table 2.1 indicates some of these shifts, along with others that have occurred since then. Clearly, technology has become an integral part of our lives and will continue to evolve, often so quickly that some people feel hard pressed to keep up. One of the implications of these types of changes is the need for flexibility. *Flexibility* is identified as one of the "habits of mind" that are required for effective thinkers (Costa & Kallick, 2000). This flexible thinking is as necessary for teachers as it is for their students in today's shifting times. Emerging and rapidly changing technologies demand individuals who are prepared to experiment, adopt, or discard technology tools as they appear, evolve, become successfully entrenched, or fall by the wayside.

Ubiquitous computing, or access to hardware giving students the ability to continually interact with digital tools and connect to the Internet, is a growing trend. Small laptops, tablets, smart phones, and other mobile devices allow ubiquitous computing. A valuable characteristic of these small devices is their portability. Students are no longer harnessed to a desktop, a classroom, or even a physical building. This freedom enables more authentic data collection, as students can take devices into the field to collect, record, and analyze information. Despite the fact that there is great potential in using mobile tools for learning, their adoption is dependent on loosening the bans that most schools currently have on them (Johnson, Smith, Levine, & Haywood, 2010; Schuler, 2009).

Internet technology is faster, multifaceted, and increasingly intelligent, as it remembers users' past actions, preferences, and history. Agents use data-mining techniques in order to learn and discover users' behaviors, and they interact with one another to share knowledge about their users. The Internet has become an almost unimaginable network of resources, and one can spend vast amounts of time browsing through websites; learning to effectively

Table 2.1 Internet Technology Trends

Moving From:	Moving To:
Narrowband	Broadband
Plain, single mode (e.g., text or speech)	Multimodal rich connectivity
Tethered (wired) access from desktop computers	Untethered (wireless) access
User adapts to the technology	Technology adapts to the user
User as solitary consumer of information	User as producer in shared, dynamic environment
Files from proprietary software housed on individual computers	Open source and cloud computing

employ these resources as true educational tools is a challenging task for educators. It is vital that we teach students the essential skills needed to become information literate citizens in a digital society.

Let's take a look at how the Internet and mobile technologies can be used to support students' investigations, along with some of the essential skills they will need.

Information Gathering with Internet Resources

In the following sections, we explore how to use the Internet as a source of information for compelling, meaningful learning. Collaborative problem- and project-based learning activities often begin with online research as a first step. Inquiry-based learning that begins with student-initiated questions leads naturally to investigation and research. The important thing to remember is that research, or searching for information, is just a step—a means to a bigger end.

Too many educators tacitly equate information searching with learning. They believe that if students are busily searching for information online, they will naturally make sense out of what they find. Yet researchers have found (Fidel et al., 1999; Schacter, Chung, & Dorr, 1998) that when students search for predetermined answers, they are not comprehending or reflecting on the meaning of what they have found. Their intention is to complete the assignment—to find the one answer that the teacher is looking for. Simply asking students to find information on the Web will probably not result in learning. Unless there is an intentional outcome, researching is a meaningless activity. Unfortunately, research often "ends with the harvesting of the data, rather than extending into the next stage of the process. While a Web hunt for close-ended questions from a website might technically be a form of research, it lacks the value of an active learning experience that can result if the information gathered is applied" (Kelly, 2000, p. 6).

Yet information searching is essential to meaning making and problem solving. In order to learn from information being sought, students must have an intention to find information that will help them solve a problem. They must have a purpose other than fulfilling the requirements of an assignment. Intentional information searching requires at least a four-step process: (a) plan, (b) use strategies to search the Web, (c) evaluate, and (d) triangulate sources (Jonassen & Colaric, 2001).

With the concept of "research as first step" firmly in mind, let's consider what it takes to become competent in using the Internet for information searches.

Searching for Information

Using the Internet as the vast online resource that it is requires multiple skills. Effective information gleaning from the Internet combines expertise in searching for information, evaluating the worth of that information, and then organizing the information to make it more readily usable.

Finding the information one needs on the Internet can be extremely challenging because of the billions of Web pages that are available. Among the concerns about the Internet as a learning tool is that there are so many interesting topics to explore and it is so easy to explore that students are often off task, following links that take them *away from* rather than *toward* their learning goal. In planning a search, students are required to identify what they need to know.

First, students should articulate their intention and verbalize what is being looked for as well as *why* that information is needed. This thought process activates knowledge that the learner already has and clarifies for the learner the dissonance that exists. Next, the learner must develop a conscious and intentional search strategy in order to locate information sources that may be useful. Selection of search terms can be a difficult process. It will be necessary for you, the teacher, to model the process of asking questions, such as who, where, when, and what, in order to identify search terms that are associated with the problem. These terms can then be developed into a search string that would be appropriate to use in a search engine.

Along with the technical skill of conducting an effective search, learners also need to develop awareness and self-regulatory skills in order to make the Internet a tool for effective learning. As they navigate the Internet, they must also be thinking about the information they encounter and how it relates to their existing knowledge. Understanding requires thinking. Browsing does not necessarily cause thinking.

A self-regulated learner who keeps his or her information-seeking goals in mind and makes good decisions can find the Web an essential information resource during intentional learning. That is, the educational secret to the Internet is intentionality. When students say, "I am looking for information to help me answer a question/build my own knowledge base/evaluate someone else's ideas/and so on," then they will likely learn from the experience. As your students visit websites that have been identified, they also need to evaluate whether the information they find there supports the students' purpose. That is, does the site contain the information that they need to fulfill their intention? Are there any ideas at the site that can be used to answer the questions they are seeking? This type of reflective thinking allows the learner to reevaluate what he or she really needs and what is missing. If the learner thinks the original search worked, then satisfaction is attained, and the searching stops. Otherwise, the learner can narrow the search by adding additional terms, expand the search by removing some of the terms, or simply scratch the original search and start over.

How can we support students in conducting intentional searches with the metacognition that keeps them focused and productive? Equipping students with the skills to search effectively is the first step in using the Internet as a source of information. The I-Search model (Tallman & Joyce, 2005) is structured to scaffold students throughout the research process, beginning with identification of topics that are personally meaningful and relevant. I-Search's inquiry-based process emphasizes metacognition, with students reflecting on the research process itself. One strategy for effective searching is understanding the different types of search tools that are available, their unique characteristics, how they work, and when a specific type is appropriate.

Search Engines and Directories   We can divide search tools into two broad categories: search engines and directories. Both search engines and directories are databases of websites, but they are constructed differently. Search engines such as Google use automated scripts known as robots (also called spiders or crawlers) that nearly constantly travel the Internet, cataloging Web pages for search engine databases. Based on an algorithm that takes many factors into account, Google ranks the Web page, which will determine its position in the listing one receives after doing a search.

Rather than searching by key words, as search engines do, directories such as Yahoo!, About, and LookSmart are databases that use a hierarchical structure, listing websites in convenient categories and subcategories. Directories are an easy place to find information when you are looking on the Web since people review the sites on them and group the sites into appropriate categories. However, this takes quite a bit of time and effort, so only a small fraction of the available sites on the Web are listed with each directory, and the "root" or main page rather than subpages is typically all that is shown. This is in contrast to a search engine that will list pages of "hits."

The Open Directory Project or DMOZ (from directory.mozilla.org, its original domain name) is an attempt to solve the problem of populating directories. DMOZ is an open-content, multilingual directory of Web links constructed and maintained by a global community of volunteer editors. By distributing responsibility for small portions of the Web among many people, DMOZ claims to be the largest, most comprehensive human-edited directory of the Web. We'll explore more social software applications like this in other chapters.

To find obscure information or all the possible sites covering a subject, you need a more in-depth search than directories offer. For this you need a search engine. Over the past few years, many smaller search engines have disappeared, with Google becoming the most popular search engine on the Web. It is, in fact, so widely used that both the *Oxford English Dictionary* and the *Merriam-Webster Collegiate Dictionary* added "google" as a verb that means using the Google search engine to find information on the Internet (Foley, 2006; Harris, 2006). In late 2010, the global information services company Experian reported the top five search engines as Google, Yahoo!, Bing, Ask, and AOLSearch. Google led with 71 percent of all searches; Yahoo! was next in line with 14 percent (www.hitwise.com/us/datacenter/main/dashboard-10133.html).

The proliferation of Google tools continues, with several specialized search engines among them. For example, Google Scholar focuses searches on scholarly literature, such as scholarly journal articles, books, theses, and peer-reviewed papers from universities, academic publishing companies, and professional organizations. Google's preferences allow a user to define the number of desired results to be returned, what language(s) are included in the pages searched, and which of three filtering levels is used. Google's advanced search allows more precise searching by limiting specific words, searching for exact wording, looking for specific file types, and searching within a designated site or domain (e.g., pearson.com, youtube, .gov, .edu). Its language tools convert search phrases, text, or entire Web pages into other languages. Wonder Wheel provides students with a visual representation of linked terms related to the search term that was entered, appearing somewhat like a concept map; those related terms can then be clicked for additional related terms, creating a dense web of possible links to explore. In Figure 2.1, the results of a search for *chlorophyll* are displayed. Notice the Wonder Wheel link on the left side of the page.

When one clicks on the Wonder Wheel link, the results from this page are displayed along with the Wonder Wheel in Figure 2.2. Next, the term *chlorophyll* was selected and expanded, resulting in the depiction shown in Figure 2.3 on page 26. Students should, of course, think about the best search terms for producing the information they are seeking; however, searching for that information is not always cut and dried. Tools like Wonder

Figure 2.1

Results from a Google Search on "Photosynthesis"

Wheel can help students consider other alternatives for expanding or refining searches, although they may also cause students to lose focus if they wander too far in a "lateral drift."

Although Google has become synonymous with searching, there are many search engines available on the Web, often using different methods of organizing and searching. Each search tool has specific features that may be best suited for particular information needs, as different search engine robots can use different methods for searching and indexing; therefore, the website results for the same search with each search engine may be different.

Figure 2.2

Results of "Photosynthesis" Search as a Google Wonder Wheel

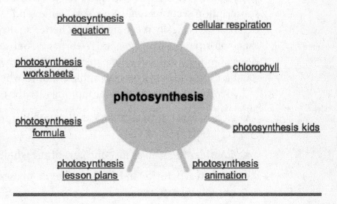

Figure 2.3

Results from Expanding "Chlorophyll" on Wonder Wheel

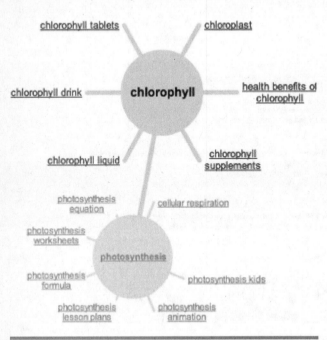

A subset of search engines is the metasearch engine. We can think of these powerful tools as a search engine clearinghouse. When a search is conducted in a metasearch engine, such as Dogpile, IxQuick, or Metacrawler, it is sent to a number of search engines, and the results from these multiple search engines are returned. Other search engine subsets include specialized engines that hunt for specific types of Internet resources, such as Newslookup.com for news, WebMD for medical information, and Whatis.com for technology topics.

Web portals, which are websites that offer both search engines and directories, typically provide customizable access to data (e.g., news, sports, entertainment) in addition to a free e-mail account. For example, Yahoo!'s newer, crawler search function is now integrated with its old directory structure and is found at Yahoo.com along with links to weather, travel, games, instant messaging, and e-mail. Other Web portal examples are Excite and Lycos.

Invisible Web   There are many searchable databases that are not directly indexed by conventional search engines (e.g., Google); to access these resources requires a direct query to the database. Some are free (e.g., AskERIC and FindArticles), some charge for access (e.g., EBSCO, GALE, ProQuest, OVID, JSTOR, and Medline), and some have both free and subscription sections (e.g., New York Times and Wall Street Journal). Information in these databases is typically more specific, of better quality, and found more quickly and efficiently than information from general Web pages. Subscription databases are searchable collections of journal articles, newspapers, citations, images, statistical data, or documents. Some databases provide only bibliographic citations whereas others provide full-text articles.

Here are some strategies for tapping into the deep or invisible Web:

- Access subscription databases through libraries or schools that pay for those subscriptions
- Consider the Web as just one part of the whole Internet
- Find an article title in ERIC or other databases and search for it with Google Scholar or other search tools

- Look for bibliographies on the Web that can be incorporated into searches for books, journal articles, or other documents

- Search for authors from books and journals

- Search for organizations and government reports

- Follow citations onto the Web

- Check e-mail addresses to contact authors for further information (Vidmar, 2003)

Feeds   It isn't always necessary to actively search out Web information, as feeds allow published website content to be automatically delivered to a user. RSS (Really Simple Syndication) was the first syndication feed format; Atom is another, less widely used format.

Feeds use a technology called XML (Extensible Markup Language) to deliver content to your desktop, an application, or a Web browser. Content could be in the form of headlines and summaries from news websites, blog or twitter feeds, YouTube videos, or podcasts. A feed is a regularly updated summary of Web content along with links to full versions of that content. The feed's text file uses XML to include information describing the content and the location of this content on the originating website. This document is then registered with one of the directories that list syndication feed sites.

To subscribe to a feed and have it display in a readable format, you'll need what's called a feed reader or aggregator. Otherwise, when you click on an RSS or Atom feed link, your browser may display a page of unformatted gibberish. There are many free and inexpensive feed readers, most of which support both RSS and Atom formats. Although feeds may be delivered to your desktop through a separate reader application (e.g., SharpReader, RSS Bandit, NetNewsWire, or NewzCrawler), Web-based readers (e.g., Bloglines, My Yahoo!, PageFlakes, Google Reader) are commonplace and simpler to use. Your Web browser may even have a built-in RSS reader. For example, the Firefox browser supports Live Bookmarks, a system that detects RSS feeds and allows users to subscribe. If a website offers an RSS feed, the Live Bookmark icon can be clicked, and the feed will appear in your bookmark list or in the Web feed reader that you designate.

While not a feed reader itself, the Rocketnews website (www.rocketnews.com) uses feeds to offer an aggregation of the latest top news stories in many categories. Similarly, Newsy (www.newsy.com) researches, analyzes, and synthesizes news stories from a variety of news outlets to create online videos with commentary. This unique news site provides users with multiple perspectives derived from numerous sources around the world.

Individualizing, Organizing, and Sharing Searches   After searching for relevant websites to gather information, one is likely to have a lot of links that need organizing! Thus, some means of organizing and saving those sites is needed.

Techniques to individualize one's searches and the saved results can help a person find and retrieve information in ways that make the most sense to that individual. Most search engines include links with directions on advanced search techniques for that particular tool, along with customized features that individualize the search experience for users.

When one creates a free Google account, the option for personalized searches is offered. Personalized searches find the results most relevant to you, based on what you've searched for in the past. This search feature also allows one to view and manage past searches and note trends in one's search activity, including top searches, most visited websites, and daily activity.

Cloud computing enables users to create bookmarks that can be accessed from any computer with Internet access rather than housing bookmarks on an individual computer's hard drive. Cloud computing takes advantage of surplus storage space on multiple servers to provide "on demand" service for users.

One type of social software (see Chapter 6) is exemplified in the growing number of social bookmarking websites that are housed "in the cloud." These sites are an increasingly popular way to locate, classify, rank, and share Internet resources. Social bookmarking services usually organize their content using tags, which can be used like key words to search for bookmarks that others have shared. These sites rank the resources according to the number of users who have bookmarked them.

When one registers for a social bookmarking service, a simple bookmarklet can be added to your Web browser. After finding a Web page you'd like to add to your list, simply select the bookmarklet, and follow the prompts for information about the page. One may add descriptive terms to group similar links together, modify the title of the page, and add extended notes for oneself or for others.

One of the earliest social bookmarking sites was Delicious (Figure 2.4). By creating an individualized list of bookmarks (defined through "tags" or key words), I can go to one

Figure 2.4

Bookmarks Saved in a Delicious Account

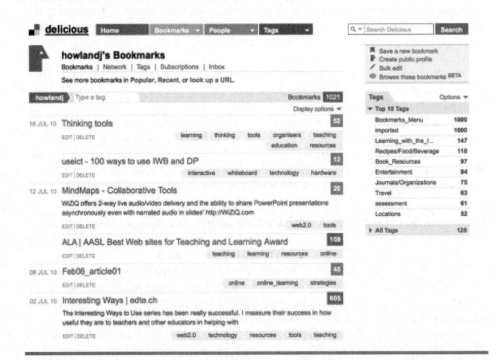

place to find current links on topics that I am interested in—in this case different kinds of cognitive tools. Each saved link on the page has been tagged with descriptive labels, making it easy to search for specific topics and categories. On the right, the "Tags" section displays the top tags assigned to bookmarked links in this account and the number of times each tag has been used.

For each bookmarked link, the small numbered box above the tags indicates the number of other users who have also saved this link. Clicking the first link, "Thinking tools," results in a page with those users' shared bookmarks (see Figure 2.5).

Subscribing to a tag will automatically update your bookmarks list with links that others have bookmarked and tagged with that label. For example, a student might be researching global warming. By adding "global warming" to her subscriptions, she will have access to many websites that other Delicious users find, tag with "global warming," and share. As with most social media sharing sites, each user has control over what is shared publicly and what is kept private. Thus, you may choose to offer public access to all your bookmarks, to selected ones, or to none. A tag bundle can organize existing tags into a group. Perhaps one has tagged various bookmarks with *global warming*, *climate*, and *ocean*. These three tags might be bundled into a group labeled *environment* as an additional management tool.

Figure 2.5

Everyone's Shared Bookmarks for "Thinking Tools" in Delicious

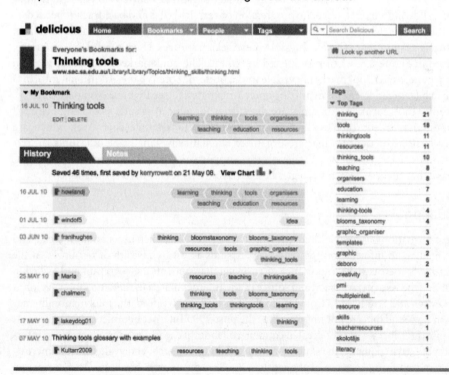

Diigo (Digest of Internet Information, Groups and Other stuff) refers to itself as a "cloud-based information management service" and offers research tools in addition to simple bookmarking (see www.diigo.com). While offering many features of a social network, Diigo's social networking is all about knowledge sharing, prompting it to label itself a "Social Information Network." Diigo enables a user to highlight text and add the equivalent of a sticky note to Web pages, which will appear when that user returns to the Web page. Annotated pages may also be shared with others. Public, private, or semiprivate groups can be formed, allowing a class or student team to collaborate on collecting, organizing, and annotating resources. The archive allows users to upload and capture a snapshot of bookmarked pages. Users can search their collections in several ways, including by highlights, sticky notes, tags, and full text of bookmarked items.

The human involvement in adding and classifying Internet resources makes social bookmarking services function somewhat like directories. However, rather than having designated employees doing the work, it is distributed among all users, similar to the Open Directory Project model. Many social bookmarking services allow users to subscribe to syndication RSS feeds based on tags in order to learn of new resources for a given topic as they are noted, tagged, and classified by other users in this continual process.

Internet browsers and add-ons can offer useful features beyond the standard bookmark or favorites list. Tabs allow new websites to open in a different tab within the same window. When saving to Firefox's bookmark folder, the option for saving all tabs into one folder is given, enhancing organization. Another organization strategy is using the browser's history feature to track searches. Firefox organizes visited Web pages in history folders, allowing a user to trace the progression of searched sites and backtrack if needed.

Zotero, somewhat similar to Diigo, is a Firefox extension that can be installed to collect, organize, cite, and share (if you choose) your research sources. Users see Zotero's interface, depicted in Figure 2.6, when it is opened in Firefox. The bookmarked websites appears in the top pane; saved bookmarks are visible in the bottom, Zotero pane. Additional information can be entered to aid in organizing and citing material (see Figure 2.7 on page 32).

Other tools for managing links are directories for educators such as eThemes (http://ethemes.missouri.edu/themes) and TrackStar (http://trackstar.4teachers.org), which are two collections of websites that are organized thematically. Finally, NoodleTools (http://noodletools.com/) is a set of online tools that supports research—including NoodleQuest, a wizard that suggests search strategies based on your answers to several questions.

Evaluating

Once information has been located, what next? The ease with which users can now create and share media and information tremendously expands access to a wealth of resources. At the same time, it increases the importance of ensuring that students are cognizant and skilled in evaluating the veracity, accuracy, and source of the Internet materials they encounter. As Johnson, Levine, and Smith said, "Contrary to the conventional wisdom, the information literacy skills of new students are not improving as the post-1993 Internet boomlet enters college. At the same time, in a sea of user-created content, collaborative work, and instant access to information of varying quality, the skills of critical thinking, research, and evaluation are increasingly required to make sense of the world" (2007). Anyone who has access to a server can

Figure 2.6

Zotero Research Tool in Firefox

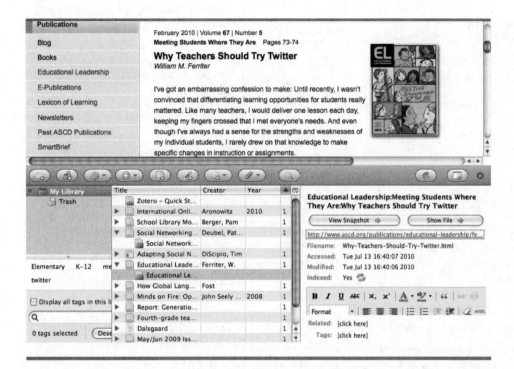

create and post Web pages. Students, often with teachers' and parents' blessings, construct their own representations by appropriating information and graphics from other websites without evaluating the viability of the ideas. There are no Internet police. Anyone can put anything on an Internet server (propaganda, pornography, and perjury), and they often do. Organizations committed to hatred are finding new voice on the Internet. It is vital that students learn how to discriminate fact from fiction, information from opinion, and reality from fantasy. So how do we determine what is or is not accurate? Knowing whether a website is reputable and contains accurate information is the next essential step in using the Internet as a source of information.

When learners locate prospective websites, they must evaluate the information contained in them. That evaluation process should engage the learner in two separate aspects of evaluation: relevancy and credibility. First, is the information on the site related to the problem? Does it contribute to the intention of the search? That is, does the site contain information that pertains to the learner's expressed intention? Does it provide an explanation, examples, alternative perspectives, or other pieces of information that the learner can use to construct his or her own knowledge?

Second, it is necessary that learners evaluate the credibility of the information. Evaluation of credibility usually involves two processes: evaluating the source of the information

Figure 2.7

Record for Individual Zotero Entry

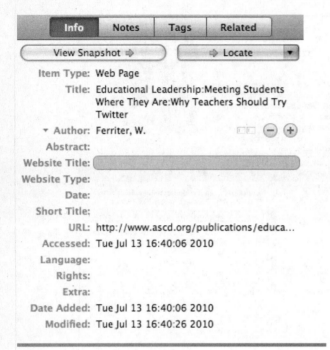

and evaluating the treatment of the subject. The teacher can model for the students the process of dissecting a website and should provide guiding questions to help students identify what to look for regarding a site's credibility. Examples of questions to evaluate the source of the information include the following:

- Who provided this information? Why?

- Does the site author have authority in that field?

- If the site is published by an organization, is it one you recognize?

- Does the organization have a vested interest or bias concerning the information presented?

- Is the site owner affiliated with an organization (such as an educational institution or a government agency) that has authority in the stated subject area?

- Is it clear when the site was developed and last updated?

- Is a bibliography or resource list included?

- Are the references used in the bibliography credible?

- How can we validate the information provided? Can we check the sources?

  Examples of questions to evaluate the treatment of the subject include the following:

- Is someone trying to sell us a product or point of view?

- What kind of site did it come from (.com = commercial, .gov = government, .edu = educational institution, or .org = nonprofit organization)? How might the source affect the accuracy? Can we believe everything that comes from the government or an educational institution?

- Is the content factual or opinion? Does the information represent theory or evidence, fact or fiction, and so on? How do we distinguish between these?

- Does it follow a logical presentation of sequence?

- Is the intended audience clear?

- Are there any gaps in logic, or is there missing information that is relevant to the subject?

- Are there political or ideological biases?

- Is this primarily an advertising or a marketing site?

- If quotes or data are provided, are they properly referenced?

- Is the language used inflammatory or extreme?

- Is the text well written? Are there misspellings, or is poor grammar used?

- How do the visuals, sound, or animation influence how we interpret the information? Do visuals and text convey the same meaning?

In asking the learner to evaluate for relevancy and credibility, you are asking him or her to engage in reflective thinking about what is really needed and what is missing. You are also asking the student to question the authority of the documents and to become more information literate by critically evaluating sources of information. A final step in this process is to triangulate the search—identify at least two other sources that verify the information found.

For more information on techniques and questions to ask in evaluating websites refer to www.lib.berkeley.edu/TeachingLib/Guides/Internet/Evaluate.html. Teachers may also want to introduce students to the easyWhois website (www.easywhois.com/), which is a free service that reports the owner of domain names. Students should be aware of "Sponsored Links" on many search results pages. These links are paid advertisements that have been purchased by companies or organizations who want to have their website links prominently displayed when you search for certain words or phrases.

Learning these critical information literacy skills should be mandatory for any students using the Internet to collect information, as they are essential 21st-century skills that encompass the ability to reason, analyze, interpret, evaluate, and draw conclusions. They are the first step as students investigate with Internet resources.

Things to Consider

Beyond developing the skills to search, manage, and evaluate Internet resources, there are other digital and information literacy issues for teachers to consider. In the next section, we discuss some of these and offer suggestions for supporting students' understanding and growth as 21st-century digital citizens.

Copyright, Fair Use, and Plagiarism   The Web has evolved into an open, social, sharing environment where media is edited, mixed, and repurposed in mash-ups, and traditional copyright laws have become limiting. The standard "all rights reserved" presented a barrier to users who wanted their works shared by others. Creative Commons, a nonprofit organization, was founded in 2001 to increase the amount of material that is legally available for others to freely use. It has worked closely with legal experts to define a range of rights and developed Creative Commons licenses that content creators may use, depending on the level of permission they wish to offer. Creators may opt out of copyright protection entirely, placing their material in the public domain (no rights reserved). For those wishing to preserve some rights, six sets of conditions are available with varying levels of accommodation and restriction. Information about the six main licenses may be found at http://creativecommons.org/about/licenses/.

Still, most Web content is copyrighted and too often is misused without proper citation. Tools to detect plagiarized material are abundant (e.g., Turnitin or http://PlagiarismDetection.org). While they may be immediately useful to teachers, it is far more beneficial to teach students the 21st-century skills they will need when they leave the artificial context of school and enter a world in which self-monitoring is expected. The ease with which one can digitally cut and paste; the prevalence of mash-ups where bits of material are modified, combined, and repurposed; the layers of copyright available through Creative Commons—all make it imperative that students learn how to identify, paraphrase, and correctly cite another's work as they create original works of their own. Plagiarism.org is an excellent website to help students learn these skills, with examples and answers to questions such as "What is plagiarism?" "What is citation?" and "How do I cite sources?" Purdue University's Online Writing Lab (http://owl.english.purdue.edu/) is another resource students can consult as they use information from other sources in developing works of their own. Teaching students to check the origins of their work in free online tools such as Viper (www.scanmyessay.com) encourages them to demonstrate habits of responsible digital citizenship. You may wish to refer to Chapter 7 for other tools that support writing.

Access Versus Safety Many schools, concerned about students encountering offensive or objectionable material on the Web, employ Internet filtering software that screens for certain words or phrases and blocks access to that site. Unfortunately, filtering software is not perfect. First, it isn't very effective in blocking sites that promote hatred, violence, or illegal drugs (Consumer Reports Staff, 2005). Second, filtering software does not consider context when deciding whether a word such as *breast* is considered objectionable. Therefore, a student researching breast cancer would find many legitimate websites unavailable.

Two avenues of thought exist about the usefulness and appropriateness of installing filtering software in schools. The first line of reasoning goes something like, "The Internet, while offering valuable information, contains dangerous and inappropriate material from which students must be protected. Filtering software will prevent them from exposure to objectionable websites." Those holding the opposite viewpoint realize that students will not be shielded forever and believe that children should be taught what to do when they inadvertently run across offensive websites. They also see an opportunity to teach effective search skills that will increase the odds of obtaining useful, legitimate sites.

The Children's Internet Protection Act (CIPA), which was passed in 2000, requires public libraries that receive federal funding to install and use Internet filtering software. Following the Supreme Court's 2003 upholding of a challenge to CIPA, the Center for Democracy and Technology published a set of guidelines to assist libraries in complying with CIPA requirements in a manner promoting free speech and robust access to information. By 2003, 96 percent of all public schools used some type of blocking software (Kleiner & Lewis, 2003). Librarians expressed concern over blocked sites that are clearly legitimate, citing the time and inconvenience of adults manually unblocking sites and fearing that students will not alert them to sites that are inadvertently blocked. They also voiced concern about the process of deciding which sites should be withheld, stating that technology specialists and software companies, rather than educators, were the decision makers (Consumer Reports Staff, 2005).

Finding moderate ground by utilizing a combination of strategies may provide a sensible solution. Filters allow the user to set levels and types of content to filter. Search sites may have built-in filters (e.g., Google's SafeSearch, Yahoo! Kids, Lycos SearchGuard, Ask for Kids). For younger students, maximum protection may be required, with less interference desired for older students. Adjusting browser settings to disallow pop-up windows can reduce unwanted Web content. However, the technologies can only go so far in addressing this issue. Perhaps the most important issue is that information literacy is an essential skill, one that teachers and parents are obligated to impart to children. Resources such as NetSmartz (www.netsmartz.org) may be useful in helping students understand critical issues of Internet use. Vicki Davis recommends teaching students five steps for online safety to protect against cyberbullying or inappropriate website material. Her recommendation to take a screenshot is notable, as a screenshot provides evidence of items that may be removed, leaving no proof.

1. *Stop.* Stop what you are doing. Don't keep clicking.

2. *Screenshot.* Take a screenshot. Save a copy and print a copy.

3. *Block.* Anyone offensive should be blocked and removed as a friend if he or she is on your friends list.

4. *Tell.* Tell your teacher or network administrator (or your parents if you are at home) about the situation and give them a copy of the screenshot. When you have a problem, do not stop speaking out until you find someone who can help you.

5. *Share.* After talking with your parents and/or teacher, if the incident is appropriate to discuss, share it with others to promote Internet safety. (http://coolcatteacher .blogspot.com/2009/09/5-steps-to-online-safety.html)

Privacy   There are trade-offs between features, functionality, an individualized experience when using the Internet, and divulging personal information. We leave a trail of digital breadcrumbs each time we perform a search, place an online order, or register on a website to receive additional services or benefits. While that data collection may seem innocuous as it occurs on an individual basis, over time an astounding amount of information about our habits, preferences, and actions is amassed. When a search engine notes the searches one performs, this enables the tool to personalize your future service, such as suggesting searches based on your past queries, yet your privacy is compromised. The more personal information you divulge to search engines or any websites, the more vulnerable you are to possible misuse of that information. Among the U.S. Computer Emergency Readiness Team's (US-CERT) suggestions for limiting the amount of personal information that can be collected by others are to browse safely, use care in supplying personal information, look for sites that use SSL to encrypt your information, and limit the use of cookies. If you are interested in learning more about spyware, Web browser security settings, cookies, and other security issues, visit the US-CERT website at www.us-cert.gov/cas/tips/ST05-008.html.

Privacy issues are critical, and users don't always have control over the confidentiality of their data or actions. In May 2006, America Online (AOL) made an unauthorized release of about 20 million key word searches conducted by hundreds of thousands of its sub-scribers from March to May. The data were posted on a special AOL research website designed for the company to learn more about people's Internet searching habits. Although no names were attached to the search requests, some of the data were revealing enough to enable the identification of the people behind the queries (Nakashima, 2006).

Perhaps surprisingly, many people now freely and intentionally offer personal infor-mation. Much of this is used to target individuals for marketing commercial products and is not seen by the general public. Social software, however, gives people the opportunity to share publicly on blogs, wikis, and social networking sites. It is essential for students to understand that the purpose, design, and functionality of networking websites such as Facebook means that the pictures, comments, and other data they post may be seen by peo-ple they did not intend as viewers. Students should be aware that information they choose to share on the Internet might also be shared with others, resulting in multiple databases containing that information.

Using Information to Build Knowledge with Open-Ended, Student-Directed Research Projects

In open-ended and student-directed research projects, students identify an area of interest, formulate a plan for obtaining needed information, and then search the Internet to access that information, generally to produce some original work using their new knowledge. *Open ended* refers to the fact that the students are encouraged to learn as much as they can about the topic rather than simply finding answers to specific questions posed by the teacher. Good teachers use these projects to help students develop strategies to determine what information is important—to develop their own set of questions. *Student directed* implies that the students are in charge, making key decisions about search strategies, about which sites from the search returns look most promising, about what to collect, and about when to initiate conversations with information providers.

The Internet is a tool for facilitating knowledge exploration by learners. Although the Internet contains a wealth of information, it is little more than a virtual depository unless that information is transformed into knowledge through meaningful, reflective, active learning activities. Sending students on scavenger hunts or providing them with collections of websites does little to promote learning unless students are searching as a means to spe-cific outcomes. When information is purposefully manipulated and reconstructed in authentic, meaningful learning tasks, the Internet becomes a powerful educational tool. Web 2.0 tools such as social bookmarking and Twitter can enlarge the potential field of information, expanding the source base and linking with other people who can offer new perspectives and experiences to broaden understanding. In the next section, we examine how well constructed WebQuests can be used to build knowledge.

Building in complex learning goals strengthens the value of Internet-based learning. Exploration is most effective when learners articulate a clear purpose for their explo-rations—that is, exploring to find information to solve a problem, resolve an argument, construct an interpretation, and so on.

The Internet can be used as a tool to develop critical-thinking skills as well as provide access to a variety of information and human resources. Riel (2000) argues, "The challenge of the knowledge-centered dimension of learning is to balance knowledge construction activities with activities that help students develop the suite of mental tools needed for this task."

Focusing Searches Using WebQuests and Student-Created WebQuests

One popular and widespread instructional technique for using Internet information is the WebQuest. Unfortunately, the strong inquiry-based foundation for WebQuests as envisioned by their creator, Bernie Dodge, has often been ignored, with many WebQuests resembling little more than electronic worksheets. Well-designed WebQuests incorporate cooperative learning, consideration of multiple perspectives, analysis and synthesis of information, and creation of original products that demonstrate knowledge gained.

A good WebQuest is an open-ended and student-directed research project, exemplifying the characteristics of meaningful learning referenced in Figure 1.1—learning that is authentic, intentional, active, constructive, and cooperative. Working in teams, students typically assume different roles and responsibilities. Assigning roles in a WebQuest or other collaborative project is a method for recognizing and differentiating individual strengths. Students may struggle with written expression, yet exhibit amazing insight when offered the chance to design—technically or artistically.

Searching for information to be used in a WebQuest activity typically begins with a list of websites that have been previously selected either through the teacher's searching or from a website such as eThemes, mentioned in an earlier section. While a great deal of the information search and evaluation processes has already been done for students participating in a WebQuest, when students create WebQuests they take the lead in selecting and researching a topic of their choice. Engaging in a well-designed teacher-created WebQuest can be a terrific learning experience, but student-created WebQuests can be of even greater value. For example, students in two Chemistry 1 Advanced Placement classes brainstormed the topic "Nuclear Issues in the 21st Century" and identified a problem (Peterson & Koeck, 2001). After teacher-led brainstorming, responses were categorized to meet the teacher's instructional objectives. Student teams chose a category to develop, with the final WebQuest being a compilation of the categories.

To develop the WebQuest, students first evaluated existing WebQuests to understand the structure. They were introduced to the GAP model (Caverly, 2000, in Peterson & Koeck, 2001):

- **G**athering information
- **A**rranging information into meaningful formats
- Using technology tools to **P**resent that new knowledge to others

Searching for and critically analyzing information were seen as especially valuable for science students in developing inductive thinking. As teams decided what to include in their portion of the WebQuest, they engaged in further critical thinking as individuals presented and defended the information they had found. When the team reached consensus, team members used Inspiration software to create concept maps of their section. Each team had one person with web development skills whose responsibility was creating the actual web file for the WebQuest. When the WebQuest was completed, these students presented it to university faculty and preservice teachers. This type of authentic project whereby students actually create a WebQuest rather than simply participate in one raises the WebQuest concept to a new level. The cognitive and social skills required for constructing WebQuests offer a motivating, deep learning experience. Students made interdisciplinary connections and were challenged intellectually. At the same time, they gained experience with technology and presentation skills—and had fun!

Both learning from *and* developing a WebQuest involve synthesizing information and applying logical thinking. However, developing a WebQuest requires students to not just respond to a problem, but to generate and define that problem. Rather than just evaluate information within preselected resources, students must determine how to search for and evaluate the worth of resources to offer others (Peterson & Koeck, 2001).

Student-produced WebQuests engage problem solving. Developing a WebQuest requires a lot of purposeful information searching to fulfill a task that is designed by the students. Producing the WebQuest requires designing the task, the activities, the interface, and the procedures. These activities demand a lot of decision making, as does evaluation of the Internet resources that will be embedded within the WebQuest. We believe that even more valuable and constructive learning occurs when students produce a WebQuest than when they participate in a WebQuest; however, teachers will need to prepare and scaffold students in their work by letting them engage in WebQuests, evaluate and discuss them, and determine criteria for well-designed WebQuests. Teachers may find Dodge's resources at http://webquest.org/ and http://questgarden.com helpful for both creating and supporting students' creation of WebQuests.

Scientific Inquiry and Experimentation

An amazing number of websites associated with inquiry tasks are available to support students' diverse interests, with applications such as Flash animations offering highly interactive learning experiences. The Edheads website (www.edheads.org), for example, uses Flash to support investigations of force and simple machines, weather, and the human body.

The Web-based Inquiry Science Environment (WISE; wise.berkeley.edu) is a free online science learning environment for students in grades 5 to 12. This website, supported by the National Science Foundation, offers a learning environment for students to examine real-world evidence and analyze current scientific controversies. Free teacher registration generates a student registration code that identifies a class, allows students to register, and creates a class account on WISE. Teachers may create original projects, copy and use existing projects, and access management tools for student assessment and feedback. WISE can be a good starting place for generating ideas and sparking areas of interest for students.

Using only a Web browser, special WISE software guides students through "evidence" Web pages that provide content, "notes" and "hints" that encourage students to reflect, and other tools for data visualization, causal modeling, simulations, online discussion with classmates, and assessment (see Figure 2.8). WISE engages students in searching for information to use in authentic, problem-solving situations.

Figure 2.8

Images of the essential features of WISE, as seen in the "What Makes Plants Grow?" project for grades 4 to 6: a browser window lists the WISE inquiry steps and evidence about plants (background), reflection notes allow the student to respond to information, and a hint (foreground) supports the students as they are answering questions.

Other WISE projects include "Cycles of Malaria," where students learn about the biology of the disease, where it is prevalent, and how it is spread. They compare three different strategies for controlling the spread of malaria. In "How Far Does Light Go?" students consider competing hypotheses about whether light goes on forever or eventually dies out. After examining a number of scenarios supporting each hypothesis, students debate the issue with their classmates. "Wolves in Your Backyard" involves students learning about wolf biology and predator–prey relationships. They survey different perspectives on wolf population control, including issues of depredation, hunting, and wildlife management (http://wise.berkeley.edu/pages/intro/wiseIntro03.html).

Teachers who used WISE projects with students report that it increases classroom interaction, reveals science as it is in the real world, and offers exciting resources that motivate kids to learn. One teacher said, "Students who were unmotivated at first demonstrated a tremendous amount of knowledge on the subject matter as they presented their evidence for the debate." Another teacher thought that WISE helped her students with critical-thinking skills, causing them to ask, "'Does this make sense?'—instead of kids tending to swallow everything and saying, 'Oh, there. It's all true.' I liked how [the project] seemed to intrigue them, and I heard some great questions from the kids [that] wouldn't have come up if they had been reading a textbook" (http://wise.berkeley.edu/pages/what_teachers_say.php).

Collecting Data with Mobile Technologies

> Mobile devices are an integral part of children's lives and they are here to stay. Our national debate must shift from whether to use these devices to support learning, to understanding how and when they might best be used. Just as *Sesame Street* introduced generations of children and their families to the potential of television as an educational medium two generations ago, today's children will benefit if mobile becomes a force for learning and discovery in the next decade. (Schuler, 2009, p. 9)

Today's students are very different from those only a few years ago in terms of their experiences with and expectations of technology. This is a digital generation—one that has no memory of life without a multitude of mobile technology tools. Mobile devices come in many forms. They may be iPods and other mp3 players, digital cameras, personal digital assistants (PDAs), small tablet notebooks, iPads, or cell phones. All these and more are part of daily life for many young people, and the lines of functionality between these devices are blurring. Cell phones and PDAs take pictures and have calendar functions; iPods record video and play podcasts and videos transferred from a laptop or cell phone. Wireless technology augments the increasing number of things one can do with these devices, as easy access to the Internet allows one to upload and download data anywhere there is an accessible wireless access point.

Prensky (2001, 2003, 2005) has labeled this generation "digital natives" and cautions those who were not born into but later adopted digital technology (the "digital immigrants") about the different language spoken by natives versus immigrants. While many "immigrants" have embraced technology as fully as the "natives," the point is well taken— we must understand the fundamental differences between the way natives and immigrants perceive, value, and use technologies. Otherwise, we risk designing learning experiences with little relevance, interest, or meaning for students.

Cell Phones, iDevices, and PDAs

Many countries, notably countries in Europe, China, Japan, and the Philippines, are using cell phones as learning tools (Prensky, 2005). Prensky states, "Cell phones have enormous capabilities these days: voice, short messaging service (SMS), graphics, user-controlled operating systems, downloadables, browsers, camera functions (still and video), and geopositioning. Some have sensors, fingerprint readers, and voice recognition. Thumb keyboards and styluses as well as plug-in screens and headphones turn cell phones into both input and output mechanisms" (p. 12). Prensky envisions cell phones as tools for accessing animations to support learning, for narrating guided tours, or to access language or vocabulary training.

When one watches how quickly and effortlessly a teenager can key in a text message on a cell phone, it's reasonable to imagine a future where innovative educators take advantage of young people's familiarity with cell phones. The Kaiser Family Foundation reported that two-thirds (66%) of all 8- to 18-year-olds own their own cell phone, up from 39 percent five years ago (Rideout, Foehr, & Roberts, 2010). These numbers can be expected to increase as cell phones become as commonplace as televisions and radios.

Teachers have reported that different types of these handheld devices can be effective tools for instruction and positively impact student motivation (Crawford & Vahey, 2002; Swan, van't Hooft, & Kratcoski, 2005; Vahey & Crawford, 2002). The relative low cost and small size of mobile devices makes them ideal for ubiquitous learning and data collection in the field. Students can gather data and display and manipulate them to test predictions using mobile devices in authentic environments. Using wireless or 3G technologies, they can access the Internet while doing fieldwork. Field notes can be recorded using text, audio, and/or video.

For several years, most handhelds used in K–12 schools were Pocket PCs, which run a form of the Windows operating system, or devices running the Palm operating system. At one time, PDAs were a fast growing segment of handhelds; however, they have been eclipsed by iPads, iPod Touch, tablets, and cell phones. Palm has discontinued its educational program and no longer supports the former PDA models that schools used, referring to them as "historical devices." Many of the applications that ran on Palm handhelds have been reworked and are now available for downloading to an iPhone, iPad, or iPod Touch. The convergence of features and emergence of smart phones with computerlike operating systems makes them an inexpensive option for many educational purposes, including investigation. Schuler (2009) said, "While it is important to understand how the latest innovations in mobile technologies—GPS, QR Codes, accelerometers, etc.—can be used for education, in order to develop scalable models, one should also consider features that will become ubiquitous. Relying on features that are more common on less expensive phones will help ensure that mobile technologies can help close rather than amplify the digital divide" (p. 34).

Perhaps the most commonly perceived problem with handheld use is the small screen size. While reading on a miniature screen seems unworkable for many adults, it appears that children don't regard it as difficult (Prensky, 2003). Most students, accustomed to the scale of portable gaming devices and of texting on cell phones, have no trouble with the small screen. However, the inexpensive keyboards that can be purchased for some devices make them more closely resemble a computer and can make data input faster and easier. Mobile devices should be synched regularly with a computer to back up information. Other management issues include the need for regular recharging, physical use and storage of the devices throughout the school day, ownership, and acceptable use policies.

Sensor Technology

Sensor technology surrounds us, from red light traffic cameras to automatic soap dispensers to sensors that are integrated into a myriad of mobile devices, including global positioning systems (GPS). A sensor is a device that receives input to which it responds by converting the data to an electrical or optical signal that is recorded in digital or analog format. Sensor technology can support scientific investigation. *Probeware*, a term describing equipment and software used to gather and analyze data, can be combined with laptops or graphing calculators for highly interactive learning experiences. For example, Vernier's LabPro offers an assortment of sensors, software, and hardware interfaces that can be combined for collecting and analyzing data. This type of package might be used with a computer, graphing calculator, handheld or GPS unit, or on its own as a remote data collector. USB connections simplify the transfer of data from probes.

Using probeware sensors and interfaces with mobile devices facilitates interactive, inquiry-based learning by providing multiple representations of data as experiments are being conducted. Probes also make scientific experiments easier for students to perform and analyze (Tinker & Krajcik, 2001). Probeware is quite visual, with real-time data displayed as tables, graphs, meters, or values. Manipulating variables is easily accomplished, with instant visible results that graphically portray relationships, rules, and principles.

Probes can be used to support learning in chemistry, biology, math, and physics. They may measure such things as temperature, pH levels, voltage, pressure, force, motion, and magnetic fields. Probes use a transducer to convert the physical phenomena to an electrical signal, which is then converted to a number by analog interface circuitry or digitally and communicated to the computer. The analog interface may either be built into the sensor or be a separate piece of equipment in between the sensor and the computer.

Digital probes contain a microcomputer chip that can calibrate information and convert measurements to digital format. The sensor attaches to a laptop via the USB port, and additional software applications can extend what happens to data once they have been transferred. Built-in Bluetooth technology is another method of data exchange. Bluetooth uses radio frequencies to transfer information between Bluetooth-compatible devices nearby, like computers, mobile phones, and other handhelds.

Wireless technology can also allow students to share data with other students as it is being collected. Imagine teams of students who are collecting information about water quality in a river. Team data might be shared by mobile devices, allowing students in the field to analyze data, look for trends, formulate hypotheses, and be guided toward other investigation. Using Documents to Go on a cell phone or PDA, students could enter data in Excel spreadsheets or share data from graphing calculators attached to probes.

GPS

The GPS, a satellite-based navigation system comprised of a network of 24 satellites, was created by the U.S. Department of Defense for military applications but was made available for civilian use in the 1980s. GPS is free and works worldwide, anytime, in any type of weather.

Garmin, a navigation and communications equipment company, describes GPS functioning as follows:

> GPS satellites circle the earth twice a day in a very precise orbit and transmit signal information to earth. GPS receivers take this information and use triangulation to calculate the user's exact location. A GPS receiver must be locked on to the signal of at least three satellites to calculate a 2D position (latitude and longitude) and track movement. With four or more satellites in view, the receiver can determine the user's 3D position (latitude, longitude and altitude). Once the user's position has been determined, the GPS unit can calculate other information, such as speed, bearing, track, trip distance, distance to destination, sunrise and sunset time and more.

Mobile devices such as cell phones are an excellent source for built-in GPS, with half the phones in the United States equipped by late 2009 (Schuler, 2009). In other cases, small GPS units may work in conjunction with other mobile devices. Separately purchased GPS devices can be used in the field, with data transfer to a laptop or, later, to a desktop computer. A standard GPS receiver not only will place you on a map at any particular location but also will trace your path across a map as you move. If you leave your receiver on, it can stay in constant communication with GPS satellites to see how your location is changing.

GPS units can be used in an interesting activity known as geocaching. Like a treasure hunt, geocaching involves physically searching for a hidden cache whose location is given through GPS coordinates on a website. The cache container contains a logbook and items as rewards; finders are asked to leave something for the next person and to record the date and time in the logbook. On its own, geocaching utilizes students' problem-solving skills, mathematical thinking, and mapping abilities. Geocaching might be combined with a study of geology, the environment, or biology. As students navigate, they may encounter plants, animals, rocks, historical sites, and any number of things that lend themselves to additional learning. Teachers often find that nature guidebooks, digital cameras, audio and/or video recorders, and notepads are useful in GPS activities. Sensor technologies are a good fit when students take to the field for geocaching or other GPS work. There are many geocaching sites online; a good place to start is Geocaching—The Official Global GPS Cache Hunt Site (www.geocaching.com). GPS units and mobile devices can also be used in conjunction with geographic information systems (GIS) (see Chapter 9).

Conducting Field Experiments

Let's explore some uses of mobile technologies to see how they have been used with students in authentic learning situations. The following examples highlight the rapidly changing nature of technology, particularly in the realm of small handheld devices. Although Palm PDAs were used for these field activities, other mobile devices could easily substitute (e.g., iPad, smart phone, laptop). One widely used PDA application was Documents to Go, which allowed users to transfer Microsoft Office files between a computer and handheld. Documents to Go and Sketchy, both used in the following example, are among the thousands of apps now available through iTunes, with more being developed every day.

Water Analysis   Water quality evaluation is frequently conducted using handheld probes (Vahey & Crawford, 2002). Students take handhelds and probes to a nearby stream or other body of water. After individual students measure different points along the streambed, data are combined by beaming them to one another or aggregating them on one unit. When students return to the classroom, handhelds are used to graph and analyze the combined data set. For many teachers, finding nearby bodies of water to sample will be relatively easy. Depending on the results of the water analysis, students might research solutions for improving water quality, hypothesize about the effects on aquatic and amphibian life, determine where runoff is originating, or design a plan for filtering water.

NatureMapping   The NatureMapping Program (http://naturemappingfoundation.org) is combining GIS (see Chapter 9) use with data collection in authentic work that connects schools with experts and communities. The program's vision is "to create a national network that links natural resource agencies, academia and land planners with local communities primarily through schools." NatureMapping incorporates species identification and data collection; data analysis, statistics, and graphics; and computers, remote sensing, GIS, local area networking, and the Internet.

Diane Petersen (2005) described some NatureMapping work done in Waterville Elementary School in Waterville, Washington. Beginning in 1999, Petersen's fourth graders began working with local farmers to collect data about short-horned lizards, an at-risk species. Farmers, who were frequently in locations where these lizards might be spotted, logged information about when and where they were seen. Later, farmers and students worked together to locate fields on maps and create tables with the data. Using aerial photographs of farmers' fields overlaid on digital maps, computer maps were then generated that depicted lizard sightings. Students also made spreadsheets to display related data. Students then generated a question, analyzed the data, and selected what was needed to graph information answering the question. Petersen describes this project as strengthening the school–community relationship. The serious, real-life contribution students are making has resulted in students who view themselves as scientists, with technology enhancing the work and partnerships. Initially, students collected data, but because the farmers were frequently in their fields and available to log information, they supplied most data in this particular case. However, students can do similar data collection, using mobile or simple logging devices to record information.

Arbor Day/Earth Day Tree Exploration   Let's look next at an effective yet easy use of mobile devices to collect field data. Suzanne Stillwell, a fourth-grade teacher at a rural school in Hallsville, Missouri, described an Arbor Day/Earth Day activity using the school grounds as her students' laboratory. Before beginning the activity, students spent three 45-minute periods practicing with the technology so they would know how to use it. They also brainstormed data they could collect from trees on the school grounds. The information they decided to collect was girth of the tree (1 meter above the ground), height of the tree's shadow (correlated to the height of the tree, if measured at the right time of day), and types of leaf and tree identification. Students used this website to help understand the measurement of the tree's shadow: http://micro.magnet.fsu.edu/primer/java/scienceopticsu/shadows.

Each partner team selected two trees on the school grounds and did the following:

1. Took a picture of the tree using the handheld cameras

2. Collected a leaf sample and took a picture of the leaf

3. Measured the girth of the tree in centimeters and recorded the information in an Excel table in Documents to Go on the handheld

4. Measured the shadow of the tree and recorded the information in an Excel table in Documents to Go on the handheld

After returning to the classroom, students beamed their information about the trees to two other teams. Each team then had information on six trees. Students uploaded the tree data to computers and made graphs showing the information of tree girth and height.

Students used their leaf samples and digital pictures to identify trees with the Missouri Department of Conservation tree manual and these online sources: www.grownative.org/index.cfm and www.mdc.mo.gov/nathis/plantpage/flora/motrees/.

Because this was one of the first projects the students had done with handhelds, they were excited about the assignment. Some of the students figured out how to put the pictures of their trees in the Excel file with the graph and data table. There was strong motivation for students to record data and share information with each other through beaming between handhelds.

Denali National Park Fire Succession Study   This last example illustrates how sensor technology can be used along with other mobile devices. In the summer of 2004, the Denali Borough School District teamed with the Eastern Area Fire Management of the National Park Service to study fire succession by monitoring the vegetation recovery in three burn areas in Alaska's Denali National Park and Preserve. Using Palm handhelds equipped with digital cameras and SmartList to Go, a program that allows one to create, view, and manage databases on a handheld, students first created a field guide of plants and animals they observed.

Next, students used a Vernier temperature sensor (ImagiWorks) and software (ImagiProbe) to measure permafrost temperature and depth at each burn site. Documents to Go software (www.dataviz.com/products/documentstogo/) enabled the creation of a Microsoft Excel spreadsheet recording temperature data and numbers of plant species found in each transect.

Handhelds were synched with a laptop to transfer and combine data for a complete count of species coverage. Participants also represented their concept of fire succession by using handhelds to draw animations on their handhelds using Sketchy (see Figure 2.9).

In each of these instances, students are engaging in active, real-life work that goes beyond the classroom to involve data collection in the field. The use of technology enables students to measure, record, manipulate, share, and represent data as they are used to answer important questions. Activities such as these place students in the role of investigating scientists and motivate them through interesting, authentic work that is relevant to their world.

Figure 2.9

Student's sketchy animation about fire succession

Source: Published by the Concord Consortium.

Finding Opinions with Online Survey Tools

We live in a culture that is saturated with market research and opinion polls to find out what people think about all kinds of things. What is your opinion regarding this candidate, this issue, this media personality? What is your favorite (fill in the blank)? How often do you purchase this product, read this magazine, or eat at this restaurant? What do you think about the latest environmental problem? What are you willing to do or do without to solve it? Sampling is done via phone, paper questionnaires, and websites.

Online survey tools enable data collection opportunities across the curriculum. These tools range in functionality, ease of use, and cost. Some are free online survey websites (e.g., Free Online Surveys); others offer tiered services ranging from a free option to paid subscription levels. Frequent users may appreciate the added features that a subscription survey site offers (e.g., SurveyMonkey, Cool Surveys, Zoomerang). Free survey sites typically limit the number of questions, responses, and/or participants that are allowed. Subscription survey tools are more likely to allow unlimited surveys, customizing options, and data analysis tools that filter results to help users find patterns in the data. Other survey tool features can include sharing of results, downloadable files for export to spreadsheets, randomizing the order of answer choices to reduce bias, and requiring responses to questions the survey creator specifies.

Some online survey tools support participants' responses in real time after the survey has been created on the survey website. An example is Poll Everywhere, which collects responses sent by cell phone text messages, Twitter, or the Web and embed that data in live charts inside PowerPoint or Apple Keynote presentations. Mobiode, another survey tool, collects responses from cell phones, displaying results in real time on the Web interface or in Excel. Although many schools currently ban cell phone use, we envision a day when students are able to use these devices to enhance learning. A student might create a presentation on the effects of a city's recycling initiative and, during the presentation, survey other students in the class to determine their recycling habits. Of course, students could respond to such questions simply with raised hands, but this method provides anonymity and automatically presents results in a graph.

A third-grade teacher described using a simple online survey to begin a nutrition unit with her students. As students answered questions about their eating habits and knowledge of nutrition, they also learned math skills. After data were collected, students created graphs depicting information such as the number of students who ate breakfast every day, how frequently students drank soda, and their favorite food selected from a list of 12 items. These results served as a springboard for discussions concerning reasons that students selected cookies as their favorite food, the influence of sugar in our diets, cause and effect, healthy eating, and how to make good food choices.

While the nutrition survey was conducted within a classroom, online surveys enable data collection from a wide audience. Students who are creating surveys themselves first need guidance in creating well-constructed survey questions. Timmerman (2003) suggests looking at examples of poorly and well-written questions, explaining the difference between open-ended and closed-ended questions, and considering how easily responses can be analyzed and graphed. Table 2.2 provides suggestions and examples for writing good surveys.

Table 2.2 Suggestions for Writing Surveys

Keep it short. Ask essential questions; avoid asking unnecessary questions	Unnecessary: How often do you eat dinner at home? What time do you eat dinner? Better: How often do you eat dinner at home?
Use simple language	Complex: With what regularity do you frequent your preferred dining establishments? Better: How often do you eat at your favorite restaurants?
Include only one concept per question	More than one concept: Do you like the color and texture of the sofa fabric? Better: Do you like the sofa fabric? or 1. Do you like the color of the sofa fabric? 2. Do you like the texture of the sofa fabric?
Avoid biased or leading questions	Biased: Don't you agree that the school year begins too early? Better: Does the school year begin too early?
Avoid confusing questions where respondents are unclear as to what is being asked	Confusing: What do you think about the beginning of the school year? Better: What is your opinion about the timing of the school year's start?
Avoid double-barreled questions that contain more than one question where respondents may agree with one but not the other.	Double-barreled: Do you agree that the school year begins too early and the school board should do something about it? Better: Does the school year begin too early? (If the participant responds yes): Should the school board address this problem?

Survey participants may be members of the originating class, students in other classes within the school or in other schools, students in other countries, teachers, or parents, depending on the purpose of the survey. Community groups or organizations could be used to identify potential respondents. For example, students might contact the Audubon Society or World Wildlife Federation for an environmental survey needing expert opinions.

When students create surveys, they engage in learning that is intentional and authentic. Identifying the purpose of a survey, making decisions about the information that is needed, formulating well-designed questions that will elicit that information, and selecting the most appropriate respondents for gaining that information entail many cognitive processes. After data are collected, students must then analyze and evaluate the results, determining trends, possible causes and effects, and other phenomena that inform their purposes. Thus, an online survey may culminate in this data analysis or it might be the beginning of a larger, more inclusive project. For more on online surveys from an assessment perspective, see Chapter 10.

Conclusion

When students are given opportunities to investigate relevant, interesting phenomena and use the information they gather to solve problems, answer their questions, or inform others, they engage in learning that has significance and value. As we have seen, technologies can support and extend student investigations. Internet resources reach far beyond text files, with audio and video, graphics, and online simulations widely available. Tools such as online survey sites offer students a mechanism for data collection from a worldwide pool of participants. We are a digital information society, which means that it is imperative that students understand the online environment—the nature of online spaces, as well as the skills to access, manage, and evaluate information found there—in order to be well-educated, intelligent, 21st-century consumers and producers of information and knowledge.

We are also a mobile society. Wireless devices can enable children to engage in flexible learning environments that permeate their daily lives (Inkpen, 1999; Soloway et al., 2001). Soloway said, "The kids these days are not digital kids. The digital kids were in the '90s. The kids today are mobile, and there's a difference. Digital is the old way of thinking, mobile is the new way" (in Schuler, 2009). Traditional lab settings that typically focus on the process of students collecting data are enhanced by the use of mobile devices that encourage analysis and problem solving. Students can collect data, display, and manipulate them to test predictions using mobile devices. While these technologies have much to offer, their value is determined largely by the way teachers integrate them into the curriculum. When thoughtfully used to promote active, reflective, complex learning, Internet and mobile technologies are at their best.

NET Standards potentially engaged by inquiry activities described in this chapter:

3. **Research and Information Fluency**
   a. Plan strategies to guide inquiry

b. Locate, organize, analyze, evaluate, synthesize, and ethically use information from a variety of sources and media

c. Evaluate and select information sources and digital tools based on the appropriateness to specific tasks

d. Process data and report results

4. **Critical Thinking, Problem Solving, and Decision Making**

a. Identify and define authentic problems and significant questions for investigation

b. Plan and manage activities to develop a solution or complete a project

c. Collect and analyze data to identify solutions and/or make informed decisions

d. Use multiple processes and diverse perspectives to explore alternative solutions

6. **Technology Operations and Concepts**

a. Understand and use technology systems

21st Century Skills potentially engaged by inquiry activities described in this chapter:

Reason Effectively

- Use various types of reasoning (inductive, deductive, etc.) as appropriate to the situation

Make Judgments and Decisions

- Effectively analyze and evaluate evidence, arguments, claims, and beliefs
- Analyze and evaluate major alternative points of view
- Synthesize and make connections between information and arguments
- Interpret information and draw conclusions based on the best analysis
- Reflect critically on learning experiences and processes

Access and Evaluate Information

- Access information efficiently (time) and effectively (sources)
- Evaluate information critically and competently

Use and Manage Information

- Use information accurately and creatively for the issue or problem at hand
- Manage the flow of information from a wide variety of sources
- Apply a fundamental understanding of the ethical/legal issues surrounding the access and use of information

Analyze Media

- Understand both how and why media messages are constructed, and for what purposes
- Examine how individuals interpret messages differently, how values and points of view are included or excluded, and how media can influence beliefs and behaviors
- Apply a fundamental understanding of the ethical/legal issues surrounding the access and use of media

Apply Technology Effectively

- Use technology as a tool to research, organize, evaluate, and communicate information

- Use digital technologies (computers, PDAs, media players, GPS, etc.), communication/networking tools and social networks appropriately to access, manage, integrate, evaluate, and create information to successfully function in a knowledge economy

- Apply a fundamental understanding of the ethical/legal issues surrounding the access and use of information technologies

Things to Think About

Here are some questions to think about as you consider using Internet resources, mobile devices, and other investigative technologies with students.

1. What are the implications for teaching and learning when these tools are included in instruction?

2. What impact will (can) mobile devices have on the curriculum?

3. How can mobile devices be used to augment your existing curriculum?

4. Who will provide the funding, support, and training for use of mobile devices?

5. Some people object to students using mobile devices, arguing that these are unnecessary, frivolous, and little more than toys. How would you respond?

6. How can we evaluate the effectiveness of these devices?

7. How will we manage student use of mobile devices?

8. What will happen if a student loses or breaks a mobile device?

9. How will mobile devices be physically cared for, especially if students take them home at night?

10. What information literacy skills do my students have?

11. What do my students need to know before engaging in Internet searches?

12. Are students' information searches conducted in a meaningful context?

13. How are students using the information they gain from Internet searches?

14. What is the Internet? Is it the computers, the programs, and multimedia documents that people store and make available, or is it the people who contribute the ideas? Or is the Internet "only minds."

15. Given the potential for students to encounter undesirable material on the Internet, what is the appropriate balance between protection and free access to information?

References

Caverly, D. C. (2000). Technology and the "Knowledge Age." In D. B. Lundell & J. L. Higbee (Eds.), Proceedings of the First Intentional Meeting on Future Directions in Developmental Education [Online] (pp. 34–36). Minneapolis: University of Minnesota, General College and The Center for Research on Developmental Education and Urban Literacy. Available: education.umn.edu/CRDEUL/pdf/proceedings/1-proceedings.pdf

Consumer Reports Staff. (2005, June). Filtering software: Better but still fallible. *Consumer Reports*, PDC 36–38. Retrieved from www.consumerreports.org/cro/electronics-computers/internet-filtering-software-605/overview/index.htm

Costa, A., & Kallick, B. (2000). *Habits of mind: A developmental series*. Alexandria, VA: Association for Supervision and Curriculum Development.

Crawford, V., & Vahey, P. (2002). *Palm Education Pioneers Program: March, 2002 Evaluation Report*. Menlo Park, CA: SRI International.

Fidel, R., Davies, R. K., Douglass, M. H., Kohlder, J. K., Hopkins, C. J., Kushner, E. J., et al. (1999). A visit to the information mall: Web searching behavior of high school students. *Journal of the American Society for Information Science, 50*(1), 24–37.

Foley, S. (2006, August 13). To Google or not to Google? It's a legal question. *The Independent.* Retrieved from www.independent.co.uk/news/business/news/to-google-or-not-to-google-its-a-legal-question-411600.html

Harris, S. D. (2006, July 7). Dictionary adds verb: To Google. *San Jose Mercury News*. Retrieved from www.mercurynews.com.

Inkpen, K. M. (1999). Designing handheld technologies for kids. *Personal Technologies Journal, 3*(1/2), 81–89.

Johnson, L., Levine, A., & Smith, R. (2007). *2007 Horizon Report*. Austin, TX: The New Media Consortium.

Johnson, L., Smith, R., Levine, A., & Haywood, K. (2010). *2010 Horizon Report: K–12 edition*. Austin, TX: The New Media Consortium Retrieved from www.cosn.org/horizon/

Jonassen, D. H., & Colaric, S. (2001). Information landfills contain knowledge; searching equals learning; hyperlinking is good instruction; and other myths about learning from the Internet. *Computers in Schools, 17*(3/4, Pt. I), 159–170.

Kelly, D. (2000). Online research skills for students. *Classroom Connect, 7*(2), 6.

Kleiner, A., & Lewis, L. (2003). *Internet access in U.S. public schools and classrooms: 1994–2002* (NCES 2004-011). Washington, DC: U.S. Department of Education, National Center for Education Statistics.

Nakashima, E. (2006, August 8). AOL takes down site with users' search data. *Washington Post*, p. D01. Retrieved from www.washingtonpost.com/wp-dyn/content/article/2006/08/07/AR2006080701150.html

Petersen, D. (2005, April). NatureMapping Takes Kids—and Technology—Outside and into Active Learning. *Edutopia*. Retrieved from www.edutopia.org/naturemapping

Peterson, C. L., & Koeck , D. C. (2001). When students create their own webquests. *Learning & Leading with Technology* 29.

Prensky, M. (2001). Digital natives, digital immigrants. *On the Horizon, 9*(5), 1–2. Retrieved July 16, 2006, from www.marcprensy.com/writing

Prensky, M. (2003). "But the screen is too small . . ." Sorry, "digital immigrants"—cell phones—not computers—are the future of education. Retrieved from www.marcprensky.com/writing/

Prensky, M. (2005). Learning in the Digital Age. *Educational Leadership, 63*(4), 8–13. Retrieved from www.siprep.org/prodev/documents/Prensky.pdf

Rideout, V., Foehr, U., & Roberts, D. (2010). *Generation M2: Media in the lives of 8- to 18-year-olds.* Kaiser Family Foundation: Menlo Park, CA.

Riel, M. (2000, September 11 & 12). New designs for connected teaching and learning. Paper presented at the Secretary's Conference on Educational Technology, Washington, DC. Retrieved from www.gse.uci.edu/mriel/whitepaper/

Schacter, J., Chung, G. K. W. K., & Dorr, A. (1998). Children's Internet searching on complex problem: Performance and process analyses. *Journal of the American Society for Information Science, 49*, 840–850.

Shuler, C. (2009). *Pockets of potential: Using mobile technologies to promote children's learning.* New York: The Joan Ganz Cooney Center at Sesame Workshop.

Soloway, E., Norris, C., Blumenfeld, P., Fishman, B., Krajcik, J., & Marx, R. (2001). Log on education: Handheld devices are ready-at-hand. *Communications of the ACM, 44*(6), 15–20.

Swan, K., van't Hooft, M., & Kratcoski, A. (2005). Uses and effects of mobile computing devices in K–8 classrooms. *Journal of Research on Technology in Education, 38*(1), 99–112.

Tallman, J., & Joyce, M. (2005, June). *What's new with the I-Search research/writing process?* Paper presented at the American Association of School Librarians 12th National Conference and Exhibition, Chicago, IL.

Timmerman, A. (2003). Survey says online survey tools have rich instructional applications. *Learning & Leading with Technology, 31*(2), 10–13, 55.

Tinker, R., & Krajcik, J. (Eds.). (2001). *Portable technologies: Science learning in context.* New York: Kluwer Academic/Plenum.

Vahey, P., & Crawford, V. (2002). *Palm Education Pioneers Program: Final evaluation report.* Menlo Park, CA: SRI International.

Web-based Education Commission. (2000). The power of the Internet for learning: Moving from promise to practice (Report). Washington, DC: U.S. Department of Education.

Experimenting with Technologies

Shutterstock

Chapter Objectives

1. Describe how microworlds support hypothesis generation

2. Show how technology simulations can support experimentation

3. Predict the effects of gaming on student performance

4. Describe how multiuser virtual environments can enhance learning

5. Describe how experimenting with different technologies support the development of NETS and 21st Century Skills

Learning to Reason Causally

In this chapter, we describe how students can use technologies to conduct experiments. Experimentation is a form of investigation or examination of factors in order to test hypotheses. As the headings in this chapter indicate, exploration involves hypothesizing, conjecturing, speculating, and testing. What does each of these mental activities have in common?

Exploring, hypothesizing, conjecturing, experimenting, speculating, and testing all require that students reason causally, that is, apply their understanding of cause-effect relationships to generate hypotheses, conjectures or speculations and test them. Causal reasoning supports two primary kinds of thinking by students. Reasoning from a set of conditions or states of an event to the possible effect(s) that may result from those states is called *prediction*. Predicting the effects of some changes in a set of conditions is the essence of scientific experimentation (or, hypothesis generation). The two primary functions of prediction are forecasting an event and testing hypotheses to confirm or refute scientific assumptions. Forecasting is used regularly by economists and meteorologists to predict changes in economic or meteorological conditions based on changes in the markets or in the weather conditions. Predictions also support experimentation; they are the hypotheses of experiments. A physicist, for example, predicts (hypothesizes) that the greater the application of a force to an object, the greater will be the change in the state of that object. Scientific predictions are empirically tested for their validity. A psychologist may predict that changes in environmental conditions, stress for example, will affect a person's behavior. Predictions assume a deterministic relationship between cause and effect, that is, that forces in the cause reliably determine an effect. Aristotle believed that everything is determined in accordance with causal rules. Prediction and hypothesizing are the basis of scientific inquiry and so supports most science standards.

When an outcome or state exists for which the causal agent is unknown, then an inference is required. That is, reasoning backward from effect to cause requires the process of inference. A primary function of inferences is diagnosis. Diagnosis is the identification of a cause, an origin, or a reason for something that has occurred. In medicine, diagnosis seeks to identify the cause or origin of a disease or disorder as determined by medical diagnosis. For example, based on symptoms, historical factors, and test results of patients that are thought to be abnormal, a physician attempts to infer the cause(s) of that illness state. Inferences are less common in school curricula than predictions, except when instruction is problem-based. Problems are as likely to be inferential as they are predictive.

Among the most important kinds of thinking that can be fostered by technology use is causal reasoning. Causal reasoning is among the most important and commonly used kinds of thinking that exist. In this chapter, we describe a number of technologies (microworlds, virtual laboratories, virtual worlds, simulations, and games) that require that students think causally while making hypotheses, conjectures, speculations, and so on.

Hypothesizing with Microworlds

The term *microworld* was coined by Seymour Papert (1980) to describe explorational learning environments that used Logo turtles to learn principles of geometry. Logo is a very simple computer programming language that provides learners with simple commands to direct the computerized turtles to create their own personal, visual worlds. Learners enter commands to manipulate a turtle on the screen in an effort to create more elaborate renderings, thus becoming familiar with "powerful ideas" underlying the turtle's operations, ideas such as variables, procedures, and recursion. The computer should be an "object to think with," according to Papert. Logo is, Papert argued, an ideal environment for creating microworlds, which are constrained problem spaces that resemble existing problems in the real world. These microworlds are generated by learners so they are inherently interesting to learners (experimenting to "see if I can do that"). Students use simple commands to construct simple objects on the screen. They can also build more complex procedures that call on simple procedures, which may call on other procedures. The resulting projects represent microworlds.

Although the theoretical rationale for Logo microworlds was strong, the procedures used to create Logo microworlds and the programming skills they require are not very generalizable. Although Logo is a syntactically simple language, it still requires several months of practice to develop skills sufficient for easily creating microworlds, and some students never become proficient. Further, many teachers are not comfortable teaching these "programming skills."

Nevertheless, the idea of microworlds as problem exploration and experimentation spaces is indeed a powerful idea. Many other microworld environments have been created that offer the exploratory advantages of Logo without the requirement of learning a programming language. They are constrained (or simplified) versions of reality that enable learners to manipulate variables and experiments within the parameters of some system. Although this kind of microworld does not always allow students to construct their own exploration spaces, they do enable learners to represent their own thinking in the ways that they explore, manipulate, and experiment with the environment.

Microworlds can assume many forms in different knowledge domains. They are primarily exploratory learning environments often in the form of simulations of real-world phenomena in which learners manipulate or create objects and test their effects on one another. "Microworlds present students with a simple model of a part of the world" (Hanna, 1986, p. 197) allowing learners to control those phenomena and construct deeper-level knowledge of the phenomena they are manipulating. Microworlds provide learners with the observation and manipulation tools necessary for exploring and testing objects in their microworld. They have proven extremely effective in engaging learners in higher-order thinking such as hypothesis testing and speculating.

There are many other fine examples of microworlds, such as ThinkerTools (White, 1993). These environments share at least two important characteristics. They usually provide single representations of phenomena, and they provide immediate feedback when learners try something out. The learner generates predictions about how some objects in the microworld will behave. Based on the prediction, the student manipulates the objects, and the microworld shows how the objects behave based on that manipulation. The way the system performs functions as feedback that the learners must interpret and use to revise their conceptual model of the domain. It is important that this feedback comes about as a natural consequence of using the microworld.

Interactive Physics

Interactive Physics (www.design-simulation.com/IP/) is a site that offers microworlds for exploring topics in physics, such as momentum, force, acceleration, and so on. Each experiment in Interactive Physics is a microworld that simulates a physical phenomenon, allowing the learner to easily manipulate several attributes of the world, such as gravity, air resistance, elasticity of bodies, and various surface parameters. More important, learners can use the tools and objects to design their own experiments to model Newtonian phenomena. Having learners design their own experiments to test a hypothesis is a key aspect of the inquiry-based science-teaching paradigm currently being promoted by most science standards.

The experiment in Figure 3.1 was developed by students using the building blocks shown on the left side of Figure 3.1 to test the effects of a one-kilogram projectile on a ten-kilogram pendulum. Learners can also change the views of the world by showing grids, rulers, vectors, axes, center of mass, and mass names. Students can turn on a tracker, which shows the motion of objects. They can also select meters, such as velocity, acceleration, momentum, various forces (friction, gravity, air), and rotation in order to measure the effects of changes in the variables that they designate. Interactive Physics is an excellent example of a microworld because the experiments are simple to create and use; students also get immediate feedback on their conceptual understanding when they run the experiment they constructed. Further, by simulating these experiments with technology, teachers and schools don't need to invest in the thousands of dollars of equipment and many hours

Figure 3.1

Experiment in Interactive Physics

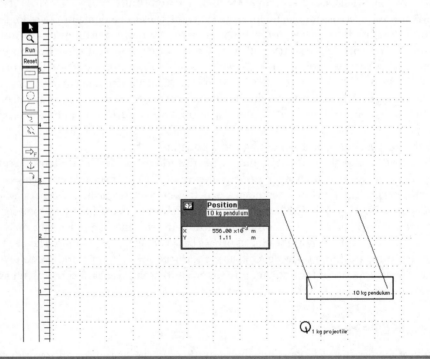

of work that would be required to set up the actual physics experiments that are contained in this environment.

SimCalc

SimCalc (www.kaputcenter.umassd.edu/projects/simcalc) is a microworld designed to introduce elementary students to calculus concepts. SimCalc consists of animated worlds and dynamic graphs in which actors move according to graphs that are defined by mathematical functions. By exploring the movement of the actors in the simulations and seeing the graphs of their activity, students begin to understand important calculus ideas. In the SimCalc activity illustrated in Figure 3.2, students match two motions. By doing so, they learn how velocity and position graphs relate to each other. Students must match the motion of the green and red graphs. To do this, they can change either graph. They iteratively run the simulation to see if they got it right. Students may also use the link to MathWorld (http://mathworld.wolfram .com) to enter their own bodily motion. For example, a student can walk across the classroom, and their motions would be entered into MathWorlds through sensing equipment. MathWorld plots their motion, enabling the students to explore the properties of their own motion.

Figure 3.2

Experiment in MathWorld

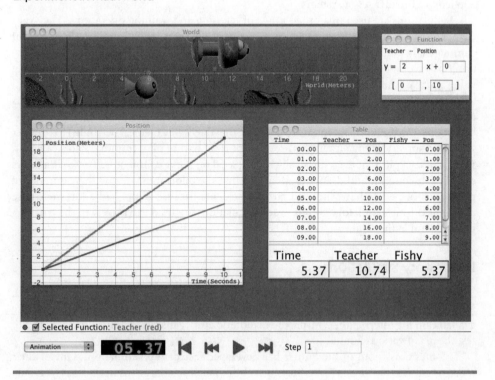

Microworlds are generally very specific to a content domain. SimCalc is useful only for supporting math learning, while Interactive Physics is useful only for testing concepts in physics. Nearly every microworld has been developed to support math and science learning outcomes. They cannot be used for any other purpose. However, they are engaging, so students usually expend a great deal of effort experimenting with specific microworlds.

Experimenting with Simulations

The next two kinds of environments that we describe are forms of simulations. Simulations are imitations of some real thing, state of affairs, or process. Simulations imitate phenomena by allowing learners to manipulate key characteristics or variables within a physical or abstract system. Because of their computational capabilities, computers are frequently used to build simulations of real-life situations. The simulation designer builds a model of the phenomena or processes that enable learners to see how the system works. By changing variables, students make predictions about the behavior of the system, a form of causal reasoning (as described early in the chapter). You may be wondering how microworlds and simulations differ. The easy answer is not much. Microworlds are a form of simulation that addresses a fairly specific phenomenon. Microworlds often provide learners with the ability to represent their own models, though not always. Simulations, on the other hand, can be applied to a broader set of systems.

Simulations are used in a broad range of teaching and training operations. They vary tremendously in detail and complexity. A search of the Internet will produce hundreds of commercially available educational simulations. For instance, numerous medical simulations exist to support medical training. These simulations typically present a patient using video and allow the medical trainee to examine the patient, order tests, make diagnoses, and test those diagnoses (inference making) by treating the simulated patient. Those patients may be presented on a computer screen or in the form of a dummy that can be manipulated. Some medical simulations are so complex that they allow medical personnel to conduct simulated surgery. Flight simulators are an important part of pilot training. Pilots can sit in simulated cockpits that even physically move based on flight commands. These simulators can present complex and dramatic situations that the pilots must deal with. A number of planeloads of people have survived airline incidents because pilots had addressed those problems during simulator training. Such simulations are used extensively in the trucking industry and in the military.

Laboratory Simulations

Among the most commonly available educational simulations are laboratory simulations. Many of these, such as the physics and chemistry lab simulation illustrated in Figure 3.3, are available on the Internet (e.g., http://phet.colorado.edu). This simulation allows learners to test the pH of various liquids.

NASA's Classroom of the Future has developed fascinating simulations. One of their most recent innovations is CyberSurgeons (http://site.cybersurgeons.net). The CyberSurgeons simulation provides an authentic way for high school students to apply science

Figure 3.3

Online Chemistry Simulation

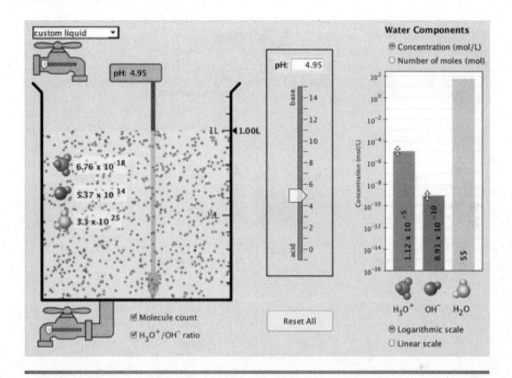

Reprinted with the permission of PhET Interactive Simulations, University of Colorado at Boulder. Access online at: http://phet.colorado.edu.

knowledge and skills. The simulation addresses numerous national and state science standards related to human body systems and the disease process. In order to complete the mission, students become part of the fictional CyberSurgeons remote trauma unit on a mercy ship. The simulated ship is equipped with a high-tech hospital and medical research capabilities, state-of-the-art high-end communications systems, and dedicated satellites to relay information. The mission is conducted through a Web/videoconference hookup from your classroom to the Challenger Learning Center at the Center for Educational Technologies at Wheeling Jesuit University in Wheeling, WV.

Before the live simulation, students learn how to analyze and apply simple datasets to medical situations. On mission day students connect live for 60 to 90 minutes with the "chief medical officer," played by a professional educator at the Challenger Learning Center. As they travel up the Amazon River, your teams of students receive alerts from research stations located in ports along the way. In real time your students will diagnose various maladies and recommend treatment (see prescription pads in Figure 3.4). The students use an array of computer tools during the mission, including a database that links symptoms,

Figure 3.4

Prescription Pads for Student CyberSurgeons

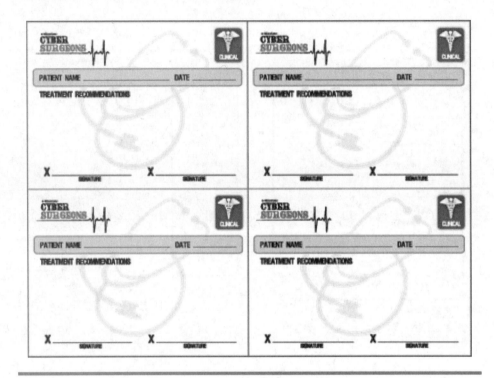

Reprinted with permission of the Center for Educational Technologies, Wheeling Jesuit University.

possible conditions, test results, and treatment options. Simulations allow students to apply what they are learning, so they understand it better.

Urban Simulations

Among the most popular and effective simulations for use in schools (especially social studies) is the urban or city simulator. City simulators were first developed for urban planners to understand how cities are likely to evolve in response to various policy decisions. They often include aspects that we frequently think of occurring in computerized games (see description of games later in this chapter). SimCity (http://simcitysocieties.ea.com/index.php) was among the first urban simulations and is now available in several versions. Students make decisions about land use and transportation. While playing SimCity, students can create characters, known as Sims, who will engage other Sims and provide players with feedback on what is going on around the city. Your Sims also experience city life. They get stuck in traffic. Players can also create mountains, valleys, and forests to surround their city as well as cause tornadoes, volcanoes, or meteor showers to challenge the community. Students may act as the mayor, who runs the city and connects their city with others in the region that are sharing or competing for resources. The mayor also dispatches emergency vehicles to deal with the natural and unnatural disasters that you create. SimCity also allows group play, computer conferences, and chat lines through the Internet. The complexity of simulations such as SimCity helps students to understand the systemic nature of organizations. Problems in SimCity are political, social, economic, historical, and cultural and cannot be solved using a single perspective. That is the nature of everyday problems that plague real cities throughout the world.

Simulation Builders

When simulations exist that meet your students' learning needs, they should be used judiciously to support meaningful learning. When they are not available (the more likely situation), then you may wish to create your own simulations. Building simulations can be a complex design and development activity, so we do not recommend the process for everyone. You need to be dedicated to the task in order to be successful. Fortunately, a number of systems have been created to help you to develop simulations. One of the best has been developed at the University of Twente in the Netherlands. Their simulation builder is called SimQuest (www.simquest.com). Don't worry. There are instructions in English. And don't forget; it's free. If you, as a teacher, do not have time to build a simulation (very understandable), your students should have no difficulties in developing a simulation. When students build the simulation, they learn more than playing a simulation.

As an example, a simulation of a sewage plant was built using SimQuest (Figure 3.5). The application is part of a series of courses about wastewater technology and can be used as a starting and end point of such a course. The students in this simulation get to operate a working sewage plant. This simulation may be useful in learning how biological processes work.

Researchers at the Massachusetts Institute of Technology (Klopfer, 2008) have developed software for constructing Augmented Reality (AR) simulations with handheld devices (http://education.mit.edu/drupal/ar). These simulations help students understand scientific concepts and principles in ecology, environmental science, geological sciences, health sciences, history, economics, local sociology, math and language arts by embedding them in lifelike situations.

Players of the outdoor game Environmental Detectives (ED) tried to uncover the source of a toxic spill. They used handheld computers with GPS to collect and analyze simulated environmental data and interviewed virtual characters. These simulations are engaging for students and are specific to their geographic location. The researchers have also created the Outdoor Augmented Reality Toolkit, a drag and drop based environment for creating AR Games.

Venturing into Games

Games are among the oldest forms of entertainment in the world. In addition to sporting games, board games, and social games, newer kinds of video and computer-based games can be used to support meaningful learning in classrooms. In this brief section, we describe how different kinds of computer games can be used in classrooms.

Figure 3.5

Simulation of Sewage Plant

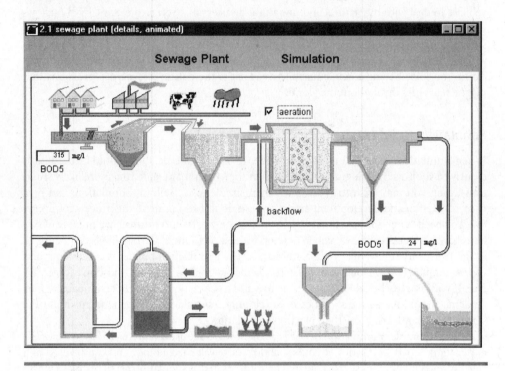

Source: van Joolingen & de Jong (2003). SimQuest. Reprinted with permission.

Among the oldest forms of computer-based educational games are quiz games, where quizzes are embedded in a quiz show context. For example, Games2Train (www .games2train.com) produces a game maker called Pick-it! for teachers to construct quiz games (see Figure 3.6). The game maker resembles the television quiz show, *Jeopardy*, allowing game players to select topics and values and play against others. The degree of meaningfulness of the learning from these games depends on the nature of the responses that are required. More often than not, quiz games require only memorization performance, although there is no reason that teachers could not add higher-order questions to the game, rather than memorization.

More complex games, such as the different versions of Sid Meier's Civilization (http:// civilization.com), engage students in complex problem solving while trying to manage their civilization. Students can select different civilizations to explore, from Sumerians to the mystical Mayans. In the game, students can map the world using satellite images. They can form armies and attack other civilizations or forge alliances with them. They can choose the form of government they wish to impose on their civilization (e.g., Fascism, Feudalism, Tribal

Figure 3.6

Pick-it! Interface

Council, and Imperialism). They can also use a well-developed trade system to manage resources, trade routes and the spread of technology. Figure 3.7 shows a number of civilizations that must learn to interact with each other peacefully or pugilistically. Civilization is obviously appropriate for social studies classes in which the teacher wants students to understand the political, military, social, cultural, and historical complexities of the world.

Games, especially complex, interactive games such as Civilization, can engage learners in very meaningful learning. Gee (2003) has identified a number of principles that underlie modern game design that can teach us a lot about learning. We list some of them here.

Active, Critical Learning Principle
All aspects of the learning environment (including the ways in which the domain is designed and presented) are set up to encourage active and critical, not passive, learning.

Semiotic Domains Principle
Learning involves mastering, at some level, semiotic domains, and being able to participate, at some level, in the affinity group or groups connected to them.

Figure 3.7

Different Cities in Civilization

Source: © 2005 Sid Meier's *Civilization III*, Firaxis Games, Take-Two Interactive, Inc.

"Psychosocial Moratorium" Principle

Learners can take risks in a space where real-world consequences are lowered.

Committed Learning Principle

Learners participate in an extended engagement (lots of effort and practice) as extensions of their real-world identities in relation to a virtual identity to which they feel some commitment and a virtual world that they find compelling.

Identity Principle

Learning involves taking on and playing with identities in such a way that the learner has real choices (in developing the virtual identity) and ample opportunities to meditate on the relationship between new identities and old ones. There is a tripartite play of identities as learners relate, and reflect on, their multiple real-world identities, a virtual identity, and a projective identity.

Practice Principle

Learners get lots and lots of practice in a context where the practice is not boring (i.e., in a virtual world that is compelling to learners on their own terms and where the learners experience ongoing success). They spend lots of time on task.

Probing Principle

Learning is a cycle of probing the world (doing something); reflecting in and on this action and, on this basis, forming a hypothesis; reprobing the world to test this hypothesis; and then accepting or rethinking the hypothesis.

Situated Meaning Principle

The meanings of signs (words, actions, objects, artifacts, symbols, texts, etc.) are situated in embodied experience. Meanings are not abstract or decontextualized. Whatever meanings are constructed are discovered bottom up via embodied experiences.

Multimodal Principle

Meaning and knowledge are built up through various modalities (images, texts, symbols, interactions, abstract design, sound, etc.), not just words.

Discovery Principle

Overt telling is kept to a well-thought-out minimum, allowing ample opportunity for the learner to experiment and make discoveries.

Not all computerized games represent these principles. Many games expose students to competition over an uninteresting task that may also engage only recall or memorization. These are good for filling classroom time, and it is likely that the students will even enjoy it. As with any technology-based activity, you must examine the nature of the task that you are engaging students in.

Immersing into Virtual Worlds

Students may also learn to interact with virtual worlds that combine many aspects of simulations and games. A virtual world is a realistic, three-dimensional computer simulation in which users identify themselves as an avatar while interacting with other users. Many virtual worlds support multiple users playing with or against each other. The simulated world appears and functions similarly to the real world. Numerous commercial virtual worlds can be used in classrooms. For instance, Entropia Universe is an economic virtual world where Entropia currency can be traded with real-world funds or used to purchase virtual land and equipment or to support a virtual person (avatar) in the Virtual Universe. Because Entropia uses a cash economy, virtual items inside the Universe actually have a real cash value (they are frequently traded on the Internet), they can be bought and sold, and the proceeds may be saved in another form of currency. Numerous virtual worlds support complex user interactions.

One of the very best multiuser virtual environments available is Quest Atlantis (http://atlantis.crlt.indiana.edu/). Quest Atlantis is a virtual world that was designed to support a

Figure 3.8

Students on a Quest in Quest Atlantis

Reprinted with permission.

variety of learning tasks for 9- to 16-year-old students that are tied to academic standards in a 3-D immersive environment (Barab, Thomas, Carteaux, & Tuzun, 2005; see Figure 3.8). Quest Atlantis combines attributes of commercial games with research-based educational practice. Quest Atlantis was designed based on the belief that play can engage children in deeper level thinking. Quest Atlantis includes 3-D worlds such as Unity World (emphasizing diversity issues), Ecology World, and Healthy World (emphasizing nutrition). Students use avatars to move through these worlds, meet other avatars, and participate in collaborative and socially responsible activities, while completing different quests. A quest is an engaging curricular task designed to be entertaining yet educational. For example, a quest in Habitat Village in Ecology World includes the following goals:

- Choose an animal that lives in your area, but you know little about
- Find out about the habits of that animal, where it lives, and what it uses for shelter
- Return to your personal digital assistant and submit a story about your animal and what it uses for shelter

Completing this quest requires that students engage in socially and educationally meaningful activities, such as conducting field studies, interviewing others, conducting research about community problems, examining current events from different perspectives, writing journals, and solving problems. While fulfilling their quests, they converse with other students as well as mentors. Thousands of students from all over the world regularly use Quest Atlantis in their classrooms.

Quest Atlantis is more than a computer game. It consists of a multiuser virtual environment that immerses children in educational tasks as part of an online adventure to save Atlantis from disaster, educational quests in that environment, unit plans for teachers, comic books, a novel, a board game, trading cards, a series of social commitments, and various characters using the environment. Research has shown that students learn significant amounts in science and social studies areas as well as gain a stronger sense of academic self-efficacy. Many virtual worlds are coming online. Here are a few others.

SparkTop (www.sparktop.org) is a site for kids with learning disabilities. Kids can find an accepting community to hang out in, low-stress opportunities to be creative, recognition for their unique talents and strengths, information on why they may struggle sometimes, and maybe just a little time to relax and have fun. It offers games, quizzes, music, message boards, animated programs and lots of positive messages, with many of the commands spoken as well as written.

Woogi World (www.woogiworld.com) is, as its website says, "a safe and engaging virtual school where elementary-age children worldwide learn age-appropriate core educational content, essential 21st-century skills, cyber safety and security, and responsible and ethical behavior that will yield academic success and the leaders of the future."

Whyville (whyville.net/smmk/nice), created by researchers and educators for 8- to 14-year-olds, "is an online virtual world dedicated to learning through exploration and communication. Our citizens come from all over the world to interact, learn, and have fun together. They participate in educational activities from math and physics to art history to economics and civics. Whyville has its own newspaper, its own Senators, its own beach, museum, City Hall and town square, its own suburbia, and even its own economy—citizens earn 'clams' by playing educational games."

The most commonly used virtual world is Second Life (http://secondlife.com), a 3-D virtual world entirely built and owned by the people in the environment. Although Second Life was developed as an entertainment medium with millions of users worldwide, it is now being used quite extensively in education, primarily in higher education. Hundreds of universities around the world conduct classes within Second Life.

In Second Life, users create an avatar who represents them in the environment. They interact with each other in virtual worlds that are constructed to support different tasks. A few examples include:

- In Manchester, England, the city council has purchased a piece of land and built a school in Second Life, where students will plan to rebuild and refurbish its real-life secondary schools (Marley, 2008).

- Dysart (2009) describes a number of fascinating applications of Second Life:
  - Pacific Rim Exchange enables students in Modesto, California schools to virtually interact with their counterparts in Japan's Kyoto Gakuen High School for cultural exchanges, culminating in an exchange project known as Skoolaborate (www .skoolaborate.com).
  - Flea Market Math at Suffern Middle School in Suffern, New York, teaches students the value of a dollar by sending them out to shop in a virtual flea market while telling them to stay within budget.
  - Kidz Connect Project enables students to engage in a series of collaborative performance and storytelling workshops, culminating in original performances by the students, some of which are produced in Second Life.

There are thousands of applications of Second Life in K–12 and university classrooms. Many simply replicate face-to-face classes because educators are not certain how to develop more innovative applications. In addition to innovativeness, a number of other problems may occur. Because people interact and communicate in virtual worlds differently than they do in face-to-face environments, a number of potential problems emerge (Pfeil et al., 2009), including:

- **Identity.** Creating their own avatar with a unique nickname provides a unique identity, which makes each participant anonymous to each other and the teacher.
- **New Communication Patterns.** It is difficult for students to know who they are corresponding with and for the teacher to evaluate student contributions.
- **New Pedagogic Roles.** Teaching in virtual worlds influences the power relationship between the student and the teacher, so it is difficult to know how much to intervene.

Conclusion

Experimenting with technologies requires that students learn to reason causally in order to make predictions about what will happen if they change some value in the game or simulation. That is important because causal reasoning is one of the most basic thinking skills that are tied to most science inquiry standards. Causal reasoning is engaged by a number of technology-based learning environments, including microworlds, simulations, games, and virtual worlds. Microworlds provide simplified representations of the world that learners may manipulate and test. These are exploratory environments that focus on a limited number of causal relationships. Simulations share many characteristics with microworlds, although they tend to be more complex, often providing multiple variables that students may manipulate. The more complex environments require a more sophisticated model underlying the simulation, making them more difficult to design and implement. Games add competition with one's self or with others. At any time of the day, hundreds of thousands of people are playing Internet-based games. Some games (not typically first-person shooter games) can appropriately support classroom-learning goals. Virtual worlds combine the characteristics of microworlds, simulations, and games into educationally driven environments that allow students to explore distant worlds and pursue learning quests. Although there are few virtual worlds available to support educational goals, they possess the greatest potential for engaging students in meaningful learning.

NET Standards potentially engaged by modeling activities described in this chapter:

1. **Creativity and Innovation**
   c. Use models and simulations to explore complex systems and issues
   d. Identify trends and forecast possibilities

4. **Critical Thinking, Problem Solving, and Decision Making**
   a. Identify and define authentic problems and significant questions for investigation
   c. Collect and analyze data to identify solutions and/or make informed decisions
   d. Use multiple processes and diverse perspectives to explore alternative solutions

5. **Digital Citizenship**
   b. Exhibit a positive attitude toward using technology that supports collaboration, learning, and productivity
   c. Demonstrate personal responsibility for lifelong learning

6. **Technology Operations and Concepts**
   a. Understand and use technology systems
   b. Select and use applications effectively and productively

21st Century Skills potentially engaged by modeling activities described in this chapter:

Reason Effectively
- Use various types of reasoning (inductive, deductive, etc.) as appropriate to the situation

Use Systems Thinking
- Analyze how parts of a whole interact with each other to produce overall outcomes in complex systems

Make Judgments and Decisions
- Effectively analyze and evaluate evidence, arguments, claims and beliefs
- Analyze and evaluate major alternative points of view
- Synthesize and make connections between information and arguments
- Interpret information and draw conclusions based on the best analysis
- Reflect critically on learning experiences and processes

Solve Problems
- Solve different kinds of nonfamiliar problems in both conventional and innovative ways
- Identify and ask significant questions that clarify various points of view and lead to better solutions

Things to Think About

1. Are inferences and predictions two sides of the same coin? If you can generate predictions, do you believe that you will necessarily be able to makes inferences just as well? Will inferences transfer equally well to predictions?

2. Doctors make diagnoses, which requires inferential thinking. What other kinds of tasks require inferences?

3. We regularly talk about the implications of some event. Can you think of implications that students may need to draw that are relevant to your learning goals?

4. Microworlds are especially effective for allowing students to generate and test predictions (hypotheses). Can you think of how students can use microworlds to test inferences?

5. If SimCalc can help third graders understand the principles of differential calculus, what kind of microworld might you design to help learners understand supply and demand?

6. Simulations have been around for decades. How do computers make them more effective?

7. Simulations allow students to fail. One view of meaningful learning is "fast-forward failure." The sooner you put students into a situation where they try something and fail, the sooner they will begin learning. Why? How could you use that principle in your own class?

8. Good simulations are hard to build. If you were building a simulation for your class, what activity would you support? What variables could students manipulate? How would they affect each other?

9. Gee (2003) identified 36 principles about why games engage meaningful learning. Do those same principles apply to simulations? Microworlds?

10. One of Gee's principles states that learning involves taking on and playing with identities. Why do you think students like to assume and test other identities?

11. Gee's principle of probing states that learning is a cycle of probing the world (doing something) and reflecting in and on this action and forming a hypothesis. Donald Schön (1983) described the reflective practitioner in his book. What do you think the characteristics of a reflective practitioner are?

12. Gee's situated learning principle is similar to the authentic characteristics of meaningful learning described in Chapter 1. How does a situation become an embodied experience?

13. Most games involve some kind of competition. When is competition good for learning? When is it harmful?

14. Virtual worlds allow students to escape their world and enter a new world with a different set of rules. Why is that so engaging?

References

Barab, S. A., Thomas, M., Dodge, T., Carteaux, R., and Tuzun, H. (2005). Making learning fun: Quest Atlantis, a game without guns. *Educational Technology Research and Development* 53(1), 86–108.

Dysart, J. (2009). Learning: The next generation. *American School Board Journal, 196*(11), 30–31.

Gee, J. P. (2003). *What video games have to teach us about learning and literacy.* New York: Palgrave Macmillan.

Hanna, J. (1986). Learning environment criteria. In R. Ennals, R. Gwyn, & L. Zdravchev (Eds.), *Information technology and education: The changing school.* Chichester, UK: Ellis Horwood.

Klopfer, E. (2008). *Augmented learning research and design of mobile educational games.* Cambridge, MA: MIT Press.

Marley, D. (2008). Pupils help create school that's just out of this world. *Times Educational Supplement* no. 4785 (April 25), 5.

Papert, S. (1980). *Mindstorms: Children, computers, and powerful ideas.* New York: Basic Books.

Pfeil, U., Ang, C. S., and Zaphiris, P. (2009). Issues and challenges of teaching and learning in 3D virtual worlds: Real life case studies. *Educational Media International, 46*(3), 223–238.

White, B. Y. (1993). ThinkerTools: Causal models, conceptual change, and science education. *Cognition and Instruction, 10*(1), 1–100.

Designing with Technologies

David Crismond, Jane L. Howland, David Jonassen

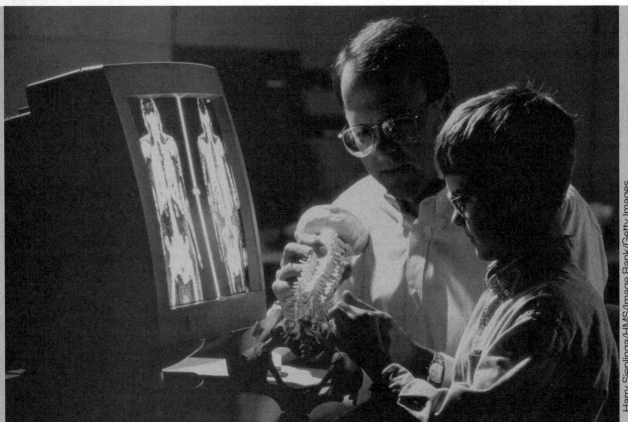

Chapter Objectives

1. Describe design and how it can engage students in meaningful learning

2. Introduce readers to technology tools that enable various types of design work

3. Describe how technology can support iterative designing and reflective thinking

4. Provide examples of technology-enhanced design projects for K–12 students

5. Describe how designing can support the development of NETS and 21st Century Skills

Learning through Design

What is design? Design is a ubiquitous activity that infiltrates all aspects of our lives. We are all designers in one way or another and most certainly are consumers of others' designs. In professional fields and personal lives, people design products, creations, processes, systems, activities, models, and a host of other outcomes. People everywhere are engaged in some form of design: writing software programs; designing a building; designing a new car or any of its 10,000 components; composing music; writing a book, play, short story, article, or poem; creating a marketing campaign for a new product; creating a new food product; designing a storefront display; decorating a home's interior or exterior; or decorating a cake. These and thousands of other tasks engage designing.

Design problems are among the most complex and ill structured of all problems that people attempt to solve (Jonassen, 2004). Many of the strategies used in problem solving are similar to those in designing (McCormick, 1998, p. 231):

Problem Solving	Designing
Define the problem	Identify a need or opportunity
Develop alternative solutions	Generate design ideas
Select the solution	Plan and make a prototype or product
Implement and evaluate the solution	Evaluate and reflect on the design

Despite the often-stated goal of finding an optimal solution that meets multiple criteria within a set of given constraints, real-world design problems can be vaguely defined or have partially stated goals and constraints, can possess multiple solutions rather than a single "right" answer, and can't be verified as correct. How you frame a design problem determines the kind of solution you create, which makes design particularly vexing to solve and hard to encode (Buchanan, 1995; Churchman, 1967). Might not even a "perfect lesson" have been taught as well in quite different ways? Ultimately, the designer must please the client, whose own views of an acceptable design may change, which can mean that the whole process of solving these ill-structured problems may begin anew.

In schools, you can find design challenges populating courses where you would expect them—in technology education, computer programming, music, math and science classes—and for those schools that offer them, in engineering and media art courses. Design is also taking center stage in a growing number of informal education settings, notably design competitions. Venues such as the FIRST Robotics and Lego design competitions (www.usfirst.org), Science Olympiad (www.soinc.org), and ThinkQuest (www.thinkquest.org) all offer four age categories in which K–12 students can participate, and all use design to motivate students to build understandings of concepts in memorable contexts—a fundamental approach to building meaningful learning in students of any age.

Drawing Designs with SketchUp

When people think of the work designers do they typically imagine a group huddled around a whiteboard drawing rapid-fire sketches of brainstormed ideas, or someone bent over a drafting table making orthographic projection drawings—those front-, side-, and top-view drawings, with sizes of parts clearly noted. Some hold that sketching and drawing are essential procedural skills that designers must be able to do (Ullman, Wood, & Craig, 1990), although others question whether this claim is true for younger designers (Bilda, Gero, & Purcell, 2006; Kimbell, 2004; Welsh & Lim, 1999) who sometimes do quite well jumping in and building simple prototypes, or using words and rough drawings to communicate their ideas.

One challenge of having students do design tasks is that many are not "graphically literate"—skilled at converting their ideas into usable graphics that can be examined and shared. A well-established technology tool, the computer-aided design (CAD) program, has been helping designers do that for some time.

The first CAD programs, developed in the early 1960s, had users wield light pens, type commands with their keyboards, and use oscilloscopes as screen displays to draw and manipulate simple lines, circles, and curves on the screen.

Today's CAD programs aid designers in visualization by enabling them to virtually build and then examine their ideas and make changes in their design's structural features, color, or surface texture. These remarkably lifelike objects can be rotated on screen, zoomed in and out so that key details can be viewed, without the need to fabricate materials or handle and use tools. During later design phases, CAD programs are useful in helping produce final drawings from which physical prototypes get made. Throughout the design process, high-quality drawings suitable for presentations can be generated using a pen that never runs out of ink, drawing lines that never waver, and writing text in the perfectly readable script that only those who put in years at the drafting table ever master.

Programs like Google's SketchUp (SketchUp.google.com) help designers visualize the buildings or rooms they created "from the ground up," specifically by starting with basic 2-D shapes and then using the "push/pull" and other tools, making 3-D objects. Floor plans become buildings, and land surveys become sculpted topographies that can be populated with trees and people. The house can be "moved" in different configurations until the designer sees a good fit between form and place. Another boon that architectural CAD systems like SketchUp provide is the capability to do a "walk-through" where users travel virtually through the designed space to get a feeling for the "built environment" before anything gets constructed.

SketchUp was at the center of a Math Science Technology Education Partnership (MSTP) curriculum development project at Hofstra University, where middle-school students applied recently learned mathematics to create bedrooms of their own design, first using SketchUp, and then building actual scale models of their rooms. The "bedroom design" curriculum used Knowledge Skill Builder (KSB) activities to give students practice working with different geometric objects useful to their bedrooms, and maintaining and staying within a given budget. Students had to calculate the floor and window areas of their rooms to meet a building code requirement that the total area of their bedroom's windows must be equal to or greater than 20 percent of the total area of the bedroom floor.

Figure 4.1

Students Design Bedroom Plans with Google's SketchUp, and Then Present the Design as a Physical Model

Courtesy Hofstra University Center for Technological Literacy

SketchUp's tools helped students measure the dimensions of their windows, adjust the size and shape of their rooms and windows, change the colors and textures of the walls and, using SketchUp's "3D Warehouse," copy and paste from among thousands of free and previously designed pieces of furniture and other artifacts into their rooms (see Figure 4.1).

A nine-year-old in Seattle, Washington, used SketchUp for a school project requiring students to draw a scale model of an apartment building. Although initially skeptical about introducing SketchUp as an instructional tool, her teacher said, "I saw a multitude of curriculum connections; geometry, measurement, logic, problem solving, art, perspective . . . the list goes on and on" (https://docs.google.com/Doc?id=dc837t9h_71f68nnbcb).

Although SketchUp was developed to help architects design buildings, it is an excellent tool for visualizing. In addition to its use in visualizing geography as described in Chapter 9, SketchUp can also help students visualize mathematical concepts, such as angles, volume, and shapes. At Laxey School, Isle of Man, John Thornley's 5- through 10-year-old students employed SketchUp to design packaging and boxes in design technology work by creating boxes in SketchUp (shown in Figure 4.2). They created artwork for the packages in another computer program, saved it as .jpg files, and then inserted the artwork into the SketchUp document. Students then used the designs they created in the software to make real boxes. Thornley's students also used SketchUp to create the lighthouses depicted in Figure 4.3 (on page 77).

Thornley said, "We use SketchUp with children as young as 5 years of age. The program needs very little introduction, children produce results very quickly and many make very rapid progress. We have found that SketchUp allows children who have difficulty expressing themselves in more conventional ways to produce work that far exceeds the expectations of their teachers. We've already had great results with children suffering from autism. SketchUp's ability to draw in perspective view makes it very easy for young children to conceptualize their thoughts" (https://docs.google.com/Doc?id=dc837t9h_69ckn7f2gv).

No-cost tutorials for SketchUp abound on the Internet. One free video tutorial produced by the Harwood Podcast Network is available as a podcast via Apple's iTunes program

Figure 4.2

Students' Packaging as Designed in
SketchUp

(www.apple.com/itunes/download), and runs on both
Mac and PC. The podcast is entitled "SketchUp: A 3-D
Toolbox" and currently houses more than 40 podcasts
that cover the basics of SketchUp (e.g., Using the Selection, Push Pull and Move tools), as well as more
advanced topics (e.g., Simple Staircase, the 3D Warehouse, and Sunlight Simulation).

Testing Designs and Building Understanding with Simulation Software

A number of National Science Foundation-funded projects have used design activities as contexts for students to
explore questions and do projects related to big ideas in
science and engineering. Teachers themselves need a
deep understanding of relevant principles of science and
engineering as well as the "device knowledge" (Johnson,
1988; McCormick, Murphy, & Davidson, 1994) of how
the systems that students are designing work (Vattam &
Kolodner, 2006).

Using simulation software (see also Chapter 3) can
support students' thinking and early design planning. In
science classrooms, simulations can help students build
mental models of how the physical world works—whether
it is the transmission of genetic traits to offspring (natural selection), the behavior of electrons as current flows
through a circuit (Ohm's law), or the movement of
objects experiencing a net force (Newtonian mechanics).
Simulations operate by running complex mathematical calculations in the background of
the software that generate a user-friendly view of some rule-driven behavior from the real
world. These programs support students in building causal explanations of how systems
work, and how elements within these systems interact with one another. When designed
well, simulations can bridge abstract theories and laws of nature with the real world, making the former more understandable, learnable, and transferable (White, 1993). Some simulation programs, like the one described next, can provide designers with fast feedback on
their design ideas and help reveal potential problems with planned devices, by showing students which designs may perform better or more poorly than others.

Trebuchet Simulator

Near the end of the school year, science teacher Doug Steinoff and technology education
teacher Craig Adams, both of Columbia, Missouri, have their Jefferson Junior High School

Figure 4.3

Students' Lighthouse Designs as Created in SketchUp

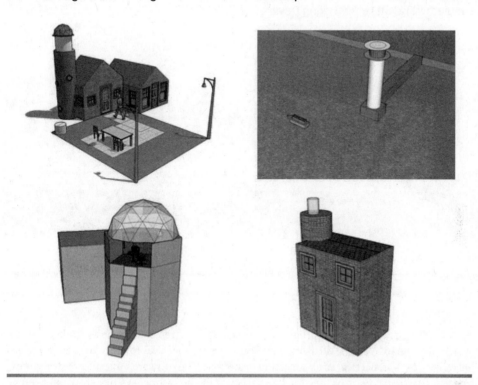

students create a gravity-powered catapult (Gurstelle, 2004) called a trebuchet (pronounced TREB-yoo-shet). The students must design and build a machine that throws a tennis ball with an attached tether so that the projectile hits a target placed between 3 and 49 meters from the device. Students must create a trebuchet that can survive not just early testing trials but also perform accurately enough for teams to earn the most points during a final design competition.

Iterative design is central to creating an effective design. For iterative design to work, students need to be able to propose ideas, build and test prototypes, diagnose and remedy problems with their interim designs, and then implement improvements quickly. A perennial problem with doing design challenges that involve lots of building—the trebuchet is made out of plywood and two-by-four lumber—is that too much project time gets consumed making and testing a single design plan, resulting in final projects that undergo too few tests and either fail outright or barely work.

A simulation program can help address this dilemma of design pedagogy, as Adams and Steinoff have found (Figure 4.4). These teachers divide students' trebuchet work into three parts: build and test a Lego model of a catapult, use a trebuchet simulator (described later) to produce early design plans, and then construct and test small and larger working prototypes.

Figure 4.4

Sequence of Design Activities for Creating a Gravity-driven Catapult: Test a Lego Model, Use a Trebuchet Simulator, and Make a Working Device

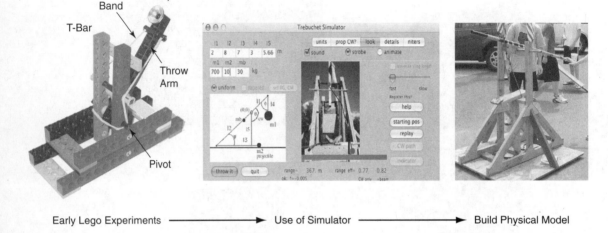

Early Lego Experiments ⟶ Use of Simulator ⟶ Build Physical Model

The Trebuchet Simulator program (www.algobeautytreb.com) enables students to run a virtual design of a device throwing a projectile before they ever touch a saw, select a counterweight, or design a trigger for an actual prototype. The software's interface is straightforward: users first type in values for key variables in the trebuchet's design (center left of screen). Users then select either the "strobe" display view, which shows a multiframe shot of the simulated test throw (Figure 4.5, center), or an animated view of it. They then click on the "throw it" button and watch the counterweight and throw arm move, the angle at which the projectile was released, and, most important, how far the ball travels ("range").

Students can use the simulator to run virtual experiments where they vary the masses for the projectile (M2) or the counterweight (M1), the length of the throw arm (L2) or counterweight arm (L1), or other parts of the trebuchet's design. Results from each test are displayed in the bottom field of the simulator's screen. By watching the "animate" view, which shows a moving stick drawing of the device in operation, students can develop a qualitative sense of how this device works and the impact that key variables have on the catapult's performance.

Steinoff and Adams have their students use the trebuchet simulator to help them make informed design decisions based on evidence, and avoid following only gut feelings or doing random guess designing. "We want them to recognize patterns to make them more successful. Their job is to manipulate those patterns to get the maximum efficiency." After conducting their virtual tests, students have in hand a set of workable dimensions for their first physical prototypes. They then can build and refine their machines with greater confidence and in less time than if they did hands-on investigations in building and testing their ideas (Klahr, Triona, & Williams, 2007).

Figure 4.5

Results from Tests on Different Designs Appear at the Bottom of the Trebuchet Simulator Program

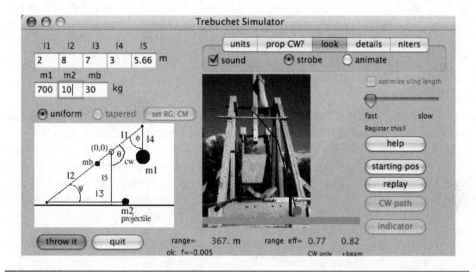

Problem Solving through the Design of Games and Animations

Software design is a content area where researchers conducted some of the early studies on the use of learning technologies to create meaningful learning environments. In fact, Seymour Papert's (1980) Logo programming language was one of the first contexts in which constructionist pedagogy was ever enacted (Kafai, 2005). Students using Logo could type computer commands and control an "evocative object" (Turkle, 1995): Logo used an on-screen turtle that made drawings on screen. By watching the turtle move and draw lines through these commands, children got the immediate feedback they needed to make debugging their programs more concrete and doable. This contrasted to kids programming with languages like BASIC, which allowed manipulation mainly of text or numbers. Studies in the 1980s showed that young children not only learned to program in Logo but also thought more reflectively and creatively (Clement & Gullo, 1984), although later research showed these gains were bound to the contexts in which students did their original work (Pea, Kurland, & Hawkins, 1985).

A number of Logo-inspired products have been developed since then, including "microworlds" that gave students creative control over multiple characters on screen, "construction kits" that enabled students to manipulate Lego bricks in the real world, and environments where students could design software for their peers (Kafai, 2005).

The process of designing games and animations draws on complex problem solving and decision making in the creation of original products, or the redesign of existing and even "classic" programs. Students must hypothesize and make predictions, create rules and test them, and learn from their initial attempts when they do not work. Students use many of the competencies promoted by 21st Century Skills and NETS as they engage in active, intentional, authentic, constructive, and cooperative learning processes (refer back to Figure 1.1). This section explores software that enables students to build their own games and simulations.

Scratch

Scratch is software that empowers users to create object-based programs that manipulate digitized video and audio. The Scratch program, which runs on most computer platforms, gives students the capability to build programs that manipulate digital images using tools similar to Photoshop's, add and replay audio tracks and music, and work with video, all while learning fundamentals in computer programming. Scratch's interface uses a Logo-styled building-block metaphor to represent programming moves. It replaces code writing with virtual programming blocks that users can insert, move and combine, and set values to variables through drop-down menus.

Scratch's creators targeted it to appeal to preteens and teenagers from different cultures, support them in creating projects they could be proud of, and, when used over time, could lead to the development of more advanced programming skills.

The main Scratch screen (Figure 4.6) has five main work areas. The "Blocks" palette to the left provides a collection of programming tools that manipulate imported digital images, sprites, and music through programming procedures ("control" commands are visible in Figure 4.6, left). In the middle-left "Scripts" area, users can drag blocks to construct sets of procedures, much as puzzle pieces can be fitted together. When procedures are not compatible, students encounter the graphical equivalent of a mismatch of puzzle parts. Scratch forces students to alter their program until they are in a form that can be implemented. Scripts manipulate "sprites," which are visible in the lower-right area. The full program is run by clicking on the green "go" flag at the right top, the results of which can be viewed in the "Stage" area.

The program's capacity to give timely feedback helps students "tinker" in productive ways and supports meaningful exposure and learning of modular programming. Simultaneously, these features allow students to produce interactive stories, animations, games, music videos, and other creative projects in the media arts. Scratch is developed by the Lifelong Kindergarten Group at the MIT Media Lab (see http://scratch.mit.edu). The program is available for free download. You may also be interested in Scratch-Ed (www.scratch-ed.org), an online space where educators can share stories, exchange resources, and ask questions.

iStopMotion and Stagecast Creator

The iStopMotion software, produced by Boinx (www.istopmotion.com), enables designers as young as elementary students to create their own animated movies and time-lapse recordings. Using a Mac computer, digital camera, or webcam, students can capture and

Figure 4.6

Scratch has Different Sections with Programming, Graphics, and Sound Tools; a Place to Compose Scripts; and a Stage (right) Where Sprites Get Animated

then compose animations frame by frame with this easy-to-learn application. When its "onion skinning" feature is turned on (Figure 4.7), the program allows for the easy juxtaposition of contiguous frames when making a movie file. This helps users produce a coherent video sequence without jerky movements from its characters, helping to limit the need for reshooting or reediting. Claymation movies can be easily made with iStopMotion. Children are capable of composing single-frame shots of the easy-to-manipulate clay figures whose evolving positions and changing shapes collectively tell a desired story.

George Rota, media specialist at Glen Lake Elementary School in Minnetonka, Minnesota, works with elementary teachers in his school to create animation and claymation movies. He introduces iStopMotion to all sixth graders at Glen Lake, who then use it to complete an extended animation project that is part of their social studies and language arts classes. Students work in groups of three or four, do research on their topics, and use index cards to create storyboards of major scenes when planning their movies. Their videos typically last from 20 to 60 seconds, not including titles and credits, which often double the total length of students' final movies.

Figure 4.7

iStopMotion's "Onion Skinning" Helps Ensure That Contiguous Frames Have Just the Right Amount of "Jump" between Each Other to Create Seamless Animations or Pans

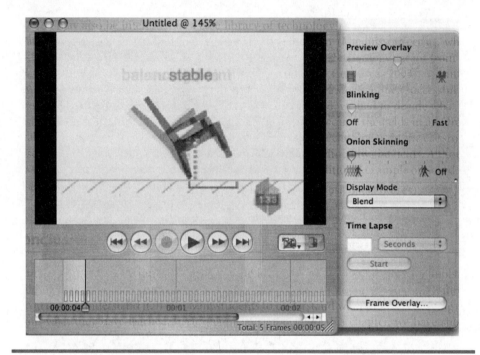

Stagecast Creator, originally developed by Apple and available for Mac, Windows, and Unix systems, is another application that enables people to create stories, games, and interactive simulations using a visual interface rather than a programming language.

AgentSheets

Developed through research at the University of Colorado-Boulder, AgentSheets aims to foster K–12 student participation in STEM fields through design of applications using its technology. AgentSheets 3 employs the use of a "Conversational Programming" model by allowing the user to create an agent (i.e., "programming buddy") who moves about in the environment that is being designed to analyze and provide feedback on not only syntax, but also semantics. The agent can help students consider the consequences of rules and conditions they are creating by providing feedback on one's logic and pointing out conceptual mistakes. This preemptive troubleshooting prompts students to experience the meaning of the commands they've written in real time and results in a highly interactive iterative design process.

AgentSheets offers a Scalable Game Design wiki (http://scalablegamedesign.cs .colorado.edu/wiki/Scalable_Game_Design_wiki) with an extensive library of teacher resources. Sample tutorial simulations (e.g., Avalanche, Contagion/Virus, Ecosystems, Electricity, Fish Farm) may be used to support concept development in math or science curriculum (e.g., probability, ratios, and exponential vs. linear growth) and data analysis by exporting simulation data for graphing, determining line of best fit, or making statistical predictions. These simulations have links to related lesson plans, learning outcomes and national standards (e.g., NETS•S, NSES, NCTM Math), sample grading strategies, detailed tutorials, and suggestions for exploring questions with the simulation. For example, the Forest Fire Design simulation allows users to study the effects of different variables on forest fires by manipulating tree density and wind direction, and how those parameters affect the probability of a fire spreading or dying out. "Making Frogger," which is based on a classic Sega-developed arcade game from 1981, asks students to redesign the original arcade game, in which a frog must overcome obstacles and predators to get across a river and reach the opposite shore. In addition to lesson plans, learning outcomes and standards, and sample grading strategies, several detailed tutorials lead one through the steps of creating very basic through more advanced levels of Frogger games. The rich resources and support that AgentSheets offers for both students and teachers increases the likelihood that students will be successful in their design work without experiencing undue frustration. In particular, the "programming buddy" may scaffold students as they problem-solve design dilemmas. These are highly instructive examples of learning not *from*, but *with*, technology.

Designing Music with Composition Software

Applications for developing songs and scores on the computer have been available since the days when microcomputing first began sporting plug-in sound cards and could produce the synthesized "voices" of various musical instruments. These programs—and their subsequent offspring, including Apple's GarageBand—display a number of music tracks on which users can enter, edit, and replay their compositions. Depending on the program, notes can be inputted via direct recordings, playing a guitar controller or MIDI keyboard attached to the computer, or doing "old-fashioned" note-by-note inputting via a mouse onto a five-line staff. Applications such as these do for music composition what word processors have done for writing—they help users who start with a blank page to enter and format material easily, and to review, revise, and save groups of notes while working toward a finished composition.

A pedagogically powerful, elegant, and free piece of software for designing music, called Impromptu, was created by MIT professor emerita of music and urban education, Jeanne Bamberger. Her program gains inspiration from the children's programming language, Logo. Impromptu's workspace (Figure 4.8) is composed of five areas and a menu bar that supports students in developing their own musical intuitions (Bamberger, 2001, 2003) while constructing tunes from groups of musical notes called "Tuneblocks." The "Tuneblocks" area is the place where music chunks or motifs can be found and stored and where collections of prefabricated blocks, based on previously transcribed musical pieces, can be loaded from the program's "catalog." Users can assign Tuneblocks a color and an

Figure 4.8

The Impromptu Program Has Five Work Areas. Three Cursor Types Found in the Tools Area Allow Tuneblocks to Be Moved, Heard, and Modified

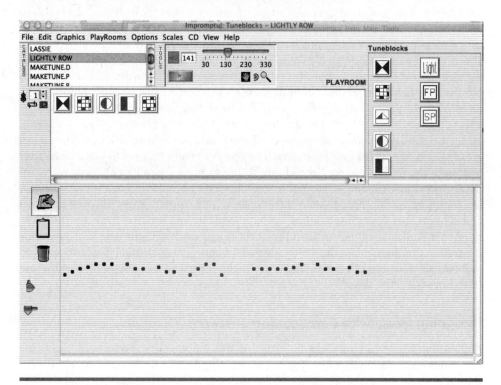

abstract pattern to help them identify one from another. They then arrange them as they wish in the "Playroom" area of the program's main window.

The key to this program's approach, seen earlier in Logo and also in Scratch, lies in how it has users—primary school aged or older—work with musical "chunks," or groups of musical sounds, rather than individual notes on a five-line score when constructing a musical piece. This enables users to grasp the composition more as a conceptual whole, as it contains far fewer parts, and each part has its own familiar sense and meaning. The immediate feedback that Impromptu gives to its users—an approach shared by many programs described in this chapter—helps users conduct their own experiments in musical meaning making. Impromptu also provides multiple representations of the collected notes contained in a row of Tuneblocks in its "Graphics" area (bottom of main window), where the relative relationship of individual notes according to pitch, rhythm, or both can be seen. The use of multiple representations has helped students build more flexible and transferable understandings since the 1980s.

Impromptu also provides a Notepad so that users can keep a running log of their process of designing music. With it, they can more easily engage in what Don Schön (1983) calls "reflective practice"—where designers frame a desired goal, create "moves" and partial solutions that are seen as experiments that attempt to reach that goal, and then review and troubleshoot the results. Such reflections can then lead to modifying the product, as well as the design goal itself (Adams, Turns, & Atman, 2003). Impromptu supports designers in having such a "conversation with materials" (Bamberger & Schön, 1991)—where they can develop, order, and make alterations to blocks of music based on intentions they have for the piece and how they hear them sound during replay.

Related Programs and Technologies: Musical Sketch Pad

The Musical Sketch Pad (http://creatingmusic.com) is an online music composition environment that is designed for use by primary school children. It provides an engaging set of tools (Figure 4.9) where children use a pencil tool to draw strings of notes that are played by a small number of instrument voices (trumpet, clarinet, piano, or drum). Each voice, represented with a different color, gets played simultaneously and can be heard at one of three different playback speeds.

An advantage of this program's music line-drawing tool is the speed with which children can enter music into the program. To edit individual notes, children must highlight sections of their newly created score and either delete them with an eraser tool or alter them with the program's inverse, reverse, or parallel tracking tools. Once drawn, however, the different voices appear as a single score rather than as separable layers. Children may find it a challenge to create musical patterns involving widely separated notes—a small trade-off considering this program's accessible interface and appeal to a younger audience.

Figure 4.9

Musical Sketch Pad

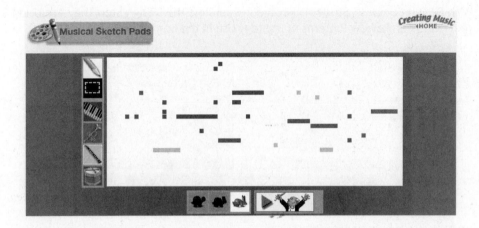

Improving Design Compass: Keeping Track of What Designers Do

Another type of software technology that supports students' design work and thinking is Design Compass (Crismond, Hynes, & Donahy, 2010), which was developed collaboratively by Tufts University and City College of New York. Using this software, students create a log of the strategies they utilize when designing. As students work in groups, one person from each team is nominated as the "recorder" and is responsible for clicking on the step that the team is doing (e.g., Brainstorm) from the design cycle that the Design Compass displays. The recorder may then enter a brief note or digital photograph on what the team sketched, built or did during that time, before clicking on another step when the team moves on to another design strategy (e.g., Research). For each click, the Compass creates an entry that it places in a spreadsheet called a "design log" that shows the time the clicks occurred, the strategy identified, and the total time spent doing the strategy. The complete log can be accessed by clicking on the program's second view tab "Graph" (see Figure 4.10, right), where users can also see a bar graph that shows how much time the team has spent on each design strategy.

The Graph view gives students feedback on how much time they spent during a project on each of the strategies, and gives them a chance to detect patterns that can help them figure out how to improve their process of design the next time they work. The software can also provide a rich set of talking points for teachers to use when they periodically visit design teams. Rather than having to rely on students' incomplete memory of what they did since the last teacher visit, all can view the sequence of steps a team has taken, read notes, and view photos showing what was done. Information regarding the Design Compass and research done with it is available at www.designcompass.org.

Figure 4.10

With Design Compass, Students Record in Real Time the Design Step They Are Using (left), and Can Review Patterns of Strategy Use in the Log View (right)

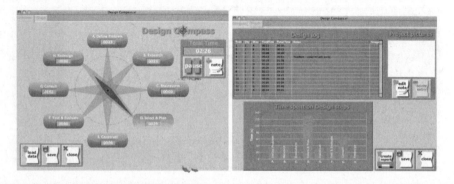

Conclusion

Many of the technologies described in this chapter show how design can better contextualize and motivate learners to explore and learn big ideas in science, mathematics, music, and computer programming. Design seems to be emerging as a new literacy for the 21st century. The last draft of the next National Science Education Standards clearly highlights engineering design as a key topic that all K–12 teachers will be asked to help their students learn: "Engineering and technology are featured alongside the natural sciences in recognition of the importance of understanding the designed world and of the need to better integrate the teaching and learning of science, technology, engineering, and mathematics" (National Research Council, July 12, 2010 draft, p. 1-1). Developing a fluency in design will become a reality as more programs are created that support designing in a variety of contexts and as teachers see themselves as designers, learn about strategies that designers have developed and honed over the years, and become conversant in the pedagogies that can make the use of design challenges effective in the classroom.

Design is not a panacea for all of education's ills, but is one additional tool for teachers to use that can give added meaning to the work students do in classrooms. As design tasks get used more often and their use is further enhanced by learning technologies, such as those described in this chapter, teachers will get the opportunity to realize more of the potential of these tasks to build transferable concepts, while instilling a joy of learning and appetite for creating innovative solutions to meaningful problems in their students.

NETS potentially engaged by design activities described in this chapter:

1. **Creativity and Innovation**
   a. Apply existing knowledge to generate new ideas, products, or processes
   b. Create original works as a means of personal or group expression
   c. Use models and simulations to explore complex systems and issues

2. **Communication and Collaboration**
   a. Interact, collaborate, and publish with peers, experts, or others employing a variety of digital environments and media
   b. Communicate information and ideas effectively to multiple audiences using a variety of media and formats
   d. Contribute to project teams to produce original works or solve problems

3. **Research and Information Fluency**
   a. Plan strategies to guide inquiry
   b. Locate, organize, analyze, evaluate, synthesize, and ethically use information from a variety of sources and media
   c. Evaluate and select information sources and digital tools based on the appropriateness to specific tasks

4. **Critical Thinking, Problem Solving, and Decision Making**
   a. Identify and define authentic problems and significant questions for investigation

b. Plan and manage activities to develop a solution or complete a project

c. Collect and analyze data to identify solutions and/or make informed decisions

d. Use multiple processes and diverse perspectives to explore alternative solutions

6. **Technology Operations and Concepts**

a. Understand and use technology systems

b. Select and use applications effectively and productively

c. Troubleshoot systems and applications

21st Century Skills potentially engaged by design activities described in this chapter:

Think Creatively

■ Use a wide range of idea creation techniques (such as brainstorming)

■ Create new and worthwhile ideas (both incremental and radical concepts)

■ Elaborate, refine, analyze and evaluate their own ideas in order to improve and maximize creative efforts

Work Creatively with Others

■ Develop, implement, and communicate new ideas to others effectively

■ Be open and responsive to new and diverse perspectives; incorporate group input and feedback into the work

■ Demonstrate originality and inventiveness in work and understand the real-world limits to adopting new ideas

■ View failure as an opportunity to learn; understand that creativity and innovation is a long-term, cyclical process of small successes and frequent mistakes

Reason Effectively

■ Use various types of reasoning (inductive, deductive, etc.) as appropriate to the situation

Use Systems Thinking

■ Analyze how parts of a whole interact with each other to produce overall outcomes in complex systems

Make Judgments and Decisions

■ Interpret information and draw conclusions based on the best analysis

■ Reflect critically on learning experiences and processes

Solve Problems

■ Solve different kinds of nonfamiliar problems in both conventional and innovative ways

■ Identify and ask significant questions that clarify various points of view and lead to better solutions

Communicate Clearly

■ Articulate thoughts and ideas effectively using oral, written, and nonverbal communication skills in a variety of forms and contexts

Collaborate with Others

- Demonstrate ability to work effectively and respectfully with diverse teams
- Exercise flexibility and willingness to be helpful in making necessary compromises to accomplish a common goal
- Assume shared responsibility for collaborative work, and value the individual contributions made by each team member

Create Media Products

- Understand and utilize the most appropriate media creation tools, characteristics, and conventions

Things to Think About

1. What makes for an engaging and effective design challenge? Do challenges with solutions that converge on a single "optimal" solution violate the spirit of exploring a design space meaningfully?

2. Which strategies in the design process could be emphasized while students are doing learning technologies-enhanced design? (Candidate topics might include doing "rapid prototyping" using simulation programs, using the Internet to do research to make better design decisions, getting faster feedback from CAD programs to support doing iterative designing and help designers visualize better what they are doing.)

3. How can students be motivated to continue exploring, revising, and refining their designs—to do meaningful iterative design—when their common refrain is, "It works, so I'm done"?

4. What trade-offs do you see with the computer-based aids described in this chapter compared to doing strictly hands-on designing? (Two downsides to using CAD systems are that students never get a feeling for the objects and don't really know when the project is finished.)

5. When and how do teachers act as designers? (Do they revise lessons after teaching them? Adapt ideas from textbooks to the needs of the class?)

References

Adams, R. S., Turns, J., & Atman, C. J. (2003). Educating effective engineering designers: The role of reflective practice. *Design Studies, 24,* 275–294.

Bamberger, J. (2001). *Developing musical intuitions: A project-based introduction to making and understanding music.* New York: Oxford University Press.

Bamberger, J. (2003). The development of intuitive musical understanding: A natural experiment. *Psychology of Music, 31*(1), 7–36.

Bamberger, J., & Schön, D. (1991). Learning as a reflective conversation with materials. In F. Steier (Ed.), *Research and reflexivity.* Newbury Park, CA: Sage.

Bilda, Z., Gero, J. S., & Purcell, T. (2006). To sketch or not to sketch. *Design studies, 27*(5), 587–613.

Buchanan, R. (1995). Wicked problems in design thinking. In V. Margolin & R. Buchanan (Eds.), *The idea of design: A design issues reader* (pp. 3–20). Cambridge, MA: MIT Press.

Churchman, C. W. (1967). Wicked problems. *Management Science, 14*(4), 141–142.

Clement, D. H., & Gullo, D. F. (1984). Effects of computer programming on young children's cognition. *Journal of Educational Psychology, 76*(6), 1051–1058.

Crismond, D., Hynes, M., & Donahy, E. (2010). "The Design Compass: A computer tool for scaffolding students' metacognition and discussions about their engineering design process." Paper presented at the AAAI Spring Symposium on Using Electronic Tangibles to Promote Learning: Design and Evaluation, Palo Alto, CA, March 22–24.

Gurstelle, W. (2004). *The art of the catapult.* Chicago: Chicago Review Press.

Johnson, S. D. (1988). Cognitive analysis of expert and novice troubleshooting performance. *Performance Improvement Quarterly, 1*(3), 38–54.

Jonassen, D. H. (2004). *Learning to solve problems.* San Francisco: Pfeiffer.

Kafai, Y. B. (2005). Constructionism. In R. K. Sawyer (Ed.), *The Cambridge handbook of the learning sciences* (pp. 35–46). Cambridge, UK: Cambridge University Press.

Kimbell, R. (2004). Ideas and ideation. *Journal of Design and Technology Education, 9*(3), 136–137.

Klahr, D., Triona, L. M., & Williams, C. (2007). Hands on what? The relative effectiveness of physical versus virtual materials in an engineering design project by middle school children. *Journal of Research in Science Teaching, 44*(1), 183–203.

McCormick, R. (1998). Problem solving and the tyranny of product outcomes. *Journal of Design and Technology Education, 1* (3), 320–341.

McCormick, R., Murphy, P., & Davidson, M. (1994). Design and technology as revelation and ritual. *IDATER '94,* 38–42.

Papert, S. (1980). *Mindstorms: Children, computers, and powerful ideas.* New York: Basic Books.

Pea, R., Kurland, D. M., & Hawkins, J. (1985). Logo programming and the development of thinking skills. In M. Chen & W. Paisley (Eds.), *Children and microcomputers: Formative studies* (pp. 193–212). Beverly Hills, CA: Sage.

Schön, D. (1983). *The reflective practitioner: How professionals think in action.* New York: Basic Books.

Turkle, S. (1995). *Life on the screen: Identity in the age of the Internet.* New York: Simon & Schuster.

Ullman, D. G., Wood, S., & Craig, D. (1990). The importance of drawing in the mechanical design process. *Computers and Graphics, 14*(2), 263–274.

Vattam, S. S., & Kolodner, J. L. (2006). Design-based science learning: Important challenges and how technology can make a difference. *Proceedings of the International Conference of the Learning Sciences,* pp. 799–805.

Welch, M., & Lim, H. S. (1999). Teaching sketching and its effect on the solutions produced by novice designers. *IDATER '99,* 188–194.

White, B. (1993). Intermediate causal models: A missing link for successful science education? In R. Glaser (Ed.), *Advances in instructional psychology* (Vol. 4, pp. 172–252). Hillsdale, NJ: Lawrence Erlbaum Associates.

Communicating with Technologies

s70/Zuma/Newscom

Chapter Objectives

1. Describe how online communication can enhance and extend student learning

2. Compare the affordances of synchronous and asynchronous communication methods

3. Identify appropriate communication methods for sharing information with others

4. Develop learning activities that use communication technologies to meet instructional goals

5. Describe how various communication tools and processes support the development of NETS and 21st Century Skills

21st Century Media Kids

Today's students are, as a group, not only technologically sophisticated but also fundamentally different than previous generations in their approaches to, use of, and relationship with media. Whereas students once were admonished against the distraction of competing sensory input, today's kids are comfortably accustomed to interacting with multiple media inputs simultaneously.

The Kaiser Family Foundation reported that in 2004, young people spent an average of 6.5 hours per day with media and, because of overlapping media use, they were actually exposed to the equivalent of 8.5 hours daily. By 2009, the average level of use had increased by over an hour per day, nearly eclipsing the amount of time spent in most adults' workdays (Rideout, Foehr, & Roberts, 2010). While young people were spending almost the same amount of time on media in 2004 as they were 5 years earlier, they increased the time spent with more than one medium simultaneously from 16 percent of the time to 26 percent of the time (Rideout, Roberts, & Foehr, 2005). That proportion grew to 29 percent by 2009, with total media exposure equaling 10 hours and 45 minutes per day. Mobile devices, such as cell phones, iPods, and handheld video players accounted for 20 percent of that consumption.

To illustrate, let's observe a 5-minute window in a typical teenager's life. Melissa is glancing at TV while listening to music on her iPod and using Facebook to instant message with a dozen friends on her laptop computer. In the background, she's checking the price of the soccer shoes she wants to order online and downloading the lyrics and guitar tabs for a new song she's heard. An audio alert lets her know that she has a new text message from Ben on her cell phone, but before she can text back a reply, the phone rings. It's her best friend, calling to ask her opinion about the new dress she's found. Melissa doesn't want to go to the mall, so Katie takes a picture of the dress with her cell phone and sends it to Melissa. In the meantime, Melissa remembers that she wants to post some of the pictures she took yesterday on her iPhone to her Flickr account.

What does this media multitasking mean for educators? K–12 students are an information-inundated generation and are used to communication that is ubiquitous and instantaneous. These behaviors have strong implications for the way we should think about the structure of classrooms, curricula, and technology use in our schools. Although little research has yet been done regarding the effects of high exposure to media on learning processes, we cannot ignore the implications of learners' proclivity to this sensory input. Doing so risks losing the attention, motivation, and interest of a new generation of students.

Chapter 6 introduces you to several ways that technology devices and Internet resources can assist in the formation and collaborative work of communities. In this chapter, we review communication technologies and related activities and programs that allow sharing and exchange of ideas both individually and as groups. Most of the technology use introduced in this chapter also contributes to community building, which is a critical element of meaningful learning as students engage in social negotiation and shared knowledge building.

The technological breakthrough that has afforded communication leading to learning communities is the Internet and related networking technologies. The Internet, particularly the World Wide Web, once primarily a source for retrieving archived information, has become the communication medium that connects scattered people and resources together. Why? In many ways, the Internet's strength lies in its decentralized nature.

The Internet is the ultimate distributed network, linking users and institutions together, allowing interactions of all kinds to occur. The Internet can become the communications vehicle that both liberates and ties learners together, including students and teachers, into coherent learning communities. While some people have feared that telecommunications would replace face-to-face interactions, there is a growing realization that, instead, technology is facilitating the means for connecting us and increasing the opportunity for building relationships and social exchanges (Rideout, Roberts, & Foehr, 2005). The overwhelming growth in social networking spaces like Facebook (www.facebook .com) demonstrates the power of these online communities to capture and support the desire that humans have to bond. How online communication affects our off-line, face-to-face relationships may depend on how deeply one immerses oneself in the online world. A teenager who isolates herself from concrete interactions with family and friends may lose important social ties. Is the increased social networking enabled by technology worth it if immediate relationships suffer? Or can online friendships provide an essential support that is difficult for some people to find in face-to-face interactions? Researchers will be investigating questions like these for some time. Rather than impose value judgments, we must critically assess the outcomes of online communication in an attempt to make the best use of new technologies.

The Internet can be part of the glue that keeps people connected—talking with each other, noticing and appreciating differences, working out divergent views, and serving as role models and audiences for one another. The education future portended by the Internet, therefore, is not isolated and targeted to individuals. Rather, it is a community-centered future in which persons are joined in working together through the power of telecommunication tools.

Exchanging Ideas Asynchronously with Discussion Boards and VoiceThread

Communication in an asynchronous online venue is different from and, in several important ways, better than face-to-face communication and other technology-based forms (e.g., telephone conversations and videoconferencing). It is true that an online discussion doesn't have the richness or, to use a computer metaphor, the *bandwidth* of a face-to-face conversation. We lose important communication cues, such as body language, tone of voice, accents, dialects, pace, pauses, and other important cues to meaning. Although this may be limiting, it may also be helpful, as authors must take more care to see that they are communicating clearly.

Paraphrasing a television commercial run by a major telecommunications vendor, on the Internet there is no race, no gender, no age, and no infirmities—only minds: people talking to people. This is certainly the case in text-based discussion boards.

Online communications are often *asynchronous* (not in real time), making them different in important ways. Howard Gardner (Gardner & Lazear, 1991; Gardner, 2000) has proposed a Theory of Multiple Intelligences, which suggests that intelligence is not a single capacity but rather a series of distinct capabilities. He suggests that rather than asking, "How smart are you?" we should ask, "How are you smart?" Some people, Gardner believes, are high in *verbal intelligence*. They are often verbally deft and capable of carrying out stimulating conversations. They tend to do well in traditional school environments. This does not necessarily mean they are the best thinkers or communicators. Other people want more time to consider an idea and formulate their responses. Rather than speaking extemporaneously, they are often minimal contributors to real-time conversations—the conversation is off to other topics before they have developed their ideas and ways to share them.

When given a chance to think and then speak, as is the case in several forms of online conversation, these people experience a new freedom and level of participation. They can be heard clearly, and the power of their responses is often impressive. When combined with the removal of biases, as already described, it becomes easy to imagine why a number of strong friendships (some crossing international borders and generations) and even romances have begun on the Internet.

Asynchronous Discussion Boards

There are both advantages and disadvantages in computer conferencing, which is defined as group discussion in which messages are stored on computers rather than being sent in real time, as with instant messaging services (Woolley, 1995). Some individuals prefer immediate response and feedback, which is not an attribute of asynchronous communication. Determining the message's content from a short subject line can be difficult, and reading discussion board postings is often quite time consuming. *Threading*, or the ability to respond to messages and have those responses clustered in sequence under the original posting, is an essential feature for online discussion boards, as it keeps messages organized and helps make the discussion relatively easy to follow. Woolley discusses several other attributes that are desirable in computer conferencing systems, including the following:

- Separate conferences for different topics, both for organization and individual interest
- Informative topic list that shows posting dates, number of responses, and titles of topics
- Search and filter tools allowing users to search messages by date, author, or key word

What advantages does asynchronous communication have over a good old-fashioned discussion? Why not just converse face-to-face rather than talking through technology? There are several reasons one might want to participate in a technology-mediated discussion. First, discussions, debates, and collaborative efforts can occur among groups of people who are co-located or at a distance. Students do not have to be in the same place to converse and learn. Many classrooms are becoming virtual—communications and learning spaces located within a networked system connecting learners all over the country and, in many cases, the world. While the immediacy of real-time chats and instant messaging has much to offer, asynchronous communication can support collaboration among learners, promoting international connections and project work. The convenience of responding to others' postings at the time one chooses becomes virtually a necessity when students are communicating with others across time zones. While a live afternoon chat at 2:00 p.m. may work well for a student in Chicago, her team member in Bangkok could find himself quite sleepy from what would be a very early 2:00 a.m. conversation in Thailand.

A second advantage is that asynchronous online communication enables learners to reflect on their ideas or responses before making them. In addition to providing opportunities to research topics and to develop arguments, online communications allow the students the opportunity to adequately present an individual or group's position. That requires reflecting on your argument before carefully presenting it. Thinking about what you are going to say before saying it is fostered by online communication.

Third—and perhaps most important—different kinds of thinking can be scaffolded in asynchronous online communications. Although in-class conversation is a powerful learning method, learners do not necessarily know how to constructively converse. Threaded discussions can guide and scaffold students as they make comments, reminding them of needed support and development, and archiving past conversations for future use.

Asynchronous discussion boards have the capacity to support classroom learning in a variety of ways. They can connect students with others beyond the immediate classroom, opening windows to new learning experiences by exposure to new ideas, cultural diversity, and unique partnerships. Asynchronous discussion boards can also serve a useful purpose within a contained classroom community by providing an outlet for extended conversations that enrich classroom activity. The 50-minute class periods so common in most secondary schools provide insufficient time for in-depth dialogue. In a typical scenario, just as students may be approaching some degree of meaningful conversation and reaching the point where significant thinking really begins, the bell signaling a change of classes sounds, abruptly halting the opportunity for learning. Collaborating and conversing on meaningful topics outside the regular school day gives students a chance to dig deeper and establishes a classroom community that exists beyond one class period. It may also connect students in separate sections of a course, broadening the range of ideas brought to the conversation.

Asynchronous discussion boards are an excellent means for supporting second-language learning. Language students can converse with native speakers from another country on mutually interesting topics (e.g., music or fashion) or among themselves on relevant topics. In this way, students are learning to communicate in the language, not just to learn about conjugations and declensions. Asynchronous discussion boards are especially effective with nonnative speakers, as it provides them with time to consider and articulate their ideas, tasks that are difficult for them to accomplish extemporaneously.

In the following sections, some applications of asynchronous discussion boards are offered.

Discussion Boards for Argumentation

We contend that synchronous discussion boards are best used to support argumentation. An argument consists of a claim (solution) that is supported by principles (warrants), evidence, and rebuttals against potential counterarguments. According to Blair and Johnson (1987), a good argument must satisfy three criteria: (1) "is there an adequate relationship between the contents of the premises and the conclusion?" (relevance), (2) "does the premise provide enough evidence for the conclusion?" (sufficiency), and (3) "are the premises true, probable, or reliable?" (acceptability). There are several reasons for using online discussion boards as a means for argumentation, which is an essential way of thinking about any discipline. Argumentation engages deeper and more mature epistemological levels of learning. It also leads to conceptual change (Asterhan & Schwarz, 2007; Baker, 1999; Nussbaum & Sinatra, 2003; Wiley & Voss, 1999). Conceptual change occurs when learners change their understanding of concepts they use and the conceptual frameworks that encompass them, reorganizing their frameworks to accommodate new perspectives. Argumentation is associated with a social constructivist conception of meaning making, where students learn through reflective interactions (arguments) that engage the social co-construction of knowledge (Driver et al., 2000; Newton et al., 1999).

There are several strategies to encourage better arguments, including refutation, synthesizing, and weighing (Nussbaum & Schraw, 2007). In the refutation strategy, an explicitly adversarial strategy, students learn to recognize alternative solutions and to rebut other arguments (What solution might someone else recommend, and how would you respond to his reasons?). In the synthesizing strategy, students try to develop a compromise position that combines merits of both sides (Is there a compromise or creative solution?). In the weighing strategy, students must learn to evaluate alternative arguments and support the stronger argument based on the weight of evidence on that side of the issue (Which side is stronger and why?). Requiring students to explain whether they really understood the lesson engages them in argumentation. Students then have access to evidence statements that enable them to reconsider their claims and present argument with more justification. Argumentation can also be supported through use of note starters, which consist of a menu of phrases from which students begin the first sentence of a discussion in an online discussion board. Oh and Jonassen (2007) found that note starters encouraged students to consider other points of view and generate more evidence.

Discussion Boards in Purposeful Community Websites

When students and teachers engage in collaborative work through websites such as ePals (www.epals.com) or ThinkQuest (see Chapter 6), they have access to several integrated communication tools, with discussion boards that are related to specific projects or are meant for more general, community dialogues.

Whereas the project-specific discussion boards can be an integral part of managing tasks and sharing ideas in collaborative project work, general discussion boards give young people the means for exchanging their thoughts on just about anything that they care to talk about with one another. Conversation centered on project work is instrumental in building knowledge in the cognitive domain; informal conversation initiated by students and focused on students' lives and personal interests has great potential not only for cognitive learning outcomes but also for constructive outcomes in the affective domain. Increasing one's knowledge, understanding, tolerance, and valuing of other individuals' customs, opinions, and beliefs can have a positive effect on students' ability to work together in collaborative groups. Informal conversations can build a foundation for future interactions that may occur in our global economy.

As technology and the growing global economy dissolve the boundaries between countries, there is a critical need to become cognizant and well informed about one another. The Brazilian student who posted a message in the ePALS "Earthquake Haiti" student forum shared his experience with an earthquake and expressed concerns about the Haitian people's recovery from the earthquake in their country (Figure 5.1). In another forum, a Brazilian student who was curious about good manners in other countries asked, "What are the 'rules' about greeting people in your country? When do you shake hands? When do you kiss? What is considered impolite in your country?" This question and its answers have important implications for cross-cultural interactions. It is not unreasonable to assume that international corporate business deals have been influenced by employees' sensitivity and knowledge of fundamental cultural expectations and rules.

Figure 5.1 illustrates the general structure of the ePALS discussion forums. Respondents to the original posting have their respective countries clearly identified by the flag displayed next to their responses. One of the unique features of ePALS is the built-in translator tool, seen in Figure 5.1, which allows users to convert messages to many languages, facilitating their usefulness to a wide audience.

Discussion Boards in Courseware

Teachers can utilize discussion through websites such as ePALS to extend and support a variety of curriculum requirements, but they may also wish to structure online conversations that take place only among members of their own classrooms. Many teachers are inte-

Figure 5.1

A Message from the ePALS Student Forums

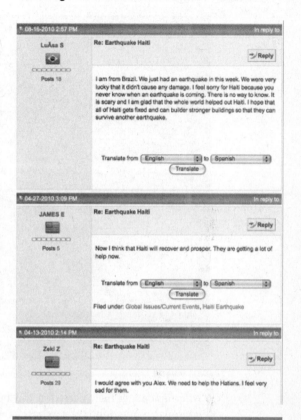

Source: ePALs.

grating the use of courseware into face-to-face classes, particularly at the secondary school level. One widely used application is the Blackboard system. This online environment provides built-in communication tools, including a discussion board. Blackboard's threaded discussion board messages may be sorted by author, date, or subject and are searchable by key words. Messages can also be selected and "collected" or compiled on one page. Although threaded discussion boards are typically thought of as text based, Blackboard also offers Voice Boards. Functioning in a similar fashion as text-based threaded discussions, Voice Boards allow students to record audio messages.

VoiceThread

VoiceThread is a Web-based application that allows people to hold an asynchronous conversation around media files, including photos, slide presentations, documents, and video. A VoiceThread may consist of a single file (Figure 5.2) or, like an album, contain a collection of media files.

Figure 5.2

VoiceThread Consisting of a Single Screen

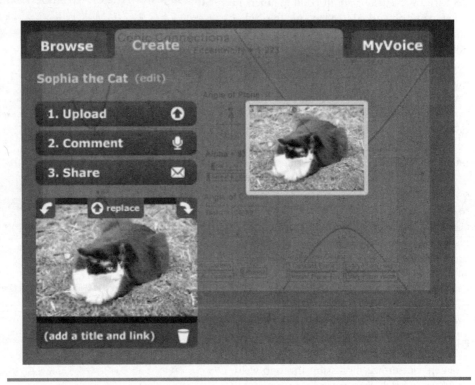

After uploading files, narration can be added to each screen by recording audio or video through a microphone or webcam, recording audio by telephone, or by typing into a textbox. Figure 5.3 depicts an existing VoiceThread with multiple screens, which are indicated by the four squares on the lower right, along with recording and navigation options. After listening to the recorded audio for this screen, visitors may leave comments, which will be indicated by icons along the side of the screen.

A simple VoiceThread might consist of a public domain picture obtained through Google, a licensed image from Flickr's Creative Commons, or a PowerPoint slide. Figure 5.4 (page 100) depicts the initial options for uploading media. Clicking "Media Sources" allows one to access media previously uploaded to Flickr, Facebook, other publicly shared VoiceThreads, or the New York Public Library's collection of more than 700,000 images.

Depending on the purpose and learning outcomes, students might critique a picture in an art class, discuss a photo of a historical or current event, or explain how an advertisement was designed to persuade an audience. Teachers can develop VoiceThreads for students' discussion or design learning activities that involve students creating their own VoiceThreads. A range of publishing options allows the VoiceThread creator to designate who can view and comment on the VoiceThread, providing levels of privacy. VoiceThread also offers several account options, from individual to classroom accounts.

Figure 5.3

VoiceThread Recording and Navigation Options

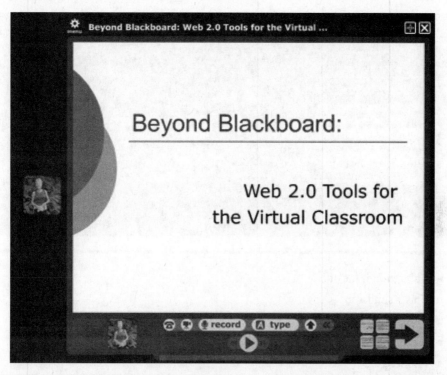

As comments are made, one can "doodle" or draw on the slide by selecting a color from a palette on the screen and using a mouse or trackpad. The doodle will only appear on the slide when that particular comment is selected for playback. This allows users to highlight or annotate the visual media as they comment on it. By selecting the moderating feature, a VoiceThread's owner may designate that comments will not automatically display; instead, the owner previews and approves them. Moderating options can also allow teachers to hold a private conversation with individual students, enabling the VoiceThread to be used as an assessment tool. Because many VoiceThreads consist of images, students have a valuable opportunity to learn about media copyright and how to cite these files. Each VoiceThread slide can have a title and description, wherein one may provide a link to the image's Web location. ImageCodr.org offers a free, online tool for determining the level of Creative Commons permission (see Chapter 2) granted for Flickr images, giving students information about images they may wish to incorporate in their VoiceThreads.

Bill Ferriter (2007) suggests that students gather facts, make connections, ask questions, and offer opinions to create worthwhile VoiceThread comments. VoiceThreads can stimulate critical thinking, as students may be prompted to compare or contrast, to evaluate, and to craft comments that can be explained and defended. Ferriter's list of sentence starters can guide students' thinking as they formulate responses.

Figure 5.4

VoiceThread Initial Options for Uploading Files

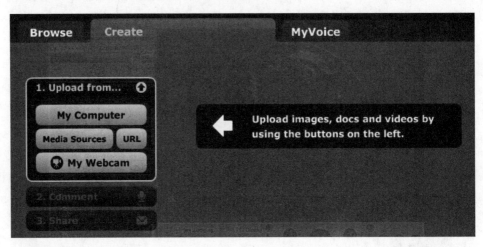

- This reminds me of . . .
- This is similar to . . .
- I wonder . . .
- I realized . . .
- I noticed . . .
- You can relate this to . . .
- I'd like to know . . .
- I'm surprised that . . .
- If I were _____, I would _____
- If _____ then _____
- Although it seems . . .
- I'm not sure that . . .

The VoiceThread Digital Library is a database of successful VoiceThread projects that are organized into categories. Here, teachers can find examples of ways to use VoiceThread with K–12 learners.

- In place of a written assessment, students created a "What do you know about Poe" VoiceThread to communicate what they had learned about Edgar Allan Poe.
- High school seniors created "A Day in the Life of . . ." as the final segment of a school wide literacy project.
- "Where I'm From" featured personally significant poems from fourth graders with their own self-portraits in the background. Students explored cultural

differences between themselves while sharing an oral presentation of their work.

- "Seventh Graders Go Green" is an interactive VoiceThread promoting environmental issues.

- A fifth-grade class used VoiceThread to create digital portfolios for student-led parent conferences. This enabled family and friends to view and comment on students' work and learning.

- Using Slave Narratives from NCLearn.org, the "Reconstruction" VoiceThread engaged eleventh graders in a study of the post-Civil War era as they responded to the experiences of freed slaves. Their teacher reported that students internalized their discussion, later using critical thinking in speculating on how freed slaves might have responded to the Great Depression and changes in society.

Things to Consider

The prevalence of Twitter and text messaging has resulted in students whose writing reflects the truncated language used with these technologies. Although use of a spellchecker may help, careful crafting of one's messages is vital. Students must understand what context and audience mean in terms of writing; teachers may want to include writing mechanics as a grading criterion. This topic could provide an excellent opportunity for generating argumentation on an asynchronous discussion board, giving students the chance to think and express their reasoning.

Online communication presumes that students can communicate—that is, that they can meaningfully participate in conversations. To do that, they must be able to interpret messages, consider appropriate responses, and construct coherent replies. Most teachers realize that not all students can engage in cogent and coherent discourse. Why can't they? For one thing, most students have rarely been asked to contribute substantive discussion in learning settings. They have often been too busy memorizing information or completing worksheets. So it may be necessary to support students' attempts to converse. Environments such as Knowledge Forum (see Chapter 6) offer the built-in structure to scaffold student discourse. When students use discussion tools that do not have these embedded supports, there are other methods teachers may use to assist students.

Salmon (2002) believes that motivated students and active, skilled moderators contribute to successful computer conferencing. Our goal is to encourage critical thinking within the discussion. Teachers must be on the lookout for conversation that remains shallow (e.g., "I agree" or "me too"), that is unfocused, or that demonstrates misconceptions, uncertainty, or imprecise thinking. There are strategies that teachers can employ to help students sharpen the focus and reach more depth in their dialogue (Collison, Elbaum, Haavind, & Tinker, 2000). To dig deeper into the ideas being generated, teachers can model use of analogies to help make connections, bring unexamined issues to the forefront, and encourage and respect multiple perspectives. Collison et al. (2000) offer the method of "full-spectrum questioning" to extract meaning from participants' conversation. The questions in Figure 5.5 demonstrate how a discussion moderator can encourage meaningful dialogue among participants in an online discussion.

Figure 5.5

Full-Spectrum Questioning from Collison et al. (2000)

Questions that probe the "so what!" response	Questions that clarify meaning or conceptual vocabulary	Questions that explore assumptions, sources, and rationale	Questions that seek to identify causes and effects or outcomes	Questions that consider appropriate action
How Relevant or Important? To whom? To what constituency? Individuals or groups? What viewpoint would impart importance? Is that me/us/them? What audience is assumed? If we knew all about this, what good would it do? **How Urgent or Interesting?** Is immediate consideration needed? Or, is the detail best left for other times or forums? Is the issue compelling, or tangentially related to my or the group's task at hand? Is the issue of intellectual merit? **What Context?** Is the issue or question part of a larger view or strategy?	**Is There Ambiguity or Vagueness?** Are terms clear or meanings commonly shared? What alternative meanings might exist? Can quantifiers be made more explicit? How much? How long? How few? To what extent? Can implicit comparisons be made explicit? **Are Concepts Held in Common?** Are terms relying on professional or technical understandings? Does meaning shift from ordinary usage to technical sense? Is persuasion confused with definition? What might be a similar example in another area?	**What Qualities Are Assumed?** Is the claim or phenomena assumed to be: Real, unique, measurable, beneficial, harmful, neutral? Might the opposite assumption be equally valid? Are biases or preconceptions evident in gender, audience, categorization? What does the speaker assume about herself or himself or the audience? **Can One Be Sure?** What evidence supports the claim? How can it be confirmed? What are reasons for belief or disbelief or assigning value? What procedures or processes give evidence for certainty? What supports any analogies?	**Primary Vs. Secondary?** Is the claim/condition a root or secondary cause or effect? Is it a trigger for other mechanisms? What are they? **Internal/External vs. Systematic Interaction?** Is the cause/effect mechanism internal or partly external to the system? What external factors affect interactions? Are reputed "causes" perhaps correlations? At what level might true causes operate? Are consequences long or short term? For whom? What limits or scenarios might apply? What are worst/best cases? What is most probable? Why? If cause/effects are connected systemically through feedback, what are the key feedback controls?	**Who Does What, How, When, with Whom, and Why?** Is there a quick fix or is a more considered view needed? Should I/we do something? Together, separately, as a group? Should it be done now? When? What is the commitment? Are those involved too close to act effectively? Are outsiders needed? Who can be engaged? What plans or strategies will be effective? What levels/conditions need addressing first? **What Comes Next?** How is effectiveness evaluated? What ongoing monitoring or re-evaluating of intervention is needed? Is there a backup plan? Who directs it? Under what conditions is operative?

Facilitating Online Learning: Effective Strategies for Moderators

Discussion moderators can scaffold students' discussion capabilities by helping them concentrate on key points, identifying the most relevant ideas, and steering the direction of the conversation to maintain its purpose. Making students aware of these communication processes as the moderator helps shape and direct the discussion can result in higher-quality subsequent postings if students understand the characteristics that contribute to constructive online discussion. Providing general guidelines such as those in Figure 5.6 can give students some common understanding as to what contributes to effective online conversations.

Depending on the situation, teachers may want to provide a forum for general discussion that is not related to the specific topics in designated forums. This allows students the opportunity to discuss things that are interesting to them yet keeps the dialogue focused on the topic's purpose in other forums. Creating a "watercooler" or "break room" forum for discussions that are unrelated to other forums may result in conversations that become equally as valuable as those the teacher plans. Teachers may create new forums based on ideas that emerge from existing forums and may involve students in deciding on areas for

Figure 5.6

Guidelines for Effective Online Discussions

- The Discussion Board should be accessed at least twice weekly (one original posting and one response is required).
- Discussion board postings should begin early in the specified discussion time frame to allow maximum interaction.
- Make your subject lines informative and descriptive. When replying to someone, change the subject line to more closely reflect your topic. That will avoid the possible scenario of having 20 replies with something like "Re: My Idea" as the subject line.
- Postings should contribute something of value. Responses such as, "Thanks for the idea. This will help a lot" or "I know just what you mean" are not appropriate postings for the forum environment. Please email other students directly if a message is not important for the entire class to read.
- Messages posted should contribute to the group's overall understanding of the topic being discussed through one or more of the following:
  - examining a topic from a new or different perspective
  - explaining issues more in-depth
  - asking relevant and effective questions
  - elaborating meaningfully on the topic
  - responding to elaborate, contradict, modify, and/or explain the original message
- Remember that without the communication cues we get when conversing face-to-face, there is a greater chance for misinterpretation. Therefore, choose your words carefully and read what you've written before you submit your posting.

discussion. Many students find that the online environment enhances the dialogue among students. As we stated previously, the structure of schools often inhibits meaningful dialogue because of time constraints. Teachers who integrate asynchronous discussion boards into their curriculum provide a solution that gives students the chance to interact beyond the confines of four walls and too few minutes.

Exchanging Ideas Synchronously with Chats and Instant Messaging

Asynchronous communication tools such as discussion boards provide the means for users to share ideas in a distributed environment, choosing when they will post messages to the board. As we showed in the previous section, there are benefits to this method of communicating; however, at times we may wish for students to communicate in a way that more closely resembles face-to-face interaction. Synchronous communication tools can provide that instant, real-time exchange of ideas.

Instant Messaging

Instant messaging is a form of real-time communication between two people that is transferred between computers connected over a network such as the Internet or between mobile devices that connect through cell networks. Originally supporting only text messages, client programs such as Skype, Google Talk, AOL Instant Messenger (AIM), and Windows Live Messenger may offer a variety of features, including support for webcams, media sharing, the ability to connect with multiple parties, and versions to install on cell phones and other mobile devices. Social networking sites such as Facebook and Course Management Systems such as Sakai and Moodle offer an instant messaging feature, as do collaborative project websites such as ePals and ThinkQuest.

Messaging software such as Skype typically gives users control over those they talk with through the use of a presence information feature, or "buddy lists." Unless a user provides his or her personal information to a directory, he or she can receive instant messages only from individuals to whom he or she has provided his or her user screen name. Each one-on-one conversation in this type of chat environment is contained in a small, separate screen. While this allows several simultaneous private conversations, users must manage several windows and conversations at once. Based on observations of young people, managing multiple conversations in an instant messaging environment is an easily learned skill. One may also invite users into a chat room, which enables shared conversation among a group of people.

Instant messaging typically increases communication and allows easy collaboration. The synchronous nature of instant messaging allows students to work together, immediately exchanging ideas with one or more individuals. Instant messaging and chats can serve as useful classroom tools for connecting students with others when real-time communication is desirable. The main consideration in choosing between instant messaging and a group chat session is whether one wishes to communicate one-to-one or with a group where several people are engaged in the same conversation. Because of the difficulty in monitoring conversations, teachers may need to carefully consider whether synchronous conversations are of benefit.

Figure 5.7

Guidelines for Safety in Online Communication

Safety Guidelines for Online Communication

- Use a pseudonym instead of your real name.
- Never give out personal information such as your last name, telephone number, home address, or parent's work address.
- Never share a password for an Internet chat room.
- Never agree to meet with someone you met in a chat room and tell your teacher if someone asks you to meet them.
- Notify your teacher if you receive an obscene or inappropriate message.
- Be aware that someone you talk with online might be pretending to be someone they aren't.
- If someone is rude or disagreeable, ignore them rather than engaging in conversation.

Informal use of instant messaging occurs outside the school day and reflects the normal activity of many young people. A vast number of kids spend time online during the evening, with instant messaging being an integral part of that activity. It is only natural that questions about homework are bandied about, with friends providing assistance to each other through instant messaging. Comparable questioning and assistance could occur among students working at a distance on collaborative projects.

Community-oriented websites such as ePALS, Global Schoolhouse, and iEARN (see Chapter 6) offer several communication tools, and using chat and/or messaging services through these sites offers an element of safety that may not be present in many venues. Because teachers will want to identify a clear purpose for student use of chat rooms and instant messaging, they may find that these purposeful websites are, at least initially, the best source for them, as conversation is centered around project work or otherwise structured to some degree. Their parameters help ensure that student use of these tools is genuinely constructive and supports learning goals.

The ability to identify the individuals involved in a chat is an important factor in determining the safety of these online conversations. Teachers may want to share the list of guidelines in Figure 5.7 with students and parents to help build awareness of ways to take advantage of the positive aspects of online communication while maintaining one's privacy and security.

Sharing Information with Presentation Technologies

Over the years, the use of PowerPoint in K–12 classrooms has become commonplace. As with any tool, its value is not inherent, but is contingent on the user. That said, the design and constraints of a tool can shape the things we do and create with it. Presentation software is often overused and, in many cases, is not used in ways that enhance learning, but rather as a means to simply retell bits of information. We will begin by considering the benefits and pitfalls of traditional presentation software. Then, we will explore some innovative ways to share ideas using social software such as Prezi and SlideShare and, finally, consider ways to utilize interactive whiteboards (e.g., SmartBoard, Promethean) effectively.

PowerPoint

Aside from being addressed in standards, being able to develop (and deliver) an effective presentation is a skill that is required not only in the later years of a K–12 education, but in many aspects of our everyday and work lives.

Presentation writing requires many of the same skills that other types of writing require: prewriting tasks such as deciding on goals, and organization and sequencing of ideas, composition of message, and editing. Microsoft's PowerPoint offers several built-in tools that can facilitate this process. We briefly describe how this product can be used to facilitate presentation writing and also discuss some of the potential downsides of the product.

Mentioning Microsoft's PowerPoint can quickly produce glazed-over eyes and a barrage of commentary about the last one hundred–slide presentation we have most recently been subjected to. The phrase "death by PowerPoint" (Bumiller, 2010) captures the stultifying nature of too many presentations, which consist of endless bullet-pointed slides that fail to convey connections or depth of thought. Certainly teachers have legitimate reasons to create and use PowerPoint presentations, but that won't teach students how to create their own presentations. In fact, it is arguable that many teachers are modeling shallow uses of presentation software themselves. However, just as with many of the other technology tools described in this book, when we put the tool into the hands of the student and ask them to create presentations, they can learn valuable skills.

PowerPoint offers several features that can help students to create effective presentations.

- *"AutoContent" wizard.* PowerPoint offers sets of "canned" slides, each for a different type of presentation (e.g., persuasive, reporting status, educational). Each set is structured with an outline of the content that ought to be included in a presentation with the general goal of the presentation type selected (e.g., reporting status).

- *Outlining.* The software offers an outline view that shows only the text and its hierarchical organization. Text can either be viewed or edited in this mode. This mode facilitates thinking about and representing presentation content in an organized hierarchy. The easily viewed outline offers teachers a quick way to see the organization of a student's presentation and provide feedback.

- *Hierarchical organization of text.* In addition to the outline view, one can easily show hierarchical relationships between text content via the use of bulleted and sub-bulleted text (text indented under the initial bullet) or numbered lists that, again, can include lists within lists. This feature provides support for presentation writers to consider the relationships between concepts on individual slides.

- *Linking.* PowerPoint supports the insertion of different types of links to other applications. Users can insert labeled links to Internet URLs or to specific locations within a Microsoft Word, Excel, or another PowerPoint document. When in presentation mode, users can jump directly from their presentation to the specified page. Given that information comes in many forms, the support of links in presentations allows learners to seamlessly bring in multiple information sources.

■ *Notes.* Users can create detailed notes for each slide to help either in the oral delivery of the presentation or to help someone who is reading the presentation at a later time to understand the slide. Teachers can draw attention to (and perhaps require the use of) this feature to emphasize the importance of creating presentation slides that contain only key points, while placing any lengthy prose into the slide notes.

PowerPoint also offers features that can distract learners from creating an effective presentation. Most of these features are focused on the visual design, graphics, and animation that are part of the presentation. Although we recognize the value of text and slide design as learning outcomes, if the primary goal is to write an effective presentation, then some students may need to be cautioned against spending too much time on the visual design features. For instance, Oppenheimer (2004) recounts the story of a student who spent 17 hours on a PowerPoint presentation of which only 7 were spent on the actual writing. Here are just a few of the potential pitfalls.

■ *Font-itus.* A term used to describe the usage of too many fonts (e.g., Arial, Comic Sans, Times New Roman) and/or too many font styles (underline, bold, italic) or sizes, or colors.

■ *Overzealous slide transitions.* PowerPoint offers the ability to have slides fade in using a checkerboard pattern, slide in from one direction or another, appear as if opening up a Venetian blinds, and on and on. Selecting one of these and using it consistently throughout a presentation may be appropriate; however, learners may be overly entranced with these effects to the point of them being a distraction.

■ *Incongruous slide templates.* PowerPoint offers many, many combinations of slide backgrounds and pre-scripted fonts, bullet types, and graphics that each combine to make a "design template." Some templates are quite abstract (e.g., digital dots) while others denote a theme (e.g., mountain top). They also vary in terms of their visual simplicity or complexity. These templates are easy to use and provide learners with a ready made set of fonts and colors that generally work together quite well. However, learners should be cautioned against choosing a template that uses graphics that don't fit with the information in the presentation, or alternatively a template that includes background graphics that conflict with their own presentation images. Fortunately, it is easy to change from one design template to another at any point during the creation of the presentation.

■ *Too many slides.* PowerPoint makes it easy to create slides; that can be both a good and a bad thing. Learners may find they create many slides where fewer more carefully designed and worded slides would be more effective.

To counteract these pitfalls, teachers can provide guidance in the form of presentation requirements. For instance, one might stipulate that presentations may only use a maximum of four different fonts and some specified number of colors or animations. Alternatively, teachers could require a phased approach to presentation development. Perhaps students are required to write the text only of their presentation initially with placeholder slides that describe in words the graph, animation, picture or other visual that will be inserted in a next draft. Teachers can then work with students on developing a clear set of presentation text before students begin to engage in the potentially distracting features of PowerPoint for inserting graphs, or animations.

Teachers may also wish to have students engage in the evaluation of existing Power-Point presentations as a learning activity for writing presentations. An Internet search will quickly provide teachers or students with a variety of presentations to study. This activity can help students together with teachers develop their own set of guidelines for how to use the features of PowerPoint to support their presentations—and as important, what to avoid.

Regardless of its potential drawbacks, putting PowerPoint into the hands of students for creating presentations is a popular activity for a wide range of grade levels. The following example illustrates how the writing aspect of creating presentations can be used within the context of other disciplines (e.g., science or history).

A suburban first-grade teacher used PowerPoint presentations as part of a research project on animals (KITE, 2001a). Students used the Internet to find and download pictures of animals; they created word problems that included their animal, gathered scientific facts about the animal and finally combined all of their unit work into a PowerPoint presentation.

Social Presentation Software: Google Presentations, SlideShare, Prezi

Web-based presentation software makes it possible to collaborate on the creation of presentations and to share them with others through the Internet. With Google Docs's Presentation component, existing PowerPoints can be uploaded or new presentations created, all of which can be shared with others for collaborating and/or viewing. Although Google Presentations allows users to collaborate on and share presentations, its features closely resemble those of PowerPoint. Figure 5.8 shows a presentation in progress.

SlideShare (www.slideshare.net) is a social media site that allows users to upload and share presentations, as well as documents and pdf files. As with Web 2.0 sites that support sharing, SlideShare gives the media owner the option to define the community for sharing, whether it is globally to the public or with a more local audience, such as a classroom. Individuals with whom the presentation is shared can leave comments, turning a static presentation into a dialogue. An added feature of SlideShare is the ability to record audio that accompanies slides.

Prezi (www.prezi.com) offers a very different interface than PowerPoint and results in a nonlinear, interactive presentation rather than a set of slides. Conceptually, this means that users have greater freedom to be creative and, without the restrictions of a linear presentation, their thinking may also be less linear. The open-ended and unique method of designing a Prezi encourages students to analyze the information they are using, make connections and consider how the visual display of information may affect the message. A Prezi enables users to show relations and context. Initially, the entire presentation appears as a graphic. One can click various parts of the graphic to jump directly to that point;

Figure 5.8

Creating a Presentation with Google Docs

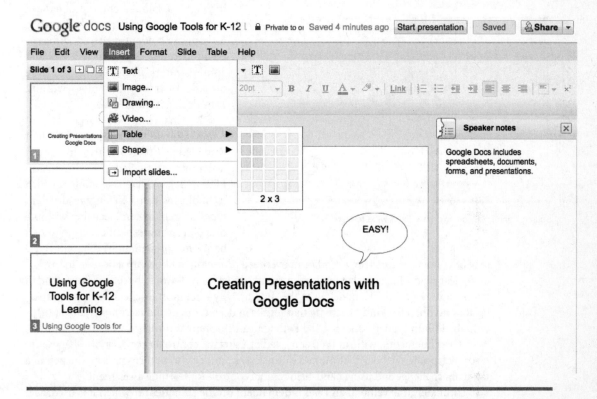

however, when creating a Prezi, the user also defines a path that can be followed by using navigation controls at the bottom of the screen, as seen in Figure 5.9. Prezis can integrate audio, video, animation, graphics, and text, making them vehicles for multimedia presentations that can use zooming and rotation to communicate messages in a nonlinear mode. The "Playing to Learn?" Prezi shown in Figure 5.9 looks like a board game, with a "Start" and "Finish." One can follow the designated path or click on individual spaces to access text, YouTube videos, and websites that illustrate the power of using games for learning. Rather than viewing a static presentation, one is actively immersed in a dynamic experience, which, in this case, is also gamelike.

Presentation Hardware: Interactive Whiteboards

The popularity of interactive whiteboards (IWB) in K–12 classrooms has skyrocketed. Unfortunately, this technology is too frequently used as little more than an electronic chalkboard or expensive overhead projector. Rather than engaging students in complex, goaldirected learning activities in which students actively collaborate, investigate, discuss, and

Figure 5.9

Playing to Learn? A Prezi by Maria Andersen

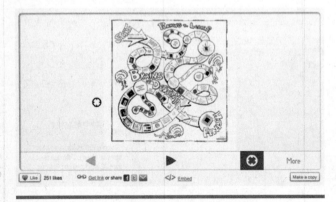

Source: http://prezi.com/rj_b-gw3u8xl/playing-to-learn

create, the nature of an IWB promotes traditional teacher-centered instruction. The IWB phenomenon serves to highlight a fundamental problem in our educational system; namely, while we espouse student-centered, differentiated learning, too often teachers and administrators are swayed by the hype of flashy or trendy technology without considering its implications.

In Chapter 1, we suggested that Technological Pedagogical Content Knowledge (TPACK) also include a learning knowledge dimension (TPLACK), with consideration of which technologies can best engage different types of thinking and learning within a discipline using a specific pedagogy. As a hardware presentation tool, an IWB may offer many features not found in an overhead projector, but how can it be used for meaningful learning? Much of what teachers currently do with IWBs would be difficult to defend in the context of a TPLACK model. Even the "interactivity" that most teachers describe is superficial rather than the kind of activity that results in deep thought and learning. Manzo (2010) described ninth graders studying the Pythagorean theorem and rules for triangle classification. Their interaction with an IWB consisted of using the controller pen to move shapes into place by tapping the board. At the end of the lesson, students took turns passing the pen in a tag-team challenge and using hand-held remote controls for learning assessment.

Ultimately, the value of an IWB is dependent on the activities for which it is used, as it is primarily a means for display. Standards-based curriculum materials are available for use with IWBs, but they should be evaluated through a "meaningful learning" lens rather than adopted universally, with no critical thinking as to their value. Too often, "canned" curriculum accompanying IWBs emphasizes the kind of learning that prepares students to achieve on standardized tests rather than developing the knowledge and skills that are necessary to succeed in a global, information-driven society.

A formal review of the effectiveness of information communication technologies included interactive whiteboards and described how they could be used to improve student learning (Kent, 2010). Kent concluded that deep understanding was promoted by activities that included high levels of ambiguity. The activities he observed in classrooms using IWBs were not enabled by use of the IWB, but would be possible without it. For example:

- Using an IWB activity, students had to arrange objects in order of importance and justify their responses.

- Students reported on current events using Internet news websites projected through an IWB. The news website included only certain aspects of the event. The teacher and students discussed issues related to the event that were not included on the website, introducing multiple ways to interpret the event.

- The IWB was used as a "task board" activity. Students interpreted magazine covers found on the Internet and analyzed the similarities and differences in the images.

Similarly, the "101 Ways to Use Your IWB and Data Projectors" wiki (http://useict.wikispaces.com/100+ways+to+use+IWB+and+DP) consists primarily of descriptions for whole-class activities such as using Skype to communicate with others, viewing websites or videos, and creating Wordle maps together.

Kathy Cassidy, a first-grade teacher, said, "I struggle hard to keep the IWB from being teacher-centered, too. We do lots of games that help with a math or science concept as a class and in small groups, but my favorite thing is to make movies on it. I have a document camera, so that helps with sharing (show and tell) time and when we look at something like plant roots together." Cassidy used an IWB as a means for students to create and share math word problems. Figure 5.10 depicts the final screen of an animation that begins with a blank screen. One of Cassidy's students narrates the simple story as he draws: "Five dogs were running around in the yard. Three more came. Five plus three equals eight." Animations were saved and uploaded to YouTube, where they were subsequently available for embedding in the class blog and wikis to share with family, friends, and others (see Chapter 6). Using an IWB to create and share original works can give students experience in presenting ideas to a group as they demonstrate math understanding.

Figure 5.10

Math Animation Created on an Interactive Whiteboard

Making Connections through Videoconferencing

Nearly 100 years ago, John Dewey commented on the dangers of a complex society that relies on schools and classrooms to convey essential knowledge and tools to its youth:

> As societies become more complex in structure and resources, the need for formal teaching and learning increases. As formal teaching and training grows, there's a danger of creating an undesirable split between the experience gained in direct association and what is acquired in school. This danger was never greater than at the present time on account of the rapid growth of the last few centuries, of knowledge and technical modes of skill. (Dewey, 1916, p. 11)

Reflecting on the state of formal education over the past several decades shows, unfortunately, that the danger Dewey warned against has, to a great extent, occurred. The schism between real-world experience and school learning is a serious concern. Technologies of various kinds can serve as bridges between schools and students' outside experiences—if they are used in the right way within a supportive context. Technologies can also link students with experts in real-life contexts through communication tools that support learning and interaction. Videoconferencing is a technology that allows two or more locations to interact simultaneously by two-way video and audio transmissions. In the following sections, some types of videoconferencing systems are discussed and ways to utilize videoconferencing to enhance learning offered.

Connecting with Experts

Interactive videoconferencing (IVC), or Web conferencing, is a technology that offers great potential for connecting students in live interactions with experts to whom they would otherwise have no access. Merrick (2005) acknowledges that teachers may be hesitant about adding a relatively unfamiliar new technology into their classrooms, especially when the current K–12 emphasis is so strongly slanted toward accountability through standardized testing. Would it not be more effective to directly teach the material on which students will be tested? We agree with Merrick that IVC can strengthen curriculum, bringing it a richness and depth that would not be possible without the expertise of professionals who are accessible through videoconferencing technology.

Teachers, particularly those in elementary classrooms who are expected to be knowledgeable in all content areas, may quickly recognize the value of the rich supplemental resources available through videoconferencing. Their curriculum can be enhanced by drawing on additional resources and on a novel approach to learning that can engage and motivate students.

Videoconferencing overcomes barriers of cost and distance since physically transporting a classroom of students to another location is often impossible. Students not only benefit from the knowledge of experts in content areas but also can practice and gain important interpersonal skills through their interactions. Moreover, videoconferencing can result in bridging gaps between schools and the community, encouraging relationships that demonstrate to students the real-life application of classroom learning.

Technical Considerations

Inexpensive desktop videoconferencing is possible through use of desktop videocameras, also called webcams. These USB devices connect to a computer that uses the Internet to link users for conferencing. Early videoconferences often resulted in rather jerky video, as data transmission was limited to the speed of slow modems. High-speed (broadband) cable and digital subscriber line (DSL) Internet connections have greatly improved the quality of desktop videoconferencing. Most computers now come equipped with a built-in videocamera. By using a built-in camera or connecting an inexpensive webcam to your computer, you can videoconference with anyone who has similar tools. In addition to the webcam and Internet connections, users simply need some type of software that supports videoconferencing (often free), computer speakers, and a microphone. Although some webcams have a built-in microphone, users may be more satisfied with the ease and quality of using a headset that combines a microphone with speaker headphones.

Many computer programs are available for participating in desktop videoconferencing. Skype is a free telephony software program that supports one-to-one phone calls through the Internet and conference calls for up to 25 people using Skype, cell phones, or landline phones. Skype uses Voice-over Internet Protocol technology that allows one to make telephone calls using a broadband Internet connection instead of a regular (or analog) phone line. With a webcam, Skype can also be used for desktop videoconferencing. Instant messaging programs such as AOL Instant Messenger, Google Talk, and MSN Messenger also allow video messages.

Applications like Microsoft NetMeeting, Elluminate, and Dimdim support multipoint data conferencing, meaning that data collaboration is possible between several people at once. Blackboard's course management software integrates Wimba tools, including Wimba Classroom, a Web conferencing application. In these Web conferencing environments, users can communicate with audio and video, talking and working together using the whiteboard or shared program features.

For more robust conferencing that can connect multiple locations, dedicated systems are often used. These systems typically feature a console that uses a high-quality remote-controlled video camera. Dedicated systems integrate all the required components into this single piece of equipment, including the control computer, speakers, necessary software or hardware for converting compressed audio and video signals, and a monitor. Polycom is one widely use dedicated videoconferencing system. Multipoint systems can allow users to connect several separate sites simultaneously.

Videoconferencing Interactions with a Geologist

First-grade teacher Kathy Cassidy uses Skype to connect her students with peers in other classrooms and with experts. During a study of rocks, students listed all the things they wanted to learn and then talked with Dr. Trish Gregg, a geologist in Oregon. "Why do some rocks look like crystals?" asked one student. The geologist explained that rocks are made of crystals, but they are sometimes too small to see without a microscope. She showed the students smooth rocks and they discussed how rivers play a role in shaping rocks. They compared bumpy rocks, heavy and light volcanic rocks, and Dr. Gregg demonstrated how a rock hammer is used to break rocks for investigating. Students brought their experiences and questions to an expert in the field, who encouraged their questioning and engaged students in a dialogue that deepened their understanding of the natural world while demonstrating the career work of a geologist.

Videoconferencing Interactions with Astronomers at Dyer

Scott Merrick facilitated the VIA Dyer (Videoconferencing Interactions with Astronomers at Dyer) program, wherein students across the country engaged in weekly videoconference presentations with scholars at Vanderbilt Dyer Observatory. He described the experience this way:

> During this series I witnessed several repeat presentations on the same topic, and one excellent example is Bob O'Dell's "Astronomical Observatories"—a fascinating overview of extra-Earth telescopes including a discussion of why they are needed.

In the ensuing question and answer sessions, I sometimes heard O'Dell receive the same or similar questions in subsequent sessions. While his answers would often be informed by his earlier ones, every time I heard him construct a new response, it was in some way different—and often more substantive, more interesting, or more age-appropriate—than the answers he had given before. Not only was he getting better at IVC, but he was also so obviously passionate and knowledgeable about his topic that he inspired genuine engagement among his audience. It was not a canned presentation; it was conversation.

For example, in the course of his presentation, O'Dell often narrated a three-minute computer-generated virtual fly-through of the Orion Nebula. While students could use Google to find and download this digital video from the Internet, with IVC they could see it and also simultaneously hear narration by the man who directed the 500-person-hour team that actually constructed the animation. O'Dell's team constructed the animation out of mathematical models and images sent back to Earth by the Hubble Space Telescope, and O'Dell himself was project scientist for the first team that undertook the design of the Hubble telescope. IVC affords students a unique opportunity to interact with someone immediately involved in current research in a given discipline. (Merrick, 2005, pp. 1–2)

A second Vanderbilt University videoconferencing initiative aimed at improving K–12 science education involved weekly videoconferences between the students and Vanderbilt faculty research scientists, physicians, postdoctoral fellows, upper-level graduate students and medical students, as well as other science professionals (McCombs et al., 2004).

Videoconferencing Interactions with Missouri Supreme Court Judges

While these examples are primarily science based, videoconferencing may be used in any content area. In Missouri, high school students gained important understanding of civics by interacting with two Missouri Supreme Court judges and a University of Missouri professor who is a constitutional expert (Heavin, 2006). During this live broadcast, in recognition of Constitution Day, panel members discussed topics chosen by the students, including the Constitution as it relates to the war on terrorism, religion in school, and drug testing and drug dogs in schools. During the broadcast, students had the opportunity to e-mail questions to the panel.

This program was provided by the Missouri Bar in cooperation with Education Solutions Global Network (ESGN), an Internet-based, video broadcast distribution network offered by the Missouri School Boards Association for education and training. It supports the delivery of digital video and audio of live events and events that have been recorded and made available "on demand." Other ESGN videoconference programming is a nature series called "Top Down: Predators and Prey," which explores the mysteries of great animal hunters and escape artists. This series originates from the Wonders of Wildlife Museum and Aquarium in Springfield, Missouri, and has connected up to 50 school districts, including ones in Alaska and Mexico.

Likewise, the Vanderbilt Virtual School connects many schools simultaneously. The school's director explains that by "using a 'bridge' at the University of Tennessee, we can connect with many schools at one time. That is very cool because students at each site can see and hear students at the other sites" (Jackson, 2005). She goes on to say,

Figure 5.11

Videoconferencing Ideas and Examples from AT&T Knowledge Network Explorer

Courses and Tutoring

- Students take classes not offered at their school, such as advanced honors, foreign language, or music courses.
- Teachers team-teach with remote teachers, sharing subject matter expertise or a unique approach to a topic.
- Students meet with tutors for enrichment, remediation, or a helpful bit of personal attention. This is great way for businesses to support schools.
- A librarian offers an introduction to library services and library tour for local schools before they come to the library.

Virtual Field Trips

- Students organize and moderate a panel discussion with a dolphin trainer, fisherman, and animal rights activist as part of an ocean unit.
- A librarian using document sharing technology, auxiliary input, or a whiteboard answers questions about research and actually demonstrates search queries using the online catalog.
- Students connect with athletes at an Olympic Training Center for advice and feedback on sports, training, and health issues.
- Students watch a play performed at a remote site followed by interaction with the actors.
- A small group interviews the author of a book the class is studying.
- Students meet with university advisors for admission counseling or interviews.
- A remote teacher or student role-plays a historical or literary figure, sharing a special experience with a larger audience.
- A graphic arts student shares a document with a professional or client for feedback and evaluation.

Multi-School Projects

- Teachers and students collaborate and exchange information with other schools in areas such as peer counseling, bilingualism, and student government.
- Students communicate with "video pals" to experience diverse cultures and ways of life, both economic and ethnic. Video pals also provide an excellent opportunity for foreign language practice.
- Schools known for outstanding programs or projects model those projects for other schools.
- Contests between schools – debates, spelling bees, or research conferences – take place via two-way video.
- Videoconferencing facilitates distributed cooperative learning, where groups at distant sites take on a learning task and teach remote peers.
- Distributed projects make use of videoconferencing technology for collaboration and communication.

(continued)

Figure 5.11 (*continued*)

Community Connections

- Town hall meetings, government hearings, school board meetings, court functions, and other government-related activities.
- Public health discussions
- Support of special interests or hobbies
- Adult education in areas such as English, literacy, job training, etc.
- Virtual author tours

One of the most touching videoconferences we had was when we first ran our Holocaust Survivors series. Mira Kimmelman, a sweet and gentle woman in her late eighties, spoke with students in six schools about her experience in Auschwitz. Although Mira's story lasted almost an hour, those elementary and middle school students sat still and did not make a sound. Following her talk, the students took turns asking her questions about Nazis, the war, her family.

Figure 5.11 offers suggestions from AT&T's Knowledge Network Explorer (www.kn.att.com/wired/vidconf/ideas.html) for implementing videoconferencing not only to connect students with experts but also for peer connections, virtual field trips, and course offerings that aren't available at all schools.

The Pacific Bell program in California (Videoconferencing for Learning) has introduced the concept of student videoconferencing groups within partner schools and has shown that videoconferencing results in positive outcomes. Specifically, videoconferencing does the following:

- Increases motivation
- Improves communication and presentation skills
- Allows students to learn to ask better questions
- Increases communication with the outside world
- Lets students learn from a primary source rather than a textbook
- Increases the depth of understanding in subject area content (www.kn.pacbell.com/wired/vidconf/intro.html)

Mark Haddon, director of education at the Smithsonian Environmental Research Center (SERC), described the Smithsonian's ventures with video conferencing. SERC's research projects are comprised of a variety of outdoor studies, including shoreline and marine life research:

> We are, in essence, a content provider to schools that have invested in video conferencing technologies. It gives students from these schools the ability to visit the Smithsonian and learn all about different types of life forms found throughout our environment, without leaving their classrooms. The fact is that many school districts are looking for content providers with good equipment because it justifies usage and encourages more schools to get involved in video conferencing. Video conferencing has developed into an excellent way for schools to provide quality education for their students, regardless of where the subject matter is located (as quoted in German, 2005).

Things to Consider

The cost of videoconferencing equipment and the needed infrastructure are certainly important considerations. While most systems are fairly easy to use, teachers will nevertheless need training before they begin scheduling videoconferences with others. Because time differences will always be a factor between distant locations, scheduling synchronous communications might tend to limit videoconferencing to partners in time zones that are not substantially different. Equipment should be checked before beginning the videoconference to ensure that everything is functioning well. During the session, mute any microphones that aren't in use to avoid distracting noise. Users should also consider basic elements such as lighting, acoustics, and the position of participants.

Beyond the technical aspects, there are several things that videoconference participants and planners can do to optimize the experience for all involved. Care should be taken to keep the technology in a support role and not to become enamored of the tool itself. As Arthur C. Clarke, British author and inventor, once said, "Before you become too entranced with gorgeous gadgets and mesmerizing video displays, let me remind you that information is not knowledge, knowledge is not wisdom, and wisdom is not foresight. Each grows out of the other, and we need them all" (Clarke, n.d.). As you plan, the essential focus should be the intended learning outcomes for your students. Think about the structure of the videoconference in relation to other learning activities. What can you do to prepare students? Is there background knowledge that will help them get the most from the videoconference and enable them to ask probing questions? Encourage students to generate questions before the videoconference. While they will undoubtedly think of questions during the session, it is advisable not to depend solely on those. Some prior thought and reflection may result in deeper inquiry than simply relying on on-the-fly questions. If possible, involve students in planning the entire session.

If students are new to this technology, they may need coaching on how to be respectful partners in the videoconferencing process. Although they see the presenter, they need to remember that they, too, are being observed. Plan for engaging interactions that go beyond the "talking head" model. There is little value in simply watching and listening to someone lecture, whereas there is significant learning potential in two-way interaction where all participants are involved in sharing information, questioning, demonstrating, and offering other activities that would otherwise be unlikely to occur.

Remember that learning doesn't end when the videoconference cameras are turned off. Plan follow-up activities that capitalize on the videoconference and involve students in analysis and constructive work that draws on and extends the videoconferencing experience.

Broadcasting with Podcasts and Internet Radio

Just as blogs now make online text publishing possible for anyone, podcasting is enabling all of us to produce the equivalent of online radio or TV programs. Two types of Internet technology deliver audio files. The first, streaming audio, delivers content that the user listens to as it is delivered, much as one would listen to a radio or TV. The second form of Internet radio, podcasting, provides audio in a form analogous to a tape recording or CD, where content is recorded and made available for future listening.

The delivery of audio files over the Internet took a giant leap with the invention of MPEG-1 Audio Layer 3 (MP3). In the mid-1990s, a compressed audio format called MP3 enabled digital streaming audio over the Internet. MP3 technology involves transforming an audio signal into a smaller digital file, allowing it to be transmitted over the Internet in a reasonable amount of time. Consider a song or recorded talk. Within the sound waves it contains, there are many more data than our ears require to make sense of the tune and words. MP3 technology samples the data and discards some of them—a trade-off between sound quality and size. Luckily, our senses don't miss the data that are discarded (unless too much gets tossed), resulting in a compressed file that is a manageable size. A Codec program or device encodes (compresses) and decodes (decompresses) the audio stream, and a server stores the data.

In addition to streaming media, another type of Internet radio has emerged. The podcast, a term that blends "broadcasting" and "iPod" (a popular portable audio device), makes audio broadcasting much simpler, allowing almost anyone to create and offer podcasts. Because streaming audio demands more advanced technology than is available at most schools, the following section focuses on podcasting.

What Is Podcasting?

One of the most rapidly expanding technologies today is podcasting. In 2005, USA Today reported that in 6 months' time, a Google search for "podcasting" had increased from a few hundred hits to 687,000 hits (Acohido, 2005). Five years later a "podcasting" search returned 14,400,000 hits. Clearly, podcasting is a popular and growing activity. In 2010, Apple expanded the availability of its podcast directory from 23 countries to 90, which added an additional 4.4 billion potential listeners (Wizzard Media, 2010).

Podcasting enables anyone to become an independent producer and distributor of audio and/or video content that can be offered worldwide through the Internet. As with blogs, there is great latitude for all kinds of publishing with podcasts.

A podcast is an audio recording that is saved as an MP3 file and made available on the Internet through RSS (Really Simple Syndication). Audio podcasts have been joined by video podcasts, which employ MP4 compression to deliver both audio and video data. Users "subscribe to" or choose the audio or video content they wish to listen to or view.

Many websites include the RSS language and podcast feeds, allowing you to request, or subscribe, to their content. For example, National Public Radio (www.npr.org) offers podcasted programming that one can automatically receive by subscribing to the RSS feed. From *National Geographic* to news and media websites such as the *New York Times*, sports channels like ESPN, the Philadelphia Museum of Art, and the Culinary Podcast Network, there is audio (and often video) content available in just about every subject imaginable.

Creating and Listening to Podcasts Software that downloads podcasts will check the RSS feeds of the podcasts you subscribe to. When a new podcast is added, the feed is updated, and the software downloads the new file to your computer. You can play this file in a Mac or Windows application (such as iTunes) on your computer. You can also have iTunes automatically synchronize and transfer the files to a mobile device, such as an iPod or iPhone that connects to your computer. While there are several podcasting applications, iTunes is most often used. It has an organized directory of podcasts you can subscribe to and, when you open iTunes, will automatically download the new editions of those podcasts.

If you have an iPod, the downloaded podcasts will synch to it when it's connected to your computer with iTunes. Smartphones (e.g., Blackberry, iPhone) with wireless Internet access can also be equipped with software that checks RSS feeds, downloads podcasts, and provides playback.

The Apple website (www.apple.com/itunes/) provides the iTunes player as a free software download. Once iTunes has been installed, select the "Podcasts" link in the Library menu. On the lower portion of the main window, you'll find a "Settings" button that gives you options for managing your podcasts. You'll also see a link to "Podcast Directory." That link accesses the iTunes music store, where you can select from many category listings. Click on the "Subscribe" button next to the podcast you want. Most podcasts offer a "Subscribe" button, but a direct URL for a podcast you've located on a web page can be entered using the "Advanced" menu in iTunes. Click on "Subscribe to Podcast" and enter the URL in the text box window.

Many other programs besides iTunes are available for listening to podcasts, including iPodderX, Juice, Playpod, and Podspider. A search for "podcast software" returns thousands of hits; the Podcasting News website has a good collection categorized into software for publishing and client software for listening to podcasts (www.podcastingnews.com/topics/ Podcasting_Software.html).

The basic technique for creating a podcast involves recording audio using a computer, microphone, and software. Free audio software such as Audacity can be used for recording and editing podcast content. For Macintosh users, Apple's GarageBand is an excellent solution. Programs like FeedBurner or Feeder can provide the necessary RSS feed, which is written in a language called XML. The MP3 and feed files are then uploaded to a Web server and a link to the podcast is listed on your web page or blog.

Podcasting in the Classroom

While there is much to be gained by listening to others' podcasts, it is an even more valuable experience for students to create their own broadcasts. As with student-created WebQuests, the cognitive requirements for designing and developing a podcast are multidimensional.

A class-created podcast offers opportunities for students to collaborate, with decision making in the forefront, as students determine the purpose and content for the podcast. Will others be involved, or will the taping consist solely of students? Are there opportunities for students to develop interview questions and bring in experts or community members to codevelop the podcast?

Student-created podcasts give students a chance to broadcast to an authentic audience and can motivate them to become experts in preparation for podcast development. Rather than regurgitating material, students should develop podcasts that contain original material or that analyze and deepen the understanding of existing material. Podcasting is a tool that supports meaningful curriculum integration, and the technical aspects of producing a podcast offer students a unique learning opportunity. Determining how to sequence material, finding or creating copyright-free music or other audio to transition between segments, practicing public speaking, and locating additional resources to extend the value of the podcast—all of these are valuable elements of podcast production.

Podcasts can also be an important component in collaborative work by enhancing the connections between students. In lieu of text-based communication, students might record personal messages to learn more about each other. Digital storytelling allows students to share experiences or create original works to record. International collaborations offer opportunities to practice second-language skills or to learn a new language. Students might also create and share music or take a walking tour of their city, recording sounds on the street. Podcasts can be used to discuss plans and ongoing work during a collaborative project and are a vehicle for sharing project outcomes with a larger audience. They give students who may be more skilled in oral communication than in written words the chance to excel.

One technique for adding value to podcasts is by extending their content through other media. A common practice is combining one's blog with his or her podcast. Ideas can be expressed in writing with a blog that contains links to other websites and to a podcast related to the blog entry. Using multimedia combines the attributes of text, audio, and video, offering users the choice of engaging different modalities.

Radio WillowWeb   At Willowdale Elementary School in Omaha, Nebraska, technology specialist Tony Vincent originated the Radio WillowWeb podcast, an online radio program/podcast created for kids by kids. Radio WillowWeb was one of the first podcasts produced by elementary students and has been used as a guide for many other schools as they embark on this technique of instructional technology use.

For one podcast, fifth-grade students created a show about sound and light that consisted of seven segments sharing students' knowledge (Figure 5.12). During the podcast, students explained how the ear works, how to protect hearing, and why color blindness occurs. Other students "interviewed" Helen Keller and reviewed "Reeko's Mad Scientist Lab," describing an experiment available there. Students shared poetry and described assistive devices for deaf and blind individuals. The "Vocabulary Theater" segment explained bioluminescence through a firefly example. Links on the podcast web page take users to related information. Radio WillowWeb can be found in the K–12 Education category in iTunes.

Our City   At the "Our City" podcast website (www.learninginhand.com/OurCity/), students from around the world are invited to submit a recording about the city they live in,

Figure 5.12

A Podcast from Radio WillowWeb

Willowcast #19

Posted April 26, 2006

Fifth graders in Ms. Sanborn's class have studied sound and light. Spencer host this show about these two important forms of energy. There are seven segments packed with interesting information:

- Ear-Regular Radio Show **by Hannah**
  - ○ Let's Hear It for the Ear!
- Interesting Interview **by Mandy**
  - ○ Helen Keller Photograph Collection
- Vocabulary Theater **by Tyler**
- Wonderful Website **by Will**
  - ○ Reeko's Mad Scientist Lab
- Did You Know? **by Stephen**
- Poetry Corner **by Shelby**
- Incredible Inventions **by Jessie**

Spotlight on Sound & Light

MP3 | 10 minutes 36 seconds | 10.2 MB

If the show doesn't play automatically, click here.

XML

with a teacher's assistance. The resulting website is a rich travelogue, with student podcasts that range from a description of huge New York city to the small village of Busy Brown Deer, Wisconsin. Students in Germany describe "Our Berlin" and sixth graders in Brunei podcast "Our Rainforest Dream." The "Our City" podcasts give listeners an inside view on geographical locations across the country from a young person's perspective. Even more important, they are a means for the students constructing the podcasts to meet content and process standards while creating a product for an audience of peers. Student developers will need to critically evaluate and choose the information they include in the podcast, write a script, locate additional resources, and engage in a variety of technical tasks.

Ram Radio   At Sandy Ridge Elementary School in North Carolina, podcasting is supplemented with "Ram Radio," a program broadcast daily through a low power transmitter that reaches 450 ft. beyond the school building. The programs are also available on the school website at http://sres.ucps.k12.nc.us/RockinTheRidge.php. A recent broadcast began with these words from the student announcer:

Good morning! You are listening to 103.3 Ram Radio, Rockin' The Ridge. Our mission statement is the ram radio podcasters of Sandy Ridge Elementary will utilize 21-century technology skills to produce a daily radio podcast. Students will learn valuable skills such as the ability to perform research, work cooperatively with others, inside and outside of the studio and finally production techniques to create a program to entertain and inform our school and community.

ColeyCasts   Brent Coley's fifth-grade students in Murrieta, California, produce Coley-Casts, highlighting their learning to share with others. ColeyCasts span the curriculum, with broadcasts related to Literature Circles Book Trailers, The Solar System, Human Body Systems, Grammar Time! and Amazing America. Coley uses these podcasts to showcase student work, share ideas with other teachers, and enhance parent-teacher-student communication. Creating the ColeyCasts is an authentic project that helps students retain the standards-based information they are learning. Coley said:

> There is nothing like the first day of school when I open up and display iTunes with my classroom's LCD projector. I point to the screen and say, "Your work is going to be here." Seeing the look on their faces when they realize they are going to create podcasts that will be available to the entire world is priceless. I leverage the fact that our podcast and website is popular, telling students that they need to do their very best work because I'm not the only one who is going to listen to what they create. I let them know that students all over the world listen to our ColeyCasts, so this global audience really helps the students work hard to produce a quality product.

Students are actively engaged in all steps of ColeyCast production. The cooperative nature of this activity is evident from the student who said, "You learn more when you're having fun. Everybody contributes their ideas to make it better." Rather than creating an artificial product seen only by the teacher and, perhaps, one's classmates, the broad audience for ColeyCasts provides authenticity. As another student expressed, "Sometimes we have people from Maine and Australia and all over the world (access the website). I think it's really cool, because it shows how interested people are." Finally, creating ColeyCasts situates students in an activity that strengthens their learning. Speaking of producing the Literature Circles Book Trailers, a student commented, "You get to go back and look at certain parts of the books. It helps me learn what we are reading." Figure 5.13 depicts a creative, original solar system podcast created by students.

In addition to student-created ColeyCasts, Coley produces StudyCasts, which are audio reviews designed to support students as they prepare for tests. Testing is an inevitable part of nearly all students' educational experience and typically contributes little to meaningful learning. Teachers who scaffold learning through resources like Study-Casts can, however, provide students with opportunities to consolidate and reflect on their learning. Teacher-created podcasts can provide guidance across the curriculum in content areas, offer advice and mentoring in building students' metacognitive skills, and bridge the gap between home and school. As a supplement to newsletters and traditional parent communication, podcasts offer an alternative that may feel more personal as a teacher speaks to families.

Getting Started with Podcasting

Coley offers Podcasting Resources (www.mrcoley.com/podcasting) for teachers interested in podcasting. This web page has guidelines, planning sheets, tutorial videos, and helpful links. For example, "How We Create a ColeyCast" describes and gives advice in four stages of the podcasting process: preproduction, recording, postproduction, and publishing. Coley said:

Figure 5.13

ColeyCast #44: The Solar System

The Solar System
The Sun, Eight Planets, and Other Celestial Objects
An Enhanced Podcast
Posted May 29, 2010

Michael hosts ColeyCast #44, an episode that is out of this world! Ever wondered which planet lies on its side, or which planet has 63 moons? Listen to this broadcast and you'll find out!

Segment Listing

- The Sun by Desarae

- Mercury by Tristan

- Venus by Tori

- Earth by Aaron

- Mars by Kiya

- Joke Time with Randi

- Jupiter by Gabe

- Saturn by Walker

- Uranus by Quinton

- Neptune by Anthony K.

- Other Objects by Angela

- Joke Time with Zachary

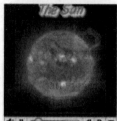

12 minutes 42 seconds

Opening and Closing Music:
"The Battle" by J. Underberg
Courtesy of Podsafe Audio

Download Instructions:
Right-click (Control-click for Mac users) on the link below, and then select "Save Target As..."

- Download ColeyCast #44
  (12.8 MB)

I would also recommend to start slowly, and not bite off more than you can chew. Don't set your goals too high, only to be disappointed later. For example, rather than setting the goal of doing a weekly podcast, perhaps choose a few topics you'd like to create a podcast about. Once you get comfortable with the process, you can then add more to your podcasting plate. In my experience, I've found it's better to begin with smaller, realistic goals. It's always easier to add more than it is to take away.

There are many websites with resources, suggestions, and educators' experiences in working with podcasting. In addition to podcasting instructions on the Apple website (www .apple.com/itunes/podcasts/), "Podcast Help" at www.speedofcreativity.org/resources/ podcast-resources offers advice and links to helpful resources. The "Podcast Directory for Educators" (http://recap.ltd.uk/podcasting/index.php) and Education Podcast Network (http:// epnweb.org) have links to school podcasts, subject podcasts, and education news podcasts. They also offer tips and resources for those interested in podcasting technology.

Tony Vincent, founder of the Radio WillowWeb podcasts, also offers the "Our City" podcast, described previously, as a way to help teachers experiment and get started with podcasting. To contribute to this website, teachers and students create the MP3 audio file and send it to Vincent at the address he provides. The RSS feed and posting is taken care of, making this a simple way for teachers to "test the waters" and explore how podcasts might be an effective addition to their curriculum. Vincent also offers downloadable examples, planning packets, and a discussion forum to help teachers' beginning podcasting efforts.

The purpose of the KidCast: Podcasting in the Classroom website (www.intelligenic .com) is to explore podcasting applications in education. One show encouraged teachers to think about how they might incorporate podcasts into their classrooms, with the host suggesting that students be asked about their experiences with podcasts. Are they consumers, producers, or both? Involving students as the podcast creators offers much more value than asking them only to passively listen to teacher-created podcasts. The "Where in the World?" podcast project combines geography, community, and culture as students create a podcast with clues about a location. Podcasts URLs are sent to the project coordinator, who updates the RSS feed. To listen to podcasts, students subscribe at www.intelligenic .com/where/rss.xml and then use deductive reasoning as they use the Internet to research the clues.

Video podcasting adds a visual element to a podcast, providing another layer of sensory stimuli and accommodating additional learning modalities. Kidcast's creator, Dan Schmit, cites these common mistakes made by teachers new to video podcasting:

- Not considering the audience as one of the first steps in developing their show
- Thinking of discrete, individual topics, rather than a larger scholarly exploration of related questions
- Putting too much time and emphasis on the production, and not enough on the quality of content and conversation in the production
- Letting questions of safety and security derail the process. Be upfront and communicate with administrators and parents about how you plan to protect identity and personal information. Be creative with your production. Talking heads aren't as interesting and are a less secure approach to student produced video.

Schmit offers these suggestions:

- Preview and review EVERYTHING before posting it. The teacher must remain the gatekeeper for the safety, truth, copyright compliance and integrity.
- Reflect on your work—try to pull new ideas for continual improvement by watching and listening to your show with a focus on constructive critique. Also, become a

subscriber to other student-produced shows. Compare and contrast your approaches and your strengths.

- Take it easy. Start small and allow yourself and your students to grow into their scholarly and technical skills. (Schmit, 2010)

When designing podcasts, encourage students to begin with a "teaser" or something to grab the audience's attention and hook them into wanting more. Break the podcast into segments and consider variety, pacing, and voice. Listen to well-designed podcasts and analyze the factors that make them successful. Not only can podcasting enhance student learning in content areas, but the very process of designing and producing a podcast offers opportunities for active learning, for collaborating, conversing, and articulating goals and the steps necessary for meeting them, in creating an authentic product for an audience. Teachers who create learning opportunities for students to use podcasting as a tool that supports meaningful learning can excite and motivate students while meeting any number of possible curriculum objectives and standards.

Conclusion

In this chapter, we have introduced you to several forms of communication that can enhance learning by exposing students to experiences they would otherwise not be afforded, by bringing the expertise and knowledge of professionals who are authorities in their fields into the classroom, and by allowing interactions between students and collaborating partners.

Online discussions, chats, blogs, and instant messaging are not meant to replace face-to-face interactions. While online communication presents opportunities for connecting people, it can also result in isolating and disconnecting us. Technologies that join us with those at a distance may interfere with our immediate relationships if they are used thoughtlessly. When a dinner partner ignores the friend sitting across from her in order to have a cell phone conversation with someone else, interaction suffers. When we ignore or neglect family members while maintaining online relationships with people at a distance, we negate the benefits of communication technologies. We have tried to show, however, that communication tools can support learners in unique ways as they engage in reasoned dialogue, collaborate with remote and diverse audiences, and learn to express themselves in writing.

Advances in technology, particularly in widespread broadband Internet access, have made it easy for users to be not only consumers of audio and video but also participants and creators of these media. We have offered reasons for integrating videoconferencing as a means of unique interactions that support learning and for podcasting, particularly when students are the creators of these broadcasts. Producing content for an authentic audience rather than merely performing for a teacher gives students meaningful learning experiences. We hope that you will reflect on the reality of media in the lives of today's young people and design creative ways that your curriculum can intersect with some of the technology ideas presented in this chapter. In the words of the futurist and author Alvin Toffler (n.d.), "The illiterate of the 21st century will not be those who cannot read and write, but those who cannot learn, unlearn and relearn."

NET Standards potentially engaged by communication activities described in this chapter:

1. **Creativity and Innovation**
    a. Apply existing knowledge to generate new ideas, products, or processes
    b. Create original works as a means of personal or group expression

2. **Communication and Collaboration**
    a. Interact, collaborate, and publish with peers, experts, or others employing a variety of digital environments and media
    b. Communicate information and ideas effectively to multiple audiences using a variety of media and formats
    c. Develop cultural understanding and global awareness by engaging with learners of other cultures
    d. Contribute to project teams to produce original works or solve problems

3. **Research and Information Fluency**
    a. Plan strategies to guide inquiry
    b. Locate, organize, analyze, evaluate, synthesize, and ethically use information from a variety of sources and media
    c. Evaluate and select information sources and digital tools based on the appropriateness to specific tasks
    d. Process data and report results

4. **Critical Thinking, Problem Solving, and Decision Making**
    a. Identify and define authentic problems and significant questions for investigation
    b. Plan and manage activities to develop a solution or complete a project
    c. Collect and analyze data to identify solutions and/or make informed decisions
    d. Use multiple processes and diverse perspectives to explore alternative solutions

5. **Digital Citizenship**
    a. Advocate and practice safe, legal, and responsible use of information and technology
    b. Exhibit a positive attitude toward using technology that supports collaboration, learning, and productivity
    d. Exhibit leadership for digital citizenship

6. **Technology Operations and Concepts**
    a. Understand and use technology systems
    d. Transfer current knowledge to learning of new technologies

21st Century Skills potentially engaged by communication activities described in this chapter:

Think Creatively

- Use a wide range of idea creation techniques (such as brainstorming)
- Create new and worthwhile ideas (both incremental and radical concepts)

- Elaborate, refine, analyze and evaluate their own ideas in order to improve and maximize creative efforts

Work Creatively with Others

- Develop, implement, and communicate new ideas to others effectively
- Be open and responsive to new and diverse perspectives; incorporate group input and feedback into the work

Make Judgments and Decisions

- Effectively analyze and evaluate evidence, arguments, claims, and beliefs
- Analyze and evaluate major alternative points of view
- Synthesize and make connections between information and arguments
- Interpret information and draw conclusions based on the best analysis
- Reflect critically on learning experiences and processes

Solve Problems

- Identify and ask significant questions that clarify various points of view and lead to better solutions

Communicate Clearly

- Articulate thoughts and ideas effectively using oral, written and nonverbal communication skills in a variety of forms and contexts
- Listen effectively to decipher meaning, including knowledge, values, attitudes and intentions
- Use communication for a range of purposes (e.g., to inform, instruct, motivate and persuade)
- Utilize multiple media and technologies, and know how to judge their effectiveness a priori as well as assess their impact
- Communicate effectively in diverse environments (including multi-lingual)

Analyze Media

- Understand both how and why media messages are constructed, and for what purposes
- Examine how individuals interpret messages differently, how values and points of view are included or excluded, and how media can influence beliefs and behaviors
- Apply a fundamental understanding of the ethical/legal issues surrounding the access and use of media

Create Media Products

- Understand and utilize the most appropriate media creation tools, characteristics and conventions
- Understand and effectively utilize the most appropriate expressions and interpretations in diverse, multicultural environments

Apply Technology Effectively

- Use technology as a tool to research, organize, evaluate, and communicate information

- Use digital technologies (computers, PDAs, media players, GPS, etc.), communication/networking tools and social networks appropriately to access, manage, integrate, evaluate and create information to successfully function in a knowledge economy
- Apply a fundamental understanding of the ethical/legal issues surrounding the access and use of information technologies

Things to Think About

1. Are multitasking media consumers really able to process all the sensory data they are taking in, or is learning being compromised?

2. How far should educators go in matching the technology used in instruction and classroom activities to the technology their students use?

3. Are online chats and instant messaging of value in the classroom? Do they add to student learning, or do they distract from "real" instruction? What is "real" instruction?

4. How can you integrate videoconferencing in your classroom? Who might you partner with to bring expert knowledge, to collaborate, or to offer new perspectives to students?

5. Can the technologies presented in this chapter be a means of engaging and involving parents in their children's schools? In what ways?

6. Does videoconferencing benefit communication by allowing participants to see each other, or does it offer little more than "talking heads"? If videoconferencing is constructive, what is it about the visual element that enhances communication?

7. Are there benefits to asynchronous, text-based communication over synchronous, face-to-face communication? In what situations?

8. Does using podcasts with students really enhance learning, or is it simply a newer version of passively delivering information?

9. In many ways, audio podcasts are akin to listening to a radio broadcast. Are radio broadcasts typically used in classrooms? Why or why not? If not, why would using podcasts be of any greater value?

10. How should libraries approach information offered through podcasts? Print media are increasingly augmented with other types of media, but how are all of them managed and made available to users?

References

Acohido, B. (2005, February 9). Radio to the MP3 degree: Podcasting. *USA Today*. Retrieved from www.usatoday.com/money/media/2005-02-09-podcasting-usat-money-cover_x.htm

Asterhan, C. S. C., & Schwarz, B. B. (2007). The effects of monological and dialogical argumentation on concept learning in evolutionary theory. *Journal of Educational Psychology, 99*(3), 626–639.

AT&T Knowledge Network Explorer (n.d.). *Videoconferencing for learning: Examples and ideas.* Retrieved from www.kn.pacbell.com/wired/vidconf/ideas.html

Baker, M. (1999). Argumentation and constructive interaction. In. J. Andriessen & P. Coirier (Eds.), *Foundations of argumentative text processing* (pp. 179–202). Amsterdam: Amsterdam University Press.

Blair, J. A., & Johnson, R. H. (1987). Argumentation as dialectical. *Argumentation, 1*(1), 41–56.

Bumiller, E. (2010, April 26). We Have Met the Enemy and He Is PowerPoint. *New York Times.* Retrieved from www.nytimes.com/2010/04/27/world/27powerpoint.html

Clarke, A. (n.d.). Retrieved from www.linezine.com/7.3/themes/q2002.htm

Collison, G., Elbaum, B., Haavind, S., & Tinker, R. (2000). *Facilitating online learning: Effective strategies for moderators.* Madison, WI: Atwood Publishing.

Dewey, J. (1916). *Democracy and education: An introduction to the philosophy of education.* New York: Macmillan.

Driver, R., Newton, P., & Osborne, J. (2000). Establishing the norms of scientific argumentation in classrooms. *Science Education, 84,* 287–312.

Ferriter, W. (2007). Using voicethread for collaborative thought. Retrieved from http://teacherleaders.typepad.com/the_tempered_radical/2007/11/using-voicethre.html

Gardner, H. (2000). *Intelligence reframed: Multiple intelligences for the 21st century.* New York: Basic Books.

Gardner, H., & Lazear, D. C. (1991). *Seven ways of knowing, teaching for multiple intelligencies: A handbook of the techniques for expanding intelligence.* Victoria, BC: Hawker Brownlow Education.

German, H. (2005). A museum on the go. *Converge Online.* Retrieved from www.convergemag.com/story.php?catid=231&storyid5100461

Heavin, J. (2006, August 16). School kids get chance to talk shop with judges. *Columbia Daily Tribune.* Retrieved from http://archive.columbiatribune.com/2006/aug/20060816news007.asp

Jackson, L. (2005, January 12). Videoconferencing deserves a second look! *Education World.* Retrieved from www.educationworld.com/a_issues/chat/chat127-2.shtml

Kent, P. (2010). ICT and Pedagogy in the Flaxmere Cluster of Schools. Australian Capital Territory Department of Education and Training. Retrieved from http://iwbrevolution.ning.com/forum/topics/pedagogically-how-iwbs-can-be

KITE. (2001a). Case 8235–1. Kite Case Library. Retrieved from http://kite.missouri.edu

Manzo, K. (2010). Whiteboards' impact on teaching seen as uneven. *Education Week Digital Directions.* Retrieved from www.edweek.org/dd/articles/2010/01/08/02whiteboards.h03.html

McCombs, G., Ufnar, J., Ray, K., Varma, K., Merrick, S., Kuner, S., et al. (2004). *Videoconferencing as a tool to connect scientists to the K–12 classroom.* Paper presented at the annual meeting of the American Educational Research Association, Montreal. Retrieved from www.vanderbilt.edu/cso/download.php?dl=file&id=62

Merrick, S. (2005). Videoconferencing K–12: The state of the art. *Innovate: Journal of Online Education, 2*(1). Retrieved from www.vanderbilt.edu/cso/download.php?dl=file&id=244

Newton, P., Driver, R., & Osborne, J. (1999). The place of argumentation in the pedagogy of school science. *International Journal of Science Education, 21,* 553–576.

NMC: The New Media Consortium and National Learning Infrastructure Initiative. (2005). *The Horizon Report.* Retrieved from www.educause.edu/LibraryDetailPage/666?ID=CSD3737

Nussbaum, E. M., & Sinatra, G. M. (2003). Argument and conceptual engagement. *Contemporary Educational Psychology, 28*(3), 384–395.

Nussbaum, E. M., & Schraw, G. (2007). Promoting argument-counterargument integration in students writing. *Journal of Experimental Education, 76*(1), 59–92.

Oh, S., & Jonassen, D. H. (2007). Scaffolding argumentation during problem solving. *Journal of Computer Assisted Learning, 23*(2), 95–110.

Oppenheimer, T. (2004). *The flickering mind: The false promise of technology in the classroom and how learning can be saved.* New York: Random House.

Rideout, V., Roberts, D., & Foehr, U. (2005). Generation M: Media in the lives of 8–18-year-olds. Kaiser Family Foundation Study Retrieved from www.kff.org/entmedia/upload/Executive-Summary-Generation-M-Media-in-the-Lives-of-8-18-Year-olds.pdf

Rideout, V., Foehr, U., & Roberts, D. (2010). Generation M2: Media in the lives of 8–18-year-olds. Kaiser Family Foundation Study. Retrieved from www.kff.org/entmedia/8010.cfm

Salmon, G. (2002). *E-tivities: The key to active online learning.* London: Kogan Page.

Schmit, D. (2010, May 19). Kidcast #62—Some Thoughts About Video Podcasting. [Web log comment]. Retrieved from www.intelligenic.com/blog/

Toffler, A. (n.d.). Retrieved from www.quotationspage.com/quotes/Alvin_Toffler/

"Wizzard Media Sees Market for Podcast Apps Explode with iTunes Expansion." Press Release, June 30, 2010. Retrieved from www.marketwatch.com/story/wizzard-media-sees-market-for-podcast-apps-explode-with-itunes-expansion-2010-06-30?reflink=MW_news_stmp

Woolley, D. (1995). *Conferencing on the web.* Retrieved from http://thinkofit.com/webconf/wcunleash.htm

Community Building and Collaborating with Technologies

Anthony Magnacca/Merrill

Chapter Objectives

1. Introduce readers to technology tools that support collaborative project work

2. Describe how technologies can facilitate the formation, growth, and activities of online learning communities

3. Identify appropriate technologies for a variety of collaborative purposes

4. Explain how knowledge-building environments support sustained inquiry and systematic reasoning

5. Describe how wikis can be used to support collaborating, designing, co-constructing, and representing knowledge

6. Describe learning activities that use technologies for connecting and collaborating with peers and experts

7. List and explain the benefits of learning communities in K–12 education

8. Describe how various collaborative tools and processes support the development of NETS and 21st Century Skills

What Is Community?

Margaret Riel once told a story about a mother explaining to her 4-year-old about the e-mail message she had sent.

> The mother explained that the words on the computer screen "go on the telephone lines just like someone talking, and a computer on the other hand is going to get them. Then that computer will send them to other computers. So my message will be sent all over the world!"
>
> The child looked up from her coloring and said, "Oh, like a talking drum."
>
> The mother, dumbfounded, finally asked, "A talking drum?"
>
> "You know, like a talking drum." The mother thought some more, and then she remembered that not long ago, an African storyteller had visited her daughter's pre-school and shown the class an African drum. When villagers wanted to get a message out to neighbors about a festival or a market, they would use the drum, and the message would be sent from village to village.

Throughout history, people have found ways to communicate with each other to support community goals and activities; they have overcome obstacles and used considerable ingenuity in doing so. From preliterate cultures to today's media-saturated society, individuals have invented and utilized technologies to support that communication. Today, people are able to connect with one another in ways that, until recently, were unimaginable.

The notion of community is used in a variety of ways and has expanded into a global view, with new technologies that are transforming our concept of community. The Internet enables communities to move beyond geographical boundaries and provides a vehicle for people around the world to interact and learn together. One-way communication that allowed idea sharing has expanded as new tools, such as wikis, blogs, video chats, Web conferencing, and social networks enable broader learning communities.

The Web has become a participatory space that no longer requires users to have technical expertise in order to contribute content. The static nature of the Web as a place to consume information has evolved into an interactive, socially connected space.

Web 2.0 is not a piece of software or anything physical; rather, it describes a fundamental shift in the nature of this second generation of the Web. At the core of Web 2.0 is a set of principles and practices intended to connect the collective intelligence of its users (O'Reilly, 2005; 2009).

Social software, a major component of Web 2.0, enables people to unite or collaborate through computer-mediated communication and to form online communities. Growing out of earlier technologies such as listservs, discussion software, and Usenet groups, the current mix of social software includes blogs, podcasting, wikis, and social networking spaces like Facebook and MySpace (Alexander, 2006). Social software, like Web 2.0, means different things to different people. At its heart, however, is the capacity to bring people together and support sharing within online communities through the use of technology. Hargadon (2010) suggests the term *educational networking* to describe educational uses of social networking technologies, recognizing that some educators may have negative views of *social networking*.

Because collaboration is an essential skill in today's workplace, some of the most important tools for education are technologies that support online collaborative environments to connect people around the world for sharing information and creating new content together (Johnson, Smith, Levine, & Haywood, 2010). The Partnership for 21st Century Skills (2009) lists Global Awareness as an essential 21st-century interdisciplinary theme, with collaboration skills as necessary outcomes for success in a global economy.

Kenneth Boulding, an economist, educator, and social scientist, once said, "We make our tools, and then they shape us" (2006; see also Boyd, 2003; Roper, 2006). This phenomenon is evident, for example, when we consider how radically our behavior and mores regarding private conversations have changed since the wide adoption of cell phones. However, as new tools enabling diverse communities to form and maintain relationships are developed, the way in which they are used may shift from the original purpose. This shifting is often shaped by the users, as technologies are revised and refined to better meet user needs. The increased sophistication and affordances of Web applications has greatly enabled this user shaping.

O'Reilly (2005), one of the early conceptualizers of Web 2.0, considered continuous improvement to be a fundamental characteristic of its development. This fluidity and common goal of improvement by a community of users is, as we shall see, also the vision of researchers and developers engaged in knowledge-building environments.

Knowledge Building with Knowledge Forum

The research-oriented Horizon Project (NMC, 2005) reported a shifting locus both of the process of constructing and sharing knowledge and of knowledge itself as a significant trend in technology. Learners are willing to participate in knowledge construction and, increasingly, expect to do so. Technologies enabling social networks and knowledge webs offer a means of constructing knowledge by facilitating collaboration and teamwork. Scardamalia and Bereiter (2005) questioned whether this knowledge-building capacity might call for a new educational science, with the unique characteristic of treating ideas as things that emerge from a sociocognitive process and that are real and can be improved. This concept of improvable ideas parallels O'Reilly's (2005; 2009) view of Web 2.0 as fluid space, continually being improved by its user community.

Scardamalia and Bereiter (1996) argue that schools inhibit, rather than support, knowledge building by: (1) focusing on individual student's abilities and learning; (2) requiring only demonstrable knowledge, activities, and skills as evidence of learning; and (3) teacher-hoarding wisdom and expertise. Students' knowledge tends to be devalued or ignored, except as evidence of their understanding of the curriculum. What students know and believe is unimportant. Or is it? Should schools focus on student knowledge, or should they support student knowledge building?

The goal of knowledge-building communities is to support students to "actively and strategically pursue learning as a goal"—that is, intentional learning (Scardamalia, Bereiter, & Lamon, 1994, p. 201). Learning, especially intentional learning by students, is a byproduct of schoolwork. To support intentional learning among students, Scardamalia and Bereiter have developed environments where students produce their own knowledge databases in their own knowledge-building community (Computer-Supported Intentional Learning Environments or CSILEs, and Knowledge Forum). Thus, student knowledge can be "objectified, represented in an overt form so that it [can] be evaluated, examined for gaps and inadequacies, added to, revised, and reformulated" (p. 201).

Knowledge Forum 4 is a knowledge-building environment that supports the collaboration process as users create and continue to improve ideas rather than simply complete tasks. True knowledge-building environments enable learning that focuses on ideas and builds deeper levels of understanding. Knowledge Forum is a collaborative database that supports a shared process of knowledge building by defining problems, hypothesizing, researching, collecting information, collaborating, and analyzing. It uses a systematic model of inquiry based on the scientific method and informed by current research in cognitive psychology.

Considerable research has been conducted on CSILE and Knowledge Forum, consistently demonstrating positive effects on learning (Scardamalia et al., 1994). Research on knowledge-building environments suggests that the sustained inquiry that is engaged in these environments results in improved scores in conceptual development as well as basic skills and a degree of student interaction that occurs regardless of ability. Gains in student confidence and the quality of student inquiry were also reported.

Using Knowledge Forum, a user community creates a database where notes are stored, ideas are connected, and knowledge is produced. Users may contribute ideas in the form of text, graphics, movies, or attachments. These ideas, which are central to the knowledge-building process, become connected, expanded, and refined as the individuals in the community question, add to, reference, and annotate each other's thoughts.

A key component of Knowledge Forum is "Rise-above" notes, which play a critical role in idea improvement. The idea of "Rise-above" is based on the philosophical concept of *dialectic*, recognizing that "the most constructive way of dealing with divergent or opposing ideas is not to decide on a winner or a compromise position but rather to create a new idea that preserves the value of the competing ideas while 'rising above' their incompatibilities" (Scardamalia, 2004, p. 7). The design of Knowledge Forum's structured environment facilitates these idea- and knowledge-building processes. Students' process of knowledge building is scaffolded through the supports that are built into the Knowledge Forum system. In Figures 6.1 and 6.2 (page 136), a group of young students is considering the problem question, "Are people machines?" Figure 6.1 shows Marta's belief that people are machines based on her reasoning that both people and machines move.

In Figure 6.2, M.M. challenges that belief (i don't agree); the opened note shows her rationale. Marta's simplistic conclusion that because people move, as do machines, this means that people are machines is refuted as M.M. states differences between people and machines.

In Knowledge Forum, students are expected to be contributors. The knowledge-building process requires them to formulate questions, define their own learning goals, acquire and build a knowledge base, and collaborate with one another. Throughout this process, information sharing occurs because of Knowledge Forum's inherent structure. Students are cued to the thinking strategies that "expert learners" demonstrate through built-in scaffolds.

Learning is not a by-product of Knowledge Forum activities; it is a direct goal. Students are encouraged to make school more meaningful by being mindful and goal directed in their pursuit of learning objectives. Like scientists, Knowledge Forum participants approach a problem, develop hypotheses or theories about the problem, and then seek to confirm, modify, or discard their theories through research, observation, and interpretation. Also like scientists, participants collaborate, review each other's work, and publish their

Figure 6.1

Knowledge Forum Note Stating a Belief

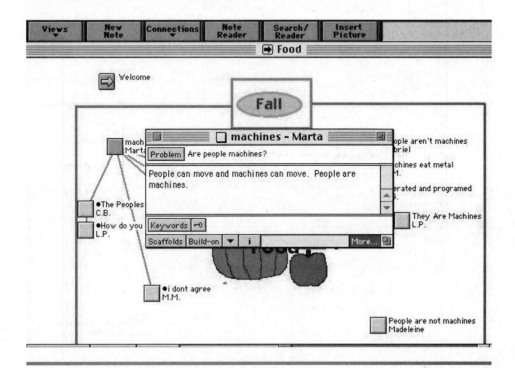

Source: Used with permission from Knowledge Forum, www.knowledgeforum.com

confirmed results. Knowledge Forum supports users in approaching information from multiple perspectives, building new connections from the knowledge.

Knowledge Forum can be applied to various subjects as it is a comprehensive model for inquiry designed to help students conceptualize and research a problem area. Knowledge Forum provides an explicit structure for engaging in thoughtful, reasoned, written discourse. Students need to practice thinking and reasoning. Written papers require reasoning, but they tend to be one-way monologues without opportunities to respond to questions from an audience. In-class oral discussions also provide reasoning opportunities, but studies show that bright students tend to dominate class discussions, leaving many students in passive roles as observers. Programs like Knowledge Forum seek to combine the best elements of writing assignments and live discussions. The communication medium is the written word, but the interactivity is similar to class discussions. Yet the programs provide more scaffolding and support for systematic reasoning than either writing assignments or class discussions: their imposed structure directs students to provide support for claims, to consider competing evidence or hypotheses, and to carefully respond to counterarguments or queries from classmates. The structured discourse that results can help students learn the norms and rules of systematic reasoning, and this in turn becomes valuable in other, less structured settings.

Figure 6.2

Knowledge Forum Note Disagreeing with Another's Belief

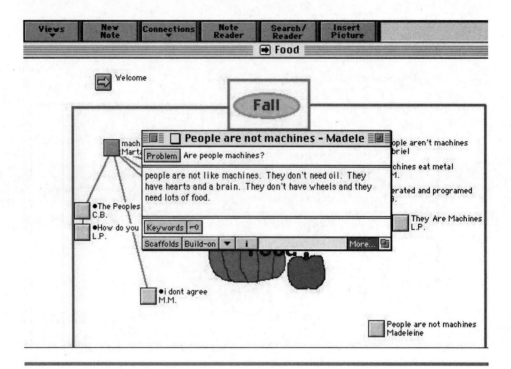

Source: Used with permission from Knowledge Forum, www.knowledgeforum.com

When students rather than the teacher or the textbook own the knowledge, they become committed to building knowledge rather than merely receiving and reprocessing it. Knowledge building becomes a social activity, not a solitary one of retention and regurgitation. Technology plays a key role in knowledge-building communities by providing a medium for storing, organizing, and reformulating the ideas that are contributed by each community member. Although these knowledge-building technology environments treat knowledge as a commodity, to the community of students it represents the synthesis of their thinking, something they own and for which they can be proud. In this sense, we believe, the goal of schools should be to foster knowledge-building communities.

Co-Constructing Knowledge with Wikis

Like Knowledge Forum, wikis offer an environment for students to join together in a knowledge-building community. A wiki is open-source server software for a website that allows users to add, remove, or edit and change available content. The fundamental characteristic of a wiki is an "edit" link allowing access to the source document. While some wikis require registration to manipulate content, others are entirely open and do not. WikiWikiWeb (http://c2.com/cgi-bin/wiki), the first wiki, was created by wiki inventor Ward Cunningham in 1995. It has a minimalist design, but other wiki systems with more structure and features have been developed (Lamb, 2004). The interface of many wikis is now like a simple what-you-see-is-what-you-get (WYSIWYG) Web authoring tool. This simplicity makes wikis a user-friendly, effective collaborative tool for constructing knowledge with others. The interactive, collaborative nature of wikis is evident in the associated discussion pages that encourage ongoing dialogue between wiki writers about wiki content, tasks that need to be completed, and other issues that arise as participants work together.

A major criticism of wikis is that because anyone can create and edit wiki pages, the content may not be accurate (Winkler, 2005). It is true that wiki contributions are not subject to review before additions or modifications are accepted. This, however, is true of all web pages and underscores the importance of making sure that students are educated in information literacy and have the skills to evaluate media. Ironically, the open-source nature of wikis may make them less susceptible to lingering inaccuracies, as there are opportunities for constant peer review of content, with users continually able to identify and correct content themselves. Wiki features, such as tabs associated with each wiki page's text, allow users to edit pages, discuss the page with other editors, and view the history and past versions of previously edited pages. Therefore, documentation of changes is freely available.

Wikipedia, the multilingual general encyclopedia wiki, strives to inform users about possible misrepresentations or biases in material posted on its pages. One may find a note on Wikipedia pages announcing that the neutrality of the section being viewed is disputed. The Talk Page then allows discussion regarding accuracy, unbiased information, and so on. This oversight and transparency, coupled with the ability to instantly correct misinformation, creates a collaborative information-building community, where all members have the opportunity to contribute.

For instance, an investigation of the accuracy of science information found only modest differences between Wikipedia and Encyclopedia Britannica (Giles, 2005). At the same time, a 12-year-old boy discovered five errors in the printed *Encyclopaedia Britannica*, which editors acknowledged (Parkinson, 2005). An editorial in the journal *Nature* (2005) urged scientists to review and edit Wikipedia topics, citing its potential to become a "free, high-quality global resource" with current, peer-reviewed information.

Wikipedia is part of the Wikimedia Foundation Inc., a nonprofit educational corporation whose goal is to develop and maintain free, open-content, wiki-based projects. A relatively recent trend in technology is finding new ways of distributing content and software, including open-source software, with flexible copyright licensing (NMC, 2005). The nonprofit Creative Commons organization (http://creativecommons.org) allows users to share their creations and to use online text and multimedia that are identified with the Creative Commons license. It is built within the current "all rights reserved" copyright law and offers a range of free, voluntary, "some rights reserved" licenses (see Chapter 2). Several Wikimedia Foundation projects utilize the options of Creative Commons licensing.

While the most widely known Wikimedia Foundation project is probably Wikipedia, the foundation also includes Wiktionary, a multilanguage dictionary and thesaurus, and Wikiquote, an encyclopedia of quotations. Wikisource is an online library of free content publications and source texts in any language. Other Wikimedia Foundation projects include Wikiversity, Wikinews, and Wikispecies.

Wikis in the Classroom

Wikis offer environments for students to engage in collaborative, co-authored work that can continually evolve and improve. Because of the high degree of sharing and revision that wikis support, there is also a high degree of critical analysis possible, as students evaluate the ideas being co-constructed, make decisions regarding their accuracy or validity, and participate in a knowledge-building community. Wikis offer collaborative environments for students not only to develop writing skills but also to engage in design work. The complex thinking required for designing an in-depth wiki publication is amplified when students work together to make decisions about content and structure.

Holocaust Wiki Project   Dan McDowell, a high school history teacher in California, developed the Holocaust Wiki Project for his students. First, the students create a family from an assigned country that was affected by the Holocaust. Dan described the project like this:

> Basically they are creating a branching simulation (think choose your own adventure) about a family in the Holocaust. They have to come up with realistic decision points, describe the pros and cons, address the consequences of each decision, and fill it in with a narrative that reflects their research on the Holocaust. Now that in itself is pretty neat, but the REALLY cool part is that they are all (about 30 different groups), putting their branching simulations into a Wiki. Using a Wiki allows them to easily create Web pages (ever try to teach Dreamweaver and academic content), edit each other's work, and easily link the pages together.

An important aspect of this wiki project is the decision-point component (see Figure 6.3) in McDowell's project design. Students are faced with complex choices whose outcomes could potentially have grave consequences on the families they have created. Students are required to analyze the results of their choices and combine that critical thinking with a demonstration of the knowledge they have gained through researching the Holocaust. This kind of deep, reflective thinking is of much greater value to students than learning activities that are designed simply to meet content standards.

Students are given the freedom to go in many different directions within the structure of McDowell's project design. This autonomy engenders creative thinking, while the wiki technology supports a classroom community where students work together in small learning groups. Wikis are simple to use not only for text editing but also for easily uploading media to the web page. A graphic of a six-pointed star that ghetto Jews were required to wear adds a supporting element to one decision-point page and represents some of the learning achieved by this student group.

First Graders' Use of Wikis   Kathy Cassidy demonstrates that wikis can be used to support meaningful learning not only with older students, but also with young learners (see Figure 6.4 on page 140). Her first graders use wikis to create collaborative stories and to convey their math learning. Four other classrooms contributed to the "Primary Math" wiki (http://primarymath.wetpaint.com/) to share their knowledge of math concepts such as patterning, symmetry, graphing, numbers, addition, and telling time. For example, students took pictures of numbers they found in their environment, such as license plates, clocks,

Figure 6.3

Decision Points Screen of the Holocaust Wiki Project

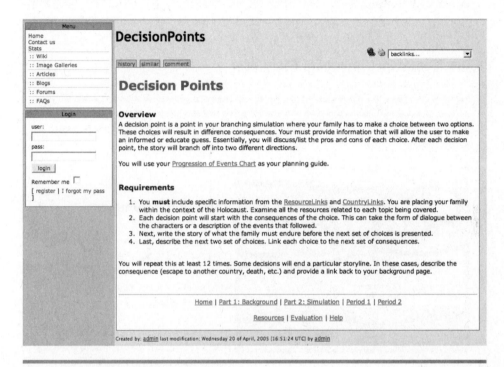

Source: Used with permission from Dan McDowell.

and soccer jerseys. They shared pictures of patterns they had found or created and embedded videos they made and uploaded to YouTube and TeacherTube (see Chapter 5).

More Uses and Suggestions for Wikis

McDowell has also used a wiki to support his students in advanced placement (AP) World History. To help students synthesize what they had studied and prepare for the end-of-year AP test, he designed a wiki project that involved students developing their own version of Wikipedia, based on the knowledge they gained throughout their year in AP World History. It is probably safe to say that the majority of AP World History students in classrooms across the country experience exam reviews that are primarily question and answer. In contrast, constructing a wiki offered a constructive, authentic, enjoyable method for students not only to review material but also to design the environment in which it would be displayed. By working collaboratively, students are able to cover much more material than would be possible with individual work, and the end result is a rich study guide resource that all students can use as they strive to pass the AP exam.

Figure 6.4

First Graders' Collaborative Story Wiki

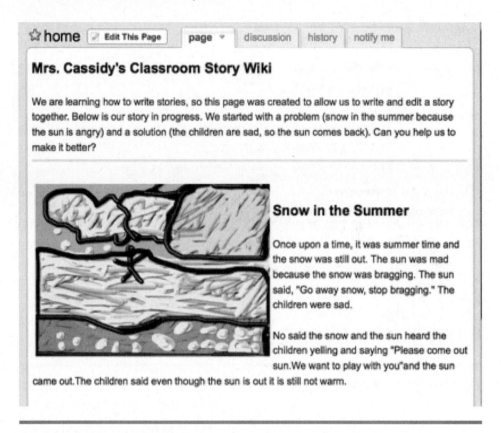

Although wikis are probably used most often to support writing in the curriculum (Lamb, 2004), the use of wikis can go well past simple writing tasks.

Novice wiki users are encouraged to learn by creating a wiki and experimenting with its features, remembering that changes are simple to make. Other suggestions are:

- Start with simple tasks
- Create a list or collection of links
- Use as an informal bulletin board
- Make an online sketch pad
- Brainstorm
- Use for planning and/or note taking

While wikis can be a valuable learning tool for collaborating, designing, co-constructing, and representing knowledge, their basic form is open ended with little built-in structure to direct students' contributions. This freedom can encourage creativity but may also result in unfocused, unproductive time spent by students unless teachers provide an overall framework for their work. The guidance and direction that McDowell provided students in the Holocaust and AP World History wiki assignments is an excellent example of effectively incorporating wikis into the curriculum.

Contributing to an existing wiki is a way to collaborate with other students in an established wiki environment. The purpose of the international "Kites Around the World" wiki project (http://globalkites.wikispaces.com) is for students to use digital media to share experiences with building and flying kites. Designing and building kites offers many possibilities for incorporating mathematical and geometry standards as students measure, use division and fractions, and determine area, perimeter and angles for their creations. Flying the kites introduces science principles such as the effect of wind direction and velocity. As students share kite traditions, they learn about different cultures. Core subjects and several 21st-century themes are incorporated in projects such as "Kites Around the World" with the possibility of combining language arts, mathematics, science, geography, history, and arts as students develop global awareness, creativity, problem-solving, communication, and digital media skills.

Building International Communities with iEARN, Global Schoolhouse, Kidlink, and ThinkQuest

World events continue to underscore the need for all citizens to understand, respect, and communicate with other cultures. Internet communities supported through websites such as Kidlink, the International Education and Resource Network (iEARN), and Global Schoolhouse allow diverse students in different geographic areas to make connections with each other, helping to create understanding and appreciation among cultures and perspectives.

The National Council for the Social Studies (1994) includes "culture" as one of ten thematic strands in social studies standards, stating:

> In a democratic and multicultural society, students need to understand multiple perspectives that derive from different cultural vantage points. This understanding will allow them to relate to people in our nation and throughout the world.

Global groups capitalize on cultural differences as a means of broadening students' perspectives and motivating learning. The new ideas and experiences that are encountered when students interact with peers in other countries and cultures can expand thinking and shape mental models that become more complex. Students may reflect on their experience as world citizens and broaden their understanding of how others live. Studies in language, geography, current events, and culture can be augmented through these groups.

iEARN Learning Circles

iEARN (International Education and Resource Network) is a nonprofit global network formed in 1988 that enables teachers and students across the world to join in collaborative project work through the power of technology. Projects culminate in some type of finished product or exhibition of learning such as art exhibits, written works, performances, and websites. In 2010, there were 2.1 million students from 125 countries engaging daily in iEARN activities.

One iEARN component, Learning Circles, supports constructive learning among a small number of schools located throughout the world through highly interactive, collaborative, project-based partnerships. Developed by Margaret Riel and a team of collaborators, Learning Circles are described as being

> small diverse, democratic groups of people (generally 6–12) who meet regularly over a specified period of time to focus their different perspectives into a common understanding of an issue or problem. The discussion takes place in an atmosphere of mutual trust and understanding. The goal is deeper understanding by the participants and their efforts are often directed towards the construction of a final product or recommendation for a course of action. (Riel, 2005)

The circle has long been used as a way to structure the meeting of a group of people, encourage members' ownership of the group's purpose and work, and recognize and value the collective wisdom of the group. Many types of learning circles exist (e.g., wisdom circles, circle time, study circles, and quality circles) that are organized as face-to-face groups. In contrast, the Learning Circles described in this section are online structures that link students and teachers internationally, tapping into the diversity of the participants as a way to build respect and understanding.

Riel (1996) likens Learning Circles to local chapters of a larger organization, like scout troops affiliated with a larger council. Local troops "set their own goals and tasks but remain connected to those who work in other locations as part of a community with shared goals and values." She describes this cooperation between local and larger levels:

> In on-line Learning Circles, as in scout troops or in a Red Cross task force, the overall task and structure is clearly defined. There are enough examples for participants to use at every step. However, the members of the circle, troop or task force know that they can take control and develop the ideas that arise from the participants. (Riel, 1996)

Learning Circles are often organized in support of a specific project or online activity, with theme-based project work that is integrated into classroom curricula. Like a task force, Learning Circles have a heavy work or activity orientation. Groups of classrooms, usually about eight, sign on to communicate and collaborate from a distance, following a time line to accomplish a defined task. The specific tasks are varied and may include research, information sharing, compilation of a database, or publishing on a common subject. The outcome of the circle is a written document, a summary, or a collection of their collaboration.

Learning Circles are an integral part of iEARN, whose goal is to connect students and teachers around the world to build understanding as they collaborate on meaningful learning projects. Learning Circles incorporate significant, intentional work within a community striving not only to complete project work but also to gain social and cultural understanding of one another in the process.

One of the Learning Circles at iEARN was "Places and Perspectives," a project that integrated history, geography, culture, and government as students broadened their perspectives by sharing knowledge with one another. Students in geography classes might collaborate on producing a travel guide, an analysis of social patterns in relation to geographical locations, or a comparison of weather patterns. A collaborative project between elementary classes could include examination of locally grown food, historical landmarks, or stories from local natives. One project involved students in Iran, Cyprus, the United States, Israel, Uzbekistan, Romania, and Egypt working together to share information and create better understanding among themselves. A student from Iran, communicating about Iranian culture and traditions, said,

> Iranian people are very friendly and hospitable. They love peace and friendship. Unfortunately because of some incorrect introduction and reflection of Iran from the media, most of the people in world do not know the real Iran and real cultures and traditions of Iran. Iran has an ancient civilization and rich culture. So, here I would like to introduce Iran in brief way, and I have attached some pictures of Iran. Hope all of you enjoy it.

A second Learning Circle, "Computer Chronicles," involves student reporters and editors from different locations working together to publish the Computer Chronicles Newspaper. This project connects students in journalism, computer publishing, English, and creative writing and has the potential for cross-curricular learning, with newspaper sections devoted to science reporting, lifestyle sections, and so on.

Learning Circles require high levels of collaboration and teamwork within participating classes and, to some extent, between classes. Much of the learning takes place as students participate in the virtual world of Internet resources. Other times, students complete off-line activities and report results to other members of their circle. The best Learning Circles specify clear work activities that require planning, execution, and reporting of activities, followed by comparison and collaboration across sites.

Learning Circles often engage in more complex activities. Unlike forums where students are tasked with discussing issues or problems, Learning Circles often have a problem-solving purpose for their existence. That purpose may involve designing some artifact (a newspaper, website, or project). To complete any of these kinds of projects, decision-making problems almost always arise, so it is safe to speculate that Learning Circles, at the very least, engage students in decision making.

The most efficient teacher within Learning Circles keeps the project going yet knows how to get out of the way when students are working well together. The teacher's critical role is one of attentive vigilance, with occasional support and intervention when obstacles threaten team progress. Teachers also need to maintain contact with other participating teachers, ensuring continuity and continuing attention to project goals.

Global Schoolhouse

Another major project supporting global learning communities is the Global SchoolNet Foundation (GSN), founded in 1984. Among several GSN initiatives is the Global Schoolhouse project (see Chapter 7). The purpose of GSN is to support 21st-century learning through content-driven collaboration. GSN supports students as they communicate, collaborate, and learn from one another and provides a location for teachers to post collaborative project ideas and find meaningful collaborative partners for their students.

GSN's Project Registry is a clearinghouse for more than 3,000 online collaborative projects that are searchable by date, age level, geographic location, collaboration type, technology tools or key word. There are 90,000 educators from 194 countries registered to participate in GSN projects.

Another aspect of GSN is "The Friendship Through Education" initiative, a coalition with several other groups including iEARN, ePALS, People To People, the U.S. Fund for UNICEF, and Worldwise Schools (a Peace Corps program). The Friendship Through Education Consortium is committed to creating both on- and off-line interactions between youth to promote a culture of peace where all human rights and dignity are respected. The initial focus after its creation in the aftermath of the September 11, 2001, terrorist attacks in the United States, was on creating links between schools in the United States and Islamic countries to "foster mutual respect and greater understanding of cultural differences." It continues to work to build strong and lasting relationships among children in the United States and in other countries and cultures by providing opportunities for online interactions (www.friendshsiptrougheducation.org).

When students participate in projects such as those offered through GSN, they experience teamwork, and have the potential to develop project management skills, engage in cross-curricular learning, and utilize technology. Andres (1995) believes that the best collaborative projects require students to "measure, collect, evaluate, write, read, publish, simulate, hypothesize, compare, debate, examine, investigate, organize, share, and report." Why should classrooms join online communities? Andres argues that students

- enjoy writing more when they are able to write for a distant audience of their peers,
- enjoy communicating with schools from different geographical locations, and
- are given opportunities to understand different cultures and so begin to consider global issues in addition to local issues.

To accomplish the active, collaborative learning envisioned by GSN, students engaged in the CyberFair initiative of GSN are encouraged to serve as "youth ambassadors" by working collaboratively with community members and using technology tools to publish a website that displays what they have learned.

A particularly successful example of this type of work comes from Technology Instructor Leanna Johnson who each year guides students in a CyberFair project. Eighth-grade students at her small Midwest school identified waste as a global problem and developed a recycling project to make a difference in their community. Figure 6.5 portrays the website they created for their "Join the Movement" project (www.stpaulgiants.com/jointhemovement/home.html). Students began by involving other classes in their school. Second graders demonstrated reuse of materials by building a miniature community from recycled boxes, paper, and milk cartons. Fourth graders created an artificial landfill and conducted an experiment to determine how quickly different types of materials would decompose. Over several months, they periodically checked the items, which included a cookie, eggshells, pizza, yarn, plastic caps and plastic wrap, wood, chalk, paper clips, Styrofoam, and a leaf. After observing the few items that decomposed, students concluded that recycling was necessary to avoid overuse of landfills.

Subsequently, students worked to install a school recycling container, which resulted in the school's ability to slash their trash pick-up by half, saving $1200 annually and keeping recyclable materials out of the landfill.

Figure 6.5

"Join the Movement" CyberFair Project Website

Next, students expanded efforts beyond their school by researching recycling in other locations. They surveyed twenty-two cities, toured a recycling transfer station and landfill, and attended a Recycling Expo. Working with their City Administrator, students collaborated on a grant to establish a recycling drop-off facility in the community. One student said, "As a result of our project work we were able to better educate our school as well as establish a recycling center in our community. With the new recycling center in place, we can ensure that the option to recycle those materials is always there."

Collaborative projects can offer opportunities to learn valuable life skills. In reflecting on her learning, one student said, "Aside from learning about recycling, I learned a lot about how the process of writing and applying for a grant goes." Students learned firsthand about local government by attending City Council meetings and working closely with the City Administrator.

Another student said, "I think the best thing about our group collaboration was all of us working together to better the community we live in. We were able to brainstorm together and feed off each other's ideas. We were able to get more done because we had so many peo-ple working together" (L. Johnson, personal communication, April 25, 2010).

Students engaged in complex, collaborative project work such as this can meet many standards and learning objectives across the curriculum as science, math, language arts, and social studies are integrated. They are also engaged in the authentic, active, constructive, intentional, cooperative characteristics of meaningful learning depicted in Figure 1.1.

Leanna Johnson: Teacher's Perspective

I am using Skype right now with a group of students who are building a website for a Global SchoolNet contest. We use Skype and Moodle to collaborate. I videoconference with them occasionally, but I mainly mentor them on the Moodle course and forums. It's important for me to allow them to pursue what they need for their project and give them advice, not commands. I try to guide them through gentle questioning. I hope to be following exactly as the 21st Century Vision suggests, to let them find what they need on their own and decide on their own what they need. I see great leadership and respon-sibility that this type of project brings about. The personal confidence the students gain is one of the elements frequently overlooked by observers of our CyberFair projects, but I get to watch the entire process and see it unfold. The students learn to conduct inter-views with adults in the community, answer questions from adults, and dialogue their activities among themselves before sharing them globally. They are incredibly nervous with interviews initially, but as the project moves forward they have no fear in speaking to anyone about their research. When I see a student gaining knowledge and personal pride in this type of learning project, it is tremendously gratifying. The benefits out-weigh the work involved. It brings all of us really close together as peers—not me, the teacher, and them, the students, but all of us together as a team. They appreciate the freedom they've had to create their own work. When we finalize, publish the website and do a press conference with the local newspaper, they completely run the interview with the reporter. (L. Johnson, personal communication, April 25, 2010)

Kidlink

Kidlink began as a grassroots project intended to interconnect as many children through the secondary school level as possible in a global dialogue. Now run by a nonprofit, user-owned organization in Sweden, the Kidlink Association's goals are to help young people understand their possibilities, set life goals, develop life skills, and find and collaborate with friends internationally. Most users are between the ages of 10 and 15. Since its inception in 1990, young people in 176 countries, from Antarctica to Finland, from Belarus to the Bahamas, have joined the conversations and projects. The Kidlink website is available in six languages, each with an adult language area manager.

When kids register on Kidlink, they receive a nickname and password. All new partici-pants are invited to introduce themselves, answering the following questions:

Question 1: Who am I?

Question 2: What do I want to be when I grow up?

Question 3: How do I want the world to be better when I grow up?

Question 4: What can I do now to make this happen?

Kidcom chat, Kidmail, and Kidlink Forum give users secure communication tools. The Kid Center is a space for participants to publish and link to Internet sites and resources that other Kidlink users might find interesting. For example, a "Recycle" page was created by one girl who asked other users to send her a Kidmail message if they wanted to help her save rainforests by recycling. Comments were added describing things others had done and sharing information about recycling.

In the Kidlink Project Center, teachers and students can actively participate in collaborative work. "What's My Number" is an ongoing project for students in elementary through secondary schools in which students create a set of clues leading to a specific number. Other students are invited to solve the math challenge. A sample challenge on the Kidlink website is:

1. The number of states in the United States of America,

2. + (plus) the strings of a Stradivarius,

3. − (minus) the number of people in a soccer field,

4. × (times) the age of the football player Maradonna when he won the World Cup in 1986.

Students may realize learning outcomes such as these from the "What's My Number" project:

- develop number sense and explore other numeration systems
- identify the multiple uses of numbers in the real world
- develop common understandings of mathematical ideas and definitions
- acquire confidence in using mathematics meaningfully
- appreciate mathematics from a multicultural perspective
- select an appropriate computational method
- formulate questions and develop problem-solving strategies
- solve word problems with a variety of structures
- estimate and judge the reasonableness of answers
- collect, organize, display, and interpret data
- demonstrate and apply the concept of measurement using various types of units
- work cooperatively
- justify their thinking
- recognize and describe patterns
- use calculators in appropriate computational situations
- use technology and the Internet as a tool for problem solving and information gathering
- value the role of math in our culture and society (See www.kidlink.org/kidspace/start .php?HoldNode=899)

Among the many other Kidlink projects are opportunities for students to contribute to a Multicultural Recipes cookbook, create e-cards for other Kidlink members to send, share a description of themselves for another Kidlink member to draw, write poetry, and compete in a "Save the Earth" contest. Although Kidlink can be used solely in one's own language, communicating with students from other countries in their native languages is one of the most constructive, authentic, and meaningful ways to study a second language that we can think of. Even if the students are communicating about their favorite movie stars or bands, they are still communicating, which is the purpose of learning a second language. Kidlink's design offers opportunities for kids to talk informally, as well as communicating for meaningful project work.

Participating in International Communities

Clearly, telecommunities open up vast new horizons to students, engendering a broader, more tolerant worldview for those involved. That should be an important goal of schools. Teachers wishing to begin using collaborative projects with students to build international understanding while meeting other curricular goals have a wealth of resources available through these well-established organizations. For example, GSN's Collaborative Learning Center contains links to collaboration tools such as blogs, chats, and instant messaging as well as information to support planning and implementing successful collaborative projects.

iEARN, GSN, and Kidlink have a long history of promoting international connections among young people. The illustrations given in this chapter are but a few of the opportunities available through these websites. For example, in addition to Learning Circles, iEARN hosts "One Day in the Life," where students can share their stories and, through "A Day in the Life: Photo Diaries," digital images of their daily experiences. iEARN also sponsors the Laws of Life Project (www.iearn.org/projects/laws.html). Youth submit essays expressing what they value most in life, describing the principles and rules that govern their lives, and sharing how those ideals were influenced and formed. Participants respond to each other, engaging in meaningful dialogue about beliefs and values and providing multiple perspectives that can expand students' thinking and help them examine, compare, and solidify their own ideas.

ThinkQuest

ThinkQuest is a password-protected, free, hosted Web-based platform for collaborative projects and competitions sponsored by the Oracle Education Foundation. ThinkQuest's project component is similar to ones previously described. The private environment with its built-in tools and support makes this an attractive, safe alternative. Figure 6.6 depicts the interface of a ThinkQuest project, "Project Rainforest." The left-hand menu reveals links to five project pages, a calendar, and a messaging tool. The pencil menu leads to areas for writing, uploading files, and tools for additional interactions with others.

The ThinkQuest International Competition requires students to apply critical-thinking, communication, and technology skills to solve a real-world problem. Each team of up to six students is guided by a coach as they develop their entry on the ThinkQuest platform. The competition requires students to present not only the solution, but the process they followed to reach their outcome. When students must reflect on and analyze their reasoning, justify actions, and explain their methods and the course of action, they are engaged in deep thinking and productive learning.

Figure 6.6

ThinkQuest "Project Rainforest"

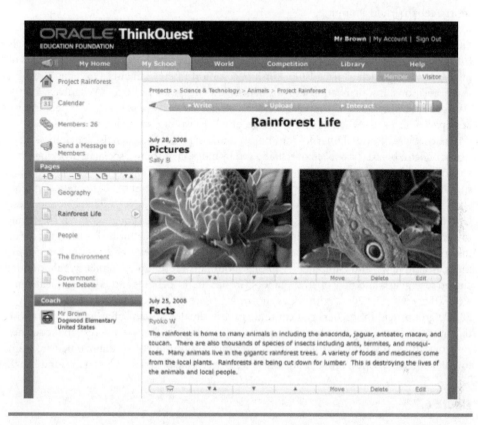

Source: www.thinkquest.org/en/projects/screenshot_popup.html?1. Used with permission from Oracle Education Foundation.

Perhaps one of the most valuable resources for teachers beginning to explore international connections with their students are the teachers who have blazed the trail. Among the supports found in global community websites are mechanisms for connecting teachers as well as students to scaffold and enhance the community experience for everyone involved.

Discussing Interests with Social (Educational) Networking Groups

People are social creatures who like to talk with each other. Generally, they talk about common interests—sports, gardening, cars, dancing, and video games—whatever objects and activities engage them. When they can, people often talk face-to-face about their interests. When they reach beyond their physical connections to find others who share their interests or to expand their discourse community, people may talk to each other at a distance through newsletters, magazines, and television shows. If you examine the magazine section in your supermarket or bookstore, you will find discourse communities focused on everything from brides to monster trucks. Cable television supports discourse networks on sports, cooking, and shopping.

The Internet has enabled people to connect synchronously and asynchronously in online social networks. A social network is defined as "a social structure made of individuals (or organizations) called 'nodes,' which are tied (connected) by one or more specific types of interdependency, such as friendship, kinship, common interest, financial exchange, dislike, sexual relationships, or relationships of beliefs, knowledge or prestige" (Wikipedia, 2010). We are all members of various social networks, which have existed for as long as people have been part of groups—whether a family, tribe, or village women's weaving collective.

Usenet was the initial Internet community and, although it is still in use today, these electronic bulletin boards have been overshadowed by blogs, chat rooms, social networking sites, and other online environments with multiple affordances beyond text. Social networking sites have increased the ability for people to not only converse, but to share photos, videos, and music with one another. In 2001, Google acquired the Deja News database, and these Usenet groups can now be found as Google Groups (http://groups.google.com). It is difficult to name a potentially interesting topic for which there is not an established conversation. For instance, Google Groups exist for people interested in boating, pets, food, arts and entertainment, health, news, and computers—among thousands more topics. Similarly, Yahoo! purchased several lists and now operates Yahoo! Groups. In its "Schools and Education" category alone, there are over 20 subgroups, as shown in Figure 6.7. One subgroup, K–12, has over 70,000 groups within it. Users can continue to drill down through subgroups to find those that are most promising for providing the desired community focus of interest. In the science category, the Astronomy Youth Group is a serious community of young people who want to talk about telescopes, celestial objects, accessories, amateur telescope making, and more.

Figure 6.7

Yahoo! Groups: Schools & Education Category

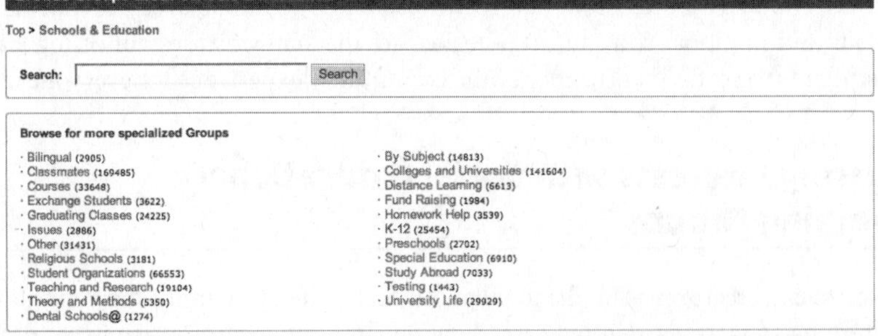

Source: © 2006 Yahoo! Inc., YAHOO! and the YAHOO! logo are trademarks of YAHOO! Inc.

The number of active and interactive discourse communities has expanded exponentially with the growth of telecommunications. These communities can now stay in constant contact about their interests.

Moodle and Ning Communities

It is indisputable that this generation is the most media saturated group of young people in history. Eight- to eighteen-year-olds now spend an average of more than seven and a half hours a day, seven days a week engaging in multiple interactions with media. This includes an average of 90 minutes using a computer for nonschool-related activities, with the greatest amount of that time spent on social networking (Rideout, Foehr, & Roberts, 2010). In just six years, Facebook has amassed over 500 million users (Ostrow, 2010). Expecting meaningful learning to occur only during the confines of a structured school day is ignoring the reality of life for today's youth. As more and more student learning is done outside of the traditional school's space and time constraints, technologies that support virtual communities are increasingly important (NMC, 2005). Social networking sites can extend learning beyond the school setting and create alternative spaces for students to interact. The transparent, ubiquitous nature of technology is taken for granted by most young people today and tremendous opportunities exist for educators who are willing to create new learning environments that engage students, allowing learner control in an authentic context.

Exploiting the popularity of social networking sites is a strategy for moving beyond the traditional boundaries of learning. Although many students are members of Facebook and/or MySpace, these communities are arguably not the best social networking sites for teachers to utilize. Social networking environments that offer a greater degree of privacy do exist and can provide a means for learning that integrates a range of 21st Century Skills, state standards, and NETS•S within specific subjects (DiScipio, 2008). However, because so many of his students were regular users of Facebook, Reuben Hoffman created a fan page for his high school sociology class. Unlike a personal page which should not be used, a fan page lists the owner as a public figure, meaning that the page's "Information" section displays the school's name and contact information rather than Hoffman's personal data. Hoffman said, "This page allows me to share what is happening in class (upcoming assignments, homework, Google Group assignments, links to photos and projects and interesting things that I find). It also allows students to share things they find. The class you are teaching is now extracurricular and not just what is happening in that hour they spend with you five days a week. They must also like the class for all of this to work. It is all about connection and collaboration. I hope to get many parents on board too. Can you imagine the discussions some families may have because you post something interesting related to the class?" (R. Hoffman, personal communication, July 27, 2010).

Leanna Johnson, whose CyberFair project was described earlier in the chapter, uses a course management system to provide an educational networking environment for students. She said:

> You might wonder why I consider Moodle an online social networking group. It isn't for me, but it *is* the main online social network for my students! They use it during school and outside of school. They use it in the summertime and on breaks and in the evenings. Moodle has been a godsend for the students and has alleviated the fear of

online stalking for our parents because the groups are peer groups and people outside the school groups cannot come in. I distinctly remember a conversation with a parent and the principal right before we implemented Moodle. The parent was concerned that students would say things or read things on Moodle that were inappropriate for school. And I said, "How is a chat module any different than note passing or comments in the bathroom or hallway or anywhere an adult isn't present?" After I explained that the Moodle administrator can view any posting at any time and everything is visible, it began to sink in that actually it was a better, more reliable place for the students than being left unsupervised in a classroom. There is accountability. They must learn that on the Internet it is possible to trace keystrokes and actions. I think the Moodle classroom is a good place to learn that. We discuss all kinds of appropriate, respectful and responsible actions required to be good citizens. It provides the opportunity for discussion. They understand much better after using Moodle to make thoughtful comments because their comments never disappear and are accessible. This is a great practice for life in general. Beyond that, though, Moodle's best feature is that it is free and only involves a download to the server. Your server host must set it up. After that, you can decide what restrictions and modules to use. The students can use forums, make glossaries, chat, add images and links, blog, and on and on. (L. Johnson, personal communication, April 25, 2010)

Johnson has created a compelling learning environment that students want to participate in—one that encourages learner control, conversation, reflection, information sharing and construction in what to students feels like an authentic, natural space. Beyond the visible learning activities, using Moodle presented a natural, authentic opportunity to discuss the kinds of digital citizenship skills and issues that are essential for today's students.

Sean Nash, a high school biology teacher, uses Ning to create a network linking students at all three high schools in his school district for a marine biology program. SaintJoe H2O (http://stjoeh2o.ning.com) is a learning network for The Saint Joseph Marine Institute, a unique high school program in the Saint Joseph School District that operates after regular school hours. Students are active in the learning network throughout the school year, with the course culminating in a two-week field study either in the Florida Keys or the Bahamas. Nash's Ning network, shown in Figure 6.8, is a space for students to connect for discussion, posting events, sharing photos and videos related to marine biology, and creating blogs. In one online discussion, Nash encouraged students to reflect on their latest class session, an introduction to coral reef formation, by asking these questions, "What new learning connected with you especially well? What 'Aha!' moments did you have where something became clear?"

In describing connections and learning that resulted from the previous session, one girl said, "I used to think that a barrier reef was the largest a reef could get. Maybe this is because there is always talk about the Great Barrier Reef off the coast of Australia. Talking about how the top of the reef would catch sand and create islands reminded me of the beach in Fort Myers. I remember walking on the beach there when I was about 8. The beach there is full of shells. The sand is basically crushed up shells." And another student wrote, "The story about the seashell is crazy! Thank you for sharing it with us. It helped me to understand how the top of the reef becomes like a beach. In class I was kind of confused about how people could live on the coral but I understand now."

The SaintJoe H2O Ning's members are not only current students, but also alumni and experts in the marine biology field. Connections on social networking sites can provide

Figure 6.8

"SaintJoe H2O" Ning Social Network

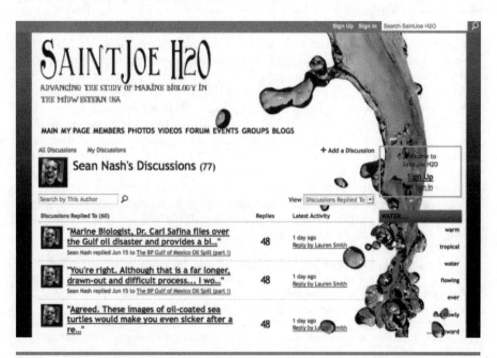

Source: Used with permission from Sean Nash.

students with experiences and knowledge they would otherwise lack. For example, a former student shared photos on the Ning of a month long research study she participated in on the Bering Sea (see http://stjoeh2o.ning.com/photo/album/show?id=2128468%3AAlbum%3A9421). In another instance, after a student posted a question on the Ning, Osha Gray Davidson, the author of "The Enchanted Braid" text that was used in past courses, sent a piece of fossilized coral.

There are different levels of Ning functionality and features. All are subscription, although Pearson Education sponsors a free Ning Mini for North America K–12 and Higher Education Ning Networks. The structure of a Ning also supports a variety of resources to enhance learning, from links to websites, videos, and live chats with experts.

Conclusion

Classrooms and schools can be communities of learners, although they often are not. Why? A community is a social organization of people who share knowledge, values, and goals. Classrooms typically are not communities because students are disconnected or are competing with one another. The students do not share common learning goals or interests.

Within classrooms, there are social communities or cliques, but their purpose is not to learn together or from one another. Rather, those cliques seek to socially reinforce their own identities by excluding others. Learning communities emerge when students share common interests. Rather than forcing students to conform to prepackaged instructional requirements, emphasis should be placed on the social and cognitive contributions of a group of learners to each other, with students collaborating and supporting each other toward commonly accepted learning goals. Learning and knowledge-building communities depend heavily on both student and teacher buy-in, responsibility, and continuing motivation as well as a rich collection of information and learning resources to support them. We believe that learning communities can be an important vehicle for reforming schools.

While the tools we've discussed have great potential for enabling communities of learners to come together for meaningful work and interaction, the sophistication of the tools themselves is not enough for success. Schools must offer the type of curriculum that requires students to collaborate, problem-solve, work in teams, manage projects, and demonstrate leadership. Project-based learning that integrates subjects, that is complex and demanding, and that requires the skills that students will need to survive and flourish in a global economy is a curriculum that can challenge students with meaningful work while meeting necessary content standards (Pearlman, 2006). Richardson (2006) says,

> The current emphasis in our educational system is on accountability and formative, standardized testing, driven largely by federal legislation. As schools struggle to produce students whose test scores compare favorably with their international peers, some people criticize the tools emerging from Web 2.0 as detrimental to student achievement. However, these collaborative, constructionist tools have much to offer and their use does not preclude students' attaining necessary curriculum content and standards.

Technologies that support community building offer great potential by providing the linkages to connect students in meaningful, collaborative learning relationships within the structure and requirements of the formal educational system. However, as with all technologies, the important consideration is not the technology itself but how well it supports and augments the learning process. Web 2.0 applications can be used for instruction, but whether they and other technologies actually promote learning depends on how thoughtfully teachers plan and make use of them.

Are learning communities just another educational fad? We think not. Seen as complex systems, networks become the mechanism that allows adaptation and change, and adaptation and change equate to learning. Thus, while a business organization "learns" by adapting to its environment, teachers and students learn when they respond and adapt to each other and to information resources. As we see in a variety of settings, adaptive change goes hand in hand with a certain kind of structure—not hierarchical, static, or centrally controlled but rather decentralized, complex, dynamic, weblike networks of collaborating contributors. When classes or groups of students function together like that, they become more capable of learning.

Individual community members—students and teachers—work independently as well as collaboratively. In doing so, innovations, insights, and solutions to problems are developed that are shared with community at large. As students and teachers continue their work, the community takes on common attributes that shape its overall character and behavior.

By jointly pooling information through the collaborative efforts demonstrated in the projects presented in this chapter, students encounter a much greater body of knowledge than would be possible if they were working within a single classroom. Perhaps even more valuable is the insight they may gain by exposure to diversity. Seeing the world through another's lens expands each individual's worldview and lays the foundation for respectful, collaborative working relationships as students grow into the adult workers and leaders of tomorrow.

NET Standards potentially engaged by collaborative activities described in this chapter:

1. **Creativity and Innovation**
   a. Apply existing knowledge to generate new ideas, products, or processes
   b. Create original works as a means of personal or group expression

2. **Communication and Collaboration**
   a. Interact, collaborate, and publish with peers, experts, or others employing a variety of digital environments and media
   b. Communicate information and ideas effectively to multiple audiences using a variety of media and formats
   c. Develop cultural understanding and global awareness by engaging with learners of other cultures
   d. Contribute to project teams to produce original works or solve problems

3. **Research and Information Fluency**
   a. Plan strategies to guide inquiry
   b. Locate, organize, analyze, evaluate, synthesize, and ethically use information from a variety of sources and media
   c. Evaluate and select information sources and digital tools based on the appropriateness to specific tasks
   d. Process data and report results

4. **Critical Thinking, Problem Solving, and Decision Making**
   a. Identify and define authentic problems and significant questions for investigation
   b. Plan and manage activities to develop a solution or complete a project
   c. Collect and analyze data to identify solutions and/or make informed decisions
   d. Use multiple processes and diverse perspectives to explore alternative solutions

5. **Digital Citizenship**
   a. Advocate and practice safe, legal, and responsible use of information and technology
   b. Exhibit a positive attitude toward using technology that supports collaboration, learning, and productivity
   c. Demonstrate personal responsibility for lifelong learning
   d. Exhibit leadership for digital citizenship

6. **Technology Operations and Concepts**
   a. Understand and use technology systems
   b. Select and use applications effectively and productively
   c. Troubleshoot systems and applications
   d. Transfer current knowledge to learning of new technologies

21st Century Skills potentially engaged by collaborative activities described in this chapter:

Think Creatively

- Use a wide range of idea creation techniques (such as brainstorming)
- Create new and worthwhile ideas (both incremental and radical concepts)
- Elaborate, refine, analyze, and evaluate their own ideas in order to improve and maximize creative efforts

Work Creatively with Others

- Develop, implement, and communicate new ideas to others effectively
- Be open and responsive to new and diverse perspectives; incorporate group input and feedback into the work
- Demonstrate originality and inventiveness in work and understand the real-world limits to adopting new ideas
- View failure as an opportunity to learn; understand that creativity and innovation is a long-term, cyclical process of small successes and frequent mistakes

Implement Innovations

- Act on creative ideas to make a tangible and useful contribution to the field in which the innovation will occur

Reason Effectively

- Use various types of reasoning (inductive, deductive, etc.) as appropriate to the situation

Make Judgments and Decisions

- Effectively analyze and evaluate evidence, arguments, claims, and beliefs
- Analyze and evaluate major alternative points of view
- Synthesize and make connections between information and arguments
- Interpret information and draw conclusions based on the best analysis
- Reflect critically on learning experiences and processes

Solve Problems

- Solve different kinds of nonfamiliar problems in both conventional and innovative ways
- Identify and ask significant questions that clarify various points of view and lead to better solutions

Communicate Clearly

- Articulate thoughts and ideas effectively using oral, written and nonverbal communication skills in a variety of forms and contexts

- Listen effectively to decipher meaning, including knowledge, values, attitudes, and intentions
- Use communication for a range of purposes (e.g., to inform, instruct, motivate, and persuade)
- Utilize multiple media and technologies, and know how to judge their effectiveness a priori as well as assess their impact
- Communicate effectively in diverse environments (including multi-lingual)

Collaborate with Others

- Demonstrate ability to work effectively and respectfully with diverse teams
- Exercise flexibility and willingness to be helpful in making necessary compromises to accomplish a common goal
- Assume shared responsibility for collaborative work, and value the individual contributions made by each team member

Access and Evaluate Information

- Access information efficiently (time) and effectively (sources)
- Evaluate information critically and competently

Use and Manage Information

- Use information accurately and creatively for the issue or problem at hand.
- Manage the flow of information from a wide variety of sources
- Apply a fundamental understanding of the ethical/legal issues surrounding the access and use of information

Create Media Products

- Understand and utilize the most appropriate media creation tools, characteristics and conventions
- Understand and effectively utilize the most appropriate expressions and interpretations in diverse, multi-cultural environments

Apply Technology Effectively

- Use technology as a tool to research, organize, evaluate, and communicate information
- Use digital technologies (computers, PDAs, media players, GPS, etc.), communication/networking tools and social networks appropriately to access, manage, integrate, evaluate, and create information to successfully function in a knowledge economy
- Apply a fundamental understanding of the ethical/legal issues surrounding the access and use of information technologies

Things to Think About

1. What responsibilities do teacher and students share in cultivating a learning community in the classroom? How can technology serve the goals of a learning community, and how might technology get in the way?

2. What are your beliefs about teaching, learning, and technology? Are you committed to designing technology-infused learning experiences that are student centered and constructivist?

3. With technology-supported learning communities, students learn different things at different speeds. How can a teacher keep track of students' various learning needs and make sure everyone is progressing well?

4. Every community has outliers—people on the margins who don't seem to fit or who struggle to participate fully. How can a teacher draw all students into the community circle? What steps can be taken to motivate students who may be reluctant to participate?

5. With the advent of virtual reality and enhanced graphical interfaces, language may become less important in communication, especially among learners of different languages. What would a virtual language look like? How would students use it to communicate?

6. Some people think that the use of blogs or wikis in classrooms is frivolous and a waste of students' time. How would you respond?

7. What are some ways that you could use the technology ideas in this chapter to support your curriculum and student learners?

8. What is your school and district's culture? Are innovative, new instructional methods and tools welcomed and embraced or does the culture reward the status quo?

9. How accommodating is your IT department? Will they work with you to overcome barriers such as firewalls that would prevent access to online tools?

10. How prepared are your students to engage in collaborative work that links them with diverse partners?

References

Alexander, B. (2006). A new wave of innovation for teaching and learning? *EDUCAUSE Review, 41*(2), 33–44.

Andres, Y. M. (1995). *Collaboration in the classroom and over the Internet*. Retrieved from www.globalschoolnet.org/gsh/teach/articles/collaboration.html

Boulding, K. (2006). *Kenneth E. Boulding*. Retrieved from http://en.wikipedia.org/wiki/Kenneth_Boulding#Quotations

Boyd, S. (2003). *Are you ready for social software?* Retrieved from www.darwinmag.com/read/050103/social.html

DiScipio, T. (2008, Sept/Oct). Adapting social networking to address 21st Century Skills. *Multimedia and Internet Schools.* Retrieved from www.mmischools.com/Newsletters/MmisXtra.aspx?NewsletterID=1719

Giles, J. (2005). Internet encyclopaedias go head to head. *Nature 438*(7070), 900–901.

Giles, J. (2005). "Wiki's wild world." Editorial. *Nature 438*(7070), 890–890.

Hargadon, S. (2010). *Educational Networking (Social Networking in Education)*. Retrieved from www.learncentral.org/group/18373/educational-networking-social-networking-education

Johnson, L. F., Levine, A., and Smith, R. S. (2009). *2009 Horizon Report*. Austin, TX: The New Media Consortium.

Johnson, L., Smith, R., Levine, A., & Haywood, K. (2010). *2010 Horizon Report: K–12 Edition.* Austin, TX: The New Media Consortium. Retrieved from www.cosn.org/horizon/

Lamb, B. (2004). Wide open spaces: Wikis, ready or not. *EDUCAUSE Review, 39*(5), 36–48.

National Council for the Social Studies. (1994). *Expectations of Excellence: Curriculum Standards for Social Studies.* NCSS Publications, *Bulletin No. 89.* Retrieved from www.socialstudies.org/standards/strands#I

NMC: The New Media Consortium and National Learning Infrastructure Initiative. (2005). *The Horizon Report.* Retrieved from www.educause.edu/LibraryDetailPage/666?ID=CSD3737

O'Reilly, T. (2009, October). *Web squared: Web 2.0 five years on.* Retrieved from http://assets.en.oreilly.com/1/event/28/web2009_websquared-whitepaper.pdf

O'Reilly, T. (2005, September 30). What *Is Web 2.0?* Retrieved from www.oreillynet.com/pub/a/oreilly/tim/news/2005/09/30/what-is-web-20.html

Ostrow, A. (2010). *It's official: Facebook passes 500 million users.* Retrieved from http://mashable.com/2010/07/21/facebook-500-million-2/

Parkinson, J. (2005, Jan. 26). *Boy brings encyclopaedia to book.* BBC News. Retrieved from http://news.bbc.co.uk/2/hi/uk_news/education/4209575.stm

Parkinson, J. (2009). xP21 Framework Defintions. The Partnership for 21st Century Skills. Retrieved June 12, 2010, from www.p21.org/documents/P21_Framework_Definitions

Pearlman, B. (2006, June). New skills for a new century. *Edutopia,* pp. 51–53. Retrieved from http://edutopia.org/magazine/ed1article.php?id=art_1546&issue=jun_06#

Richardson, W. (2006). *Blogs, wikis, podcasts, and other powerful Web tools for classrooms.* Thousand Oaks, CA: Corwin.

Rideout, V., Foehr, U., & Roberts, D. (2010). *Generation M2: Media in the lives of 8- to 18-year-olds.* Kaiser Family Foundation: Menlo Park, CA.

Riel, M. (1990). Cooperative learning across classrooms in electronic Learning Circles. *Instructional Science, 19*(6), 445–466.

Riel, M. (1996, January). *The Internet: A land to settle rather than an ocean to surf and a new "place" for school reform through community development.* Retrieved from www.globalschoolnet.org/gsh/teach/articles/netasplace.html

Riel, M. (2005). *The teacher's guide to learning circles.* Retrieved from www.iearn.org/circles/lcguide/p.intro/a.intro.html

Roper, D. (2006). *Quotes from Kenneth Ewert Boulding.* Retrieved from www.colorado.edu/econ/Kenneth.Boulding/quotes/q.body.html

Scardamalia, M. (2004). CSILE/Knowledge Forum. In *Education and technology: An encyclopedia* (pp. 183–192). Santa Barbara, CA: ABC-CLIO.

Scardamalia, M., & Bereiter, C. (1996). Adaptation and understanding: A case for new cultures of schooling. In S. Vosniadou, E. De Corte, R. Glaser, & H. Mandl (Eds.), *International perspectives on the design of technology-supported learning environments* (pp. 149–163). Hillsdale, NJ: Lawrence Erlbaum Associates.

Scardamalia, M., & Bereiter, C. (2005). Does education for the knowledge age need a new science? *European Journal of School Psychology, 3* (1), 21–40.

Scardamalia, M., Bereiter, C., & Lamon, D. (1994). The CSILE Project: Trying to bring the classroom into World 3. In K. McGilly (Ed.), *Classroom lessons: Integrating cognitive theory and classroom practice* (pp. 201–228). Cambridge, MA: MIT Press.

Wikipedia (2010). *Social network.* Retrieved from http://en.wikipedia.org/wiki/Social_network

Winkler, C. (2005). Are wikis worth the time? *Learning and Leading with Technology, 33*(4), 6–7.

Writing with Technologies

Scott Cunningham/Merrill

Chapter Objectives

1. Introduce readers to technology tools that can help learners visually organize their writing and that can meaningfully support creative writing

2. Describe how blogs can be used to meaningfully support writing

3. List and explain the potential benefits of using blog tools to support writing

4. Describe applications of technology tools that allow learners to publish their writing on the Internet

5. Describe applications of technology tools that allow learners to engage in collaborative writing

6. Describe applications of technology tools that allow learners to engage in peer feedback on writing

7. Describe the limitations of these technologies

8. List NETS and 21st Century Skills that can be addressed by the technology-based writing activities in this chapter

Although all the learning tasks we address in this book are important, teaching students to write well is fundamental to not only many school-based tasks but a myriad of everyday and work tasks from personal communication with friends and family to written reports that are still common in the business world. Further, the "language arts" remain a core subject in the 21st Century Skills framework (Partnership for 21st Century Skills, 2004). And if these aren't enough reasons to invest efforts into improving writing instructional activities, in our current climate of "accountability" and high-stakes testing, national and state standards alike place a high degree of emphasis on writing outcomes (National Council of Teachers of English, 1996).

As teachers are well aware, many students of all ages struggle with both learning to write well, as well as learning to enjoy (or at least not dislike) writing. Writing, in fact, may have been one of the first core learning outcomes addressed by technology. Even though we are so accustomed to using them we may not even consider their impact, word-processing packages had and continue to enable the creating and editing of the written word. Because they are so accepted and commonly used in most aspects of schooling, we don't address word processors in this chapter—but do focus on more current technology tools for supporting both individual and collaborative writing.

Even though it may seem that writing is being reduced to 140 character "tweets," we maintain that substantive writing is still required to function in today's society. Writing itself is a complex activity composed of many component tasks (Flower, Schriver, Carey, Haas, & Hayes, 1989):

- Setting goals
- Planning
- Idea organization
- Composition of text
- Editing

The technology tools we discuss address these tasks in varying ways. We address the various components of writing and how technology can support them in both individual and collaborative settings.

Supporting Writing Organization, Planning, and Reflection on Writing through Visualization Tools

Organizing ideas before beginning to write is commonly accepted as an important part of the writing process. This section describes several technology tools that support this activity by helping learners to externally visualize writing structures.

Visually Organizing Ideas with Concept Maps

Concept mapping is an activity that requires learners to draw visual maps of concepts connected to each other via lines (or links). Concept maps—sometimes referred to as semantic networks or cognitive maps—provide learners with a tool for representing the semantic structure of domain knowledge and in turn linking those structures to existing mental structures (see Chapter 8). Creating a concept map involves identifying important concepts, arranging those concepts spatially, identifying relationships among those concepts, and labeling the nature of the relationships among those concepts. As we describe next, this process can be applied to the planning and analysis of written products.

Concept maps can be drawn by hand using simple artifacts such as cards and string, paper and pencil or sticky notes. However, a variety of computer-based semantic networking software enables much easier (and arguably more powerful) production of concept maps. Several computer-based concept mapping tools are available (Wetzel, 2010). See Table 7.1 for a sample list of such tools.

These programs provide visual and verbal screen tools for developing concept maps. These tools enable learners to identify the important ideas or concepts in a knowledge domain and interrelate those ideas in multidimensional networks of concepts by labeling the relationships between those ideas. The tools vary in their features and some—such as CMap and Inspiration—are more focused on educational applications than others.

Concept maps are composed of nodes (concepts or ideas) and links (statements of relationships) connecting them. In computer-based concept maps, nodes are represented as information blocks, cards or in some cases with pictorial icons made available by the program (e.g., "paleontologist" in Figure 7.1) and the links are labeled lines (e.g., "studied by" in Figure 7.1). We note that when choosing a concept mapping or semantic networking computer program, educators should make sure the program supports the labeling of links as the creation of descriptive link labels is a critical part of the creation of maps.

Table 7.1 Sample Concept Mapping Software Tools

C-Map http://cmap.ihmc.us	Free mapping tool available for all hardware platforms (e.g., Mac or PC); appropriate for users of all ages; available in 17 languages. Because it is free and easy to use, it has a growing user base; look forward to more K–12 applications and examples.
Inspiration/Kidspiration www.inspiration.com	Popular tool that runs on both Macs and PCs. Kidspiration is the version for younger learners. Both tools are visually appealing but do not offer some features that can better support knowledge organization and idea development. For instance, all maps must be created on a single page and learners may focus excessively on choosing pictorial icons instead of on organizing and creating meaningful links between nodes.
MindMeister www.mindmeister.com	Online tool available in a free and for-fee version. An "academic" subscription version offers support for unlimited number of maps and the ability to collaborate on maps. Does not support labeled links between nodes.
Visual Thesaurus www.visualthesaurus.com	A specialized mapping tool for providing a visual thesaurus look-up of the words related to one that you enter.

Figure 7.1

Sample Concept Map Created with Semantica

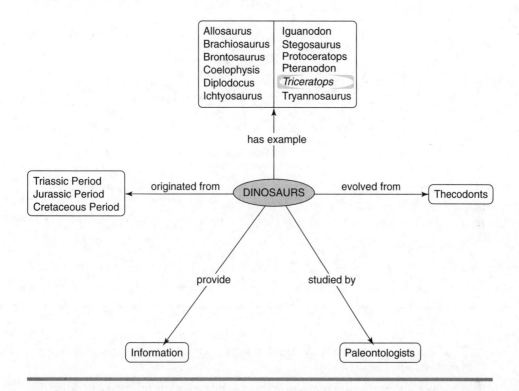

For the writing process, concept maps can function as effective intentional planning tools, as well as analysis tools. When students are planning a paper or a speech, they can create concept maps to both help generate and organize their ideas. Even children as young as kindergartners can use mapping tools like Kidspiration—the K–5 version of Inspiration—to write their own books (Bafile, 2009). Further, some claim that the visual nature of the tool helps kids get their ideas down and thus get beyond the fear of the "blank page" that sometimes accompanies writing activities (Bafile, 2009).

Although concept maps can be used in several ways in the writing process, Anderson-Inman and Horney (1996) describe steps for using a concept mapping activity for brainstorming as a precursor to organization and actual writing. This activity is designed to be completed by students working collaboratively and the use of a computer projector enhances students' ability to see the map progress and thus aid in collaboration.

1. Students generate ideas quickly and without evaluating them. One student is designated as a "recorder" and generates associated nodes and links within the concept mapping software (see Figure 7.2a). Tools such as Inspiration offer quick keyboard sequences for creating nodes quickly.

Figure 7.2a

First Draft of Concept Map

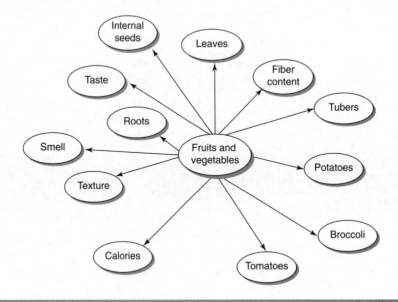

2. Students arrange the existing ideas into clusters. Nodes are dragged around the screen into clusters (see Figure 7.2b).

3. Students elaborate the newly organized map so that it is more functional in aiding the writing of the paper, report, or presentation. Such elaboration may include editing of duplicate ideas, adding more links to create a more well-connected map (and eliminating isolated or nearly isolated nodes), or refining link descriptions (see Figure 7.2c on page 166).

Concept maps can also be used as an initial support or template for structuring different types of writing activities. While there are other tools designed to support specific writing forms (e.g., NoodleTools, noodletools.com, for supporting research note writing) concept maps have the advantage of supporting multiple writing forms with one tool. Figure 7.3 (page 167) shows a map template that students could *start* with for constructing a persuasive argument; similar templates are available with many concept mapping packages for writing activities such as developing a research topic, organizing a presentation, or writing a bibliography. We caution teachers that such map templates must be used carefully as our experience indicates that students may limit their own maps to a simple replacement strategy of the nodes in the templates. If templates are used, students should see how a template is transformed into a completely developed map for the type of writing in question.

To summarize, the power of using concept mapping as a precursor to writing is that the process requires students to actively evaluate and organize their ideas as they are generating

Figure 7.2b

Concept Map Arranged into Clusters

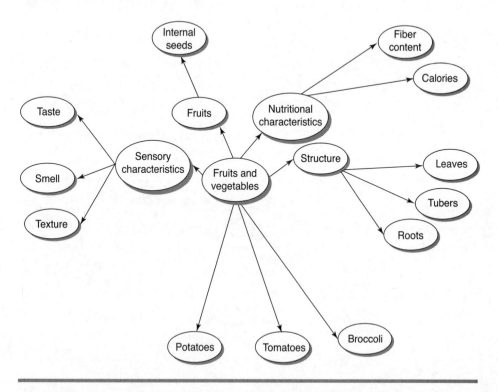

them. To create concept maps, students need to first identify important concepts and represent them in the software along with the relationships between the concepts. That means they must synthesize sources of information to identify the ideas that are important to the goal of their writing.

Rather than simply *defining* these concepts, students need to describe how they relate to the other ideas that they have identified. They will then elaborate on these relationships in their written product. This process can be enhanced by collaboration with other students. We also note that the organization task supported by creating concept maps can be applied to any type of writing (e.g., research reports, prose, poetry) but slightly different accompanying lessons. Lastly and from a more practical standpoint, the visual nature of the mapping tools helps students keep track of what they have created so far; and further allows easy "editing" or changing of the organization before it is turned into prose.

Note that we posit that the greatest power of this tool is only achieved when students generate their own maps and create labeled links to describe the relationships between their nodes. Teachers may initially help students learn the software, provide sample maps and provide ongoing feedback on student-generated maps, as well as provide examples or create

Figure 7.2c

Elaborated Concept Map

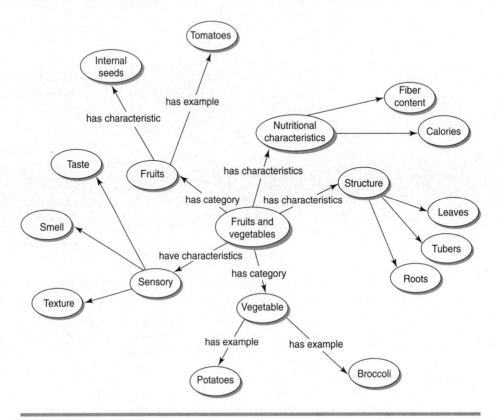

interactive lessons for turning a completed map into written prose (e.g., teachers may wish to start with "translating" a map or a portion of a map into a single paragraph). However, unless students generate their own maps and links (either individually or collaboratively) they will not actively need to organize and evaluate the ideas they are considering for their writing activity. Our experience has shown that when teachers show students how to construct the maps, student maps tend to look the same. Teachers can then prompt students or ask them questions about the underlying semantic relationships that they are trying to convey to help them clarify these relationships, edit them when necessary, and produce a more useful map. Such prompting and feedback activities will lead to a map that can more readily be translated into a written product.

Visualizing Ideas and Word Use

Tools like concept maps can help students organize their thoughts and ideas before and during the process of writing. As described, one of the strengths of concept maps is that they provide a visual representation of how ideas in a writing task are interrelated. The

Figure 7.3

Concept Map Template for a Persuasive Argument

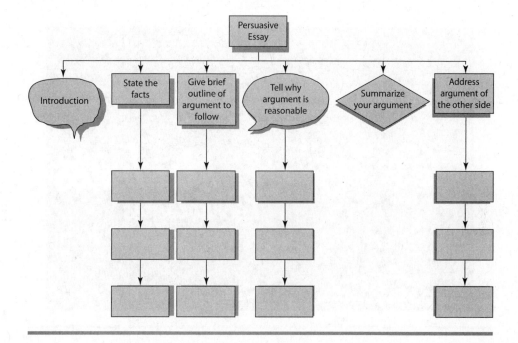

"externalization" of a learner's ideas about how to organize concepts to be written about can help him or her confront that organization and more easily reorganize.

Another visualization tool that may be helpful in the writing process is Wordle (www .wordle.net). Wordle is a free, online tool for creating "word clouds" from text provided by the user. Wordle creates images of the text based on the frequency of each word in the provided text. Figure 7.4 shows a Wordle cloud generated from text from the first chapter of this book.

Wordle is based on tag clouds; tag clouds are applications that allow users to "tag" or mark content in a document and then produce a boxed set of clickable words. A tag cloud though is composed of tags only—that someone has "marked" on the text. The creator of Wordle decided to leave behind the tags and create a visual image of the text based only on word counts.

Wordle is fairly straightforward in its functionality. It does just what it says it does—creates an image based on the count of each word in a provided text. The word you use the most is shown in the biggest font in the created image. So, referring to Figure 7.4, we can see that the text selected from Chapter 1 of this book emphasizes "learning" and "students" to pretty much equal degrees. You can save Wordle images as PDFs or take screenshots of them. Many Wordle images are also published in the online gallery; but teachers are cautioned that these images are not vetted. Users can make minor adjustments to their images on characteristics such as color schemes and fonts.

Figure 7.4

Wordle Cloud Example

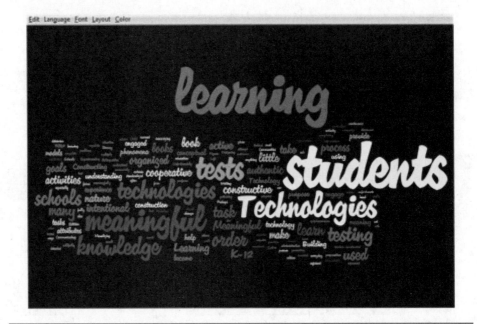

Wordle can be used just for fun of course, but also as a tool to promote reflection and conversation about the text. Not all applications support writing (for instance, some are more focused on text *analysis*) but the following are examples that are focused on writing.

In her classroom blog site, classroom teacher Mrs. Reed describes how she had her first graders use Wordle as a follow-up activity on adjectives (http://mrsreedsvirtualclassroom .blogspot.com/2010/01/wordle_28.html). Her students first generated 20 adjectives to describe a single noun. Then, they each used Wordle to create a visual representation of the noun and accompanying adjectives. Figure 7.5 shows one student's representation of the adjectives associated with the noun *hamsters*. One can imagine that the teacher might have used these Wordle images as a basis for discussion between students and with her as the teacher. Such discussions could help clarify word meanings, spellings, and usage misconceptions such as classifying verbs (e.g., plays) as an adjective.

Another teacher used Wordle clouds as a way to help her students engage in poetry writing (NA, 2008; http://twowhizzy.blogspot.com/2008/06/wordle-thinking-about-time-poems-and.html). She started by creating a Wordle image of a poem that illustrated several characteristics of poems: a repetitive two-line structure and a poetic rhythm achieved via a series of nouns and onomatopoeic verbs. The teacher argues that the children can better "see" some of these structures when they study the Wordle poetry "skeleton" in conjunction with reading the poem.

Figure 7.5

Wordle Image of Noun *Hamsters* and Additional Adjectives

The teacher then moves students into their own poetry writing based on the structures they have learned about via the Wordle-supported lesson. They begin simply by changing noun and verb phrases and move forward from there. And similar to Mrs. Reed's example, students also create Wordle images of their own poems and use these images to discuss both frequently used words (those that appear the largest in the Wordle image) as well as less frequently used words—noting that perhaps the latter category might be considered for writing revisions.

The creator of Wordle however also clearly describes some of the tool's limitations. Teachers and learners alike should be aware of how the following limitations can impact how Wordle can be used and its results interpreted (Feinberg, 2010):

- *The size of the words is "naïve."* Wordle doesn't take into account word length when creating its image. Thus when two words of different lengths are used the same number of times, the longer word will take up more space in the map, which may make it appear as if it were used more frequently—when this is not the case.

- *Color is meaningless in the Wordle image.* Color does not communicate anything about the importance or frequency of any word but is used only for visual appeal and to provide visual contrast between words. A similar caveat applies to Wordle fonts, which are also only for aesthetics.

- *Wordle images are not comparative.* Wordle counts words but that does not make it an appropriate tool for comparing texts as word frequencies do not reveal the structure or the complete meaning of the writing.

Although we do not propose Wordle as a tool that would be a singular focus in a writing activity, as the prior examples show, it could provide the basis for conversations between peers or students and teachers. In a recent survey of Wordle users nearly two-thirds of respondents indicated that they had "learned something new about the text" in their use of Wordle and over half indicated they had "confirmed their understanding" of the text (Viégas, Wattenberg, & Feinberg, 2009).

Supporting Creative Writing and Publishing with Technology

Like many middle school students, Eileen Skarecki's Columbia Middle School students in New Jersey read the popular adolescent novel, *The Pigman*. In Skarecki's words, the novel "leaves the reader hanging." Her response? Have students write a final chapter, and post the submissions on the Internet for others to read and respond to.

The National Commission on Writing posits that using technology tools can help motivate writers because often an aspect of technology-based writing is publishing the writing in some form (Lenhart, Madden, Macgill, & Smith, 2007). All the tools in this chapter provide some type of innovative, yet meaningful, support for different aspects of writing. But perhaps the greatest growth in writing-related technologies are those that allow one to *publish* one's creative written work on the Internet. For instance, a recent study from the Pew Research Centers shows that 64 percent of teenagers who are online have participated in at least one content-creating activity on the Internet. Further, 28 percent have created their own online journal or blog—an increase from 19 percent in 2004 (Lenhart et al., 2007). This trend is all part of what one media and culture expert calls the "society of authorship" (Rushkoff, 2004) where any person with Internet access can contribute his or her ideas to the body of materials on the Internet.

This simple activity of placing one's work on the Web for public access inspires many students to take their work more seriously and to engage in a level of reflection about their work that is otherwise rare. It may also cause them to write with a purpose, to think critically about what they write, to read what others have produced, and to compare their own work to the work of others. In addition to this new level of reflection inspired by Web publishing, it is possible to design activities that cause students to be more reflective—to think about their work and the work of others in ways that lead to academic growth. The next few sections of this chapter explore how the creative process of writing can be supported and meaningfully enhanced with technology tools—some of which support this creative process and others that simply provide a public forum for student work—which may in and of itself lend to the students' development.

Using Blogs to Publish Ideas

Blogs—short for "web logs"—are a means of enhancing and supporting meaningful communication between learners. A blog—with its read and write functionalities—typifies Web 2.0. Says a technology coordinator for a Florida school district, "Blogs started Web 2.0 as we know it, and brought us into the era of the read/write Web" (as cited in Riedel, 2010). A blog is a type of website that allows for the easy creation, updates, and nearly instant publishing of content of the author's choosing (Richardson, 2010). When blogs were first introduced, they were predominantly intended to be simply personal diaries without any between-user interaction or commenting. This initial lack of interaction is what differentiated them from wikis.

However, since those early days, the purpose and function of blogs have evolved with many blogs now being highly interactive spaces. Readers post responses to blog entries, creating opportunities for dialogue rather than a one-sided monologue. Blog writers can link to multiple websites, including links to other blogs that might substantiate or refute the opinions expressed in one's own blog. The structure of blogs is reverse chronology, with the most recent entry appearing at the top of the blog webpage. Common features of blogs include the ability to add permanent links allowing other websites to link directly to one's blog, archiving of posts, features that post a link from a currently browsed site directly to a user's blog, and the ability to add a search engine to a blog, making it possible for users to search blog content. The public and published nature of blogs, plus the ability to comment on another's blog post, makes them a powerful communication tool, but the primarily written-word nature of blogs can help support writing tasks as well.

Why Blog?

The uses of blogs in educational settings are varied and range from an entry portal to a particular teacher's classroom to individually based student writing products. For instance, a student might take on the persona of a character from a novel or a historical situation and create blog posts in that persona. Before providing some in-depth examples of blog educational applications, let's briefly examine the underlying rationales for using blogs. Like the uses of blogs, the purported reasons for using them are quite varied. In a recent publication, Richardson (2010) proposes several potential instructional benefits of students participating in blogging activities some of which are summarized and illustrated with examples here:

- *Providing classroom experiences beyond the "walls" of the classroom.* The Internet-posted nature of blogs provides the opportunity for students to connect with other learners, and experts, who may not be available within their own class or building settings. High school teacher Micah Mathis describes that he used his "mhs psychology blog" (www.mhspsychology.blogspot.com) with his students to help get them to further research material that they did not cover directly in class. He formatted the blog posts in such a way that his students had to do extra research via the Internet or apply some of the concepts they learned in class to the real world in order to participate.

- *Posting on a blog may appeal to different learning styles.* This argument is similar to other asynchronous forms of expression (e.g., online discussion forums); students who may be reluctant to speak up in class may find a "voice" in blog postings that can be made on their own time. Ultimately, this may allow for more complete participation by all students. Mathis's other objective was to encourage students who wouldn't normally participate in class discussions. Some students had a fear of talking in public or felt time pressures in class to express their feelings and thoughts. Mathis said, "It allowed students who needed more processing time to respond to have as much as they needed to participate in the class's online discussion."

- *Blogging could enhance the expertise of the blogger on the targeted subject.* Referring back to Figure 1.1, blogging can engage several—if not all—of the characteristics of meaningful learning (e.g., active, constructive, intentional, authentic, cooperative). If a student is developing a blog on, say, the benefits and costs of recycling in her community, the act of constructing blog postings can require her to develop and synthesize expertise in that domain. Richardson (2010) argues that the student is actually creating a "database" of knowledge on the topic. We may not go so far as to agree with that (as a blog is not keyed or indexed like a database), however creating blog postings can be a mechanism for student knowledge construction and synthesis as he or she researches and makes her points in the blog. Further, the necessity of replying to postings—and perhaps revising or defending one's position—could result in knowledge revision, or conceptual change which has been shown to be a powerful form of learning.

- *Blogging and the evidence of outside readers and their comments can be motivating to writers.* Anne Davis, an elementary teacher whose fourth- and fifth-grade students wrote blogs that were read by high school students who mentored them, reported, "Having an outside audience really made a difference to them. They couldn't believe that someone else would care what they wrote" (Falloon, 2005).

Other potential benefits from blogging have been proposed and include promoting self- and critical reflection, promoting collaboration and the development of virtual communities between learners (Cook & Schwier, 2008), and promoting analogical thinking (Eide Neurolearning Blog, 2005).

Before moving on to some examples of the creative ways blogging is being used in educational settings to support writing, we feel it necessary to point out that while there is great enthusiasm for the potential benefits of blogging, the research on the impact of blogging on students is in its infancy and most data at this point is strictly anecdotal. A couple of notable exceptions are recent studies from the Pew Internet and American Life Project that showed that teen bloggers are more prolific than their counterparts (Lenhart et al., 2007), and a study with a small sample of high school bloggers that found they felt blogging helped them to better articulate their ideas, and that blogging helped them to *begin* writing their papers (Ramaswami, 2008). Given the difficulty of the "blank page," this latter result is somewhat notable.

Examples of Writing and Publishing with Blogs

Bob Sprankle, a former third- and fourth-grade teacher at Wells Elementary in Wells, Maine, is a 2005 Edublog Award winner. "Room 208," his class blog site (http://bobsprankle .com/blog/index.html), illustrates how young writers use personal blogs to publish and share their ideas with each other as well anyone in the blogosphere (see Figure 7.6). In her blog, Elizabeth has posted a story she wrote: "The Hamster and the Mouse." Elizabeth also posted a drawing of a dragon.

The community of viewers who visited Elizabeth's blog provided her with lots of positive feedback. For instance, one reader commented on the way Elizabeth portrayed the emotion of fear in the dragon and suggested that she might write a story about this drawing. This type of "motivational" feedback is one of the strengths of blogs for young writers.

Figure 7.6

Blog Entries of Elizabeth's Picture and Story

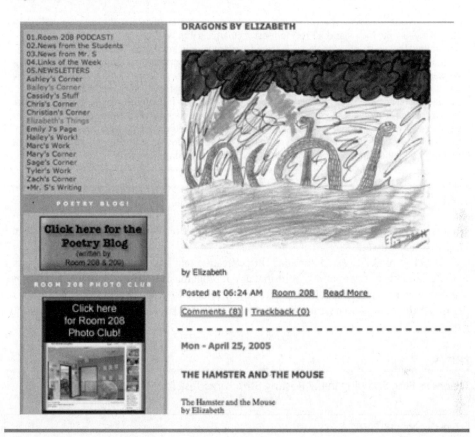

Many have difficulty starting a writing task or are concerned that no one is interested in what they write. Such feedback can affirm young writers' concepts of themselves as conveyors of ideas, engage them in conversation with a purposeful community of other writers, and encourage learners to reflect on their work.

When considering blogging to develop writing skills, Richardson (2010) describes how blogging—when done effectively and thoroughly—may be considered "connective writing." He describes connective writing as a writing form that "forces those who do it to read carefully and critically, that demands clarity and cogency in its construction, that is done for a wide audience, and that links to the sources of the ideas" (p. 28). The Newly Ancient blog (www.newlyancient.com) from an individual teenaged blogger in the Northeast United States illustrates some aspects of "connective writing." Figure 7.7 shows a posting that discusses his hopes for then President-elect Obama.

The example illustrates how such blog writing must start with reading and synthesis. Although the blogger does express personal ideas and hopes ("I hope President-elect

Figure 7.7

Newly Ancient Posting Illustrating Connective Writing

One of my favorite things about President-elect Obama is that he is the first president to truly understand the power of technology—to a large extent, it got him elected. Already, he is beginning to bring his powerful technology platform into government. I hope by that the end of his term we will see government data opened up with accessible and non-proprietary formats (like XML) which can be accessed by all citizens. The availability of this data will truly give news organizations, technologists, and students new ways to easily and effectively monitor government activity. Ethan Bodnar has written an excellent letter which reflects these principles and offers specific advice on what to do. Thankfully, these changes can easily be implemented, given the right team, and are (or should be) decidedly nonpartisan. I hope President-elect Obama learns from his success with technology on the campaign trail and brings that same edge to government.

Obama . . .") the posting does much more than that as the posting proposes a premise and links to other sources.

The class blog, "Te Ao O Tamaki" (http://teaotamaki.blogspot.com), from a school in New Zealand illustrates a more traditional use of blogging as a central place where students' classroom work is published, improved, and commented on. The teacher posting shown in Figure 7.8 illustrates two characteristics of how blogs can successfully be used in classes.

Figure 7.8

Teacher's Blog Showing Initial Posting Structures Task for Students

Tuesday, May 18, 2010

Year 10 Cultural Perspectives: Text 1—Boy Overboard/Themes

Write one paragraph on what YOU think is the most important idea in the novel *Boy Overboard*.

In your paragraph you need to make sure that you follow the Paragraph Structure that we have been working on as a class.

1. S—statement.

2. E—explain your statement.

3. E—example of your statement [quote].

4. E—explain what your example shows.

By doing this, you will be giving yourself preparation on what to write for your formal essay for the novel.

Work hard and enjoy!

First, the teacher has provided structure for the week's blogging activities that involves a writing assignment associated with a book the class is reading (see Figure 7.8). He clearly articulates that their initial posting should include the five elements of writing a good paragraph that they have been studying in class. Second, he has provided an additional purpose for the blog posting—that it will help them to prepare to write their formal essay about this novel. The blog continued to build on the novel reading task over the next few weeks providing students with further opportunities to work on their analysis of the novel, post their thoughts, receive feedback and then ultimately write the paper the teacher mentions.

Any learning activity can benefit from reflection. Our last blog classroom example from Anne Davis—a fifth-grade teacher in the southern United States—exemplifies how a classroom blog helped these students reflect on what they had learned about the writing process via their blogging activities (Richardson, 2010). At The Write Weblog (http://itc.blogs.com/thewriteweblog), every student has blogged and reflected on the blogging impact on writing over the space of about two to three months. Figure 7.9 shows an excerpt from two postings; one from "Alejandro" and another from "Maria" reflecting on blogging and writing.

Returning to ideas presented earlier in this chapter, we recall that students' lack of confidence in writing is often an impediment to developing their writing skills. Maria in particular seems to be aware of specific strategies she has learned—that of using "your voice." Although these posts do not provide proof of Alejandro's or Maria's improved writing skills, even the belief that they have improved—as they've expressed—may be considered a positive outcome.

Figure 7.9

Student Blog Postings Reflecting on Writing and Blogs

Long Live Blogs

I had read a story on Inappropriate Comments made by Mrs. Davis. I was surprised that other people don't trust other people can have a chance to write in blogs. Besides, if we get a bad comment we can just delete it with a click of a button. Those people that don't trust us are wrong that we can't blog because blogs are what make people better at writing. I also think that we should be able to blog because ever since the weblog group started blogging, all of us have improved on our writing skills. Also, once I saw on CNN that people are getting bad grades on writing. Weblogs will help you on your writing skills and help you be a better writer. The people that want to end blogs should at least give us chance to explain to them that blogs are helpful because you can express your feelings and problems. . . .

I Have Learned A Lot!

I have learned many things throughout the year from weblogs. When I first came to weblog group I really didn't like writing as much as I do now. The biggest deal for me that I have learned is to use your voice. I have learned that my voice counts in my writing. When you use your voice in your writing it shows your personality. In your own writing you should always write about your opinion. I've also learned how to organize my weblog and how to make it the way I feel it should be. . . . If I had the chance to write on weblogs next year in 6th grade I would love to . . .

Finally, we note that all of these blog examples—that we consider illustrate positive points—go beyond some typical but limited uses of blogs (e.g., journaling only, only posting assignments, or simply posting links) that may not realize the potential of the tool. As Richardson (2010) describes, the potential strength of blogs is to not only communicate, but to connect, and such blogging activities require more effort. Our next section briefly provides some considerations for creating blogging tasks that promote meaningful learning.

What to Consider When Using Blogging

Although blogs can give students a wide audience for their writing, art, and other creative works, their unstructured format may result in postings that have little educational value for the students constructing them. To ensure that students are using blogs in ways that support significant learning, teachers need to clearly define the intended objectives for learning and determine whether a blog is the best instructional tool for meeting those objectives. Perhaps the objective is simply for students to engage in informal personal writing, but more than likely teachers will need to provide some guidance and structure to help students meet more complex objectives. For instance, even though some of our blog writing examples are from elementary students, Richardson (2010) suggests that the more advanced analytical thinking required of ongoing blogging activities (such as the Newly Ancient blog, Figure 7.7) may not be feasible for younger students.

By letting students choose their blog entry purpose or structure, their blog writing may be scaffolded such as was illustrated in the "Te Ao O Tamaki" blog. Spammers and other unwanted visitors can be avoided by using blog programs that require a secure log-in. Teachers must provide guidelines and clearly communicate the guidelines along with the reasons for security concerns. Students' blog entries should be identified by only first names, pseudonyms, or other nonidentifiable labels. Previewing student blog entries before posting can also help teachers feel comfortable with the content and safety of blogging, especially if a public forum is used. Lastly, providing a scoring guide or other means for communicating expectations can help students use blogs more effectively (see Chapter 10 on assessment).

Finally, there are many online blog sites that allow educators to create blogs for their students. Blogspot, EduBlogs, Bloglines, and Blogger are just a few, but the landscape of these tools is constantly changing. If you are looking for blogging software, we suggest you talk to your colleagues, but also refer to such resources as the following. These sites all provide lists of blogging software as well as some annotations on their features (e.g., privacy or filtering controls built in for students).

> Kathy Schrock's Guide for Educators, http://school.discoveryeducation.com/ schrockguide/edtools.html (look under Web 2.0 tools)
> 50 Blogging Tools for Teachers, www.teachingtips.com/blog/2008/07/21/50-useful-blogging-tools-for-teachers

Other Internet Publishing Tools

Clearly the growth of the use of blogs in educational settings has been tremendous over the last couple of years, but they are not the only tool available for learners wishing to publish

their ideas on the Web. Kidscribe describes itself as a "bilingual site for kid authors" (www
.brightinvisiblegreen.com/kidscribe). It is a simple website that was created to provide
young writers with a forum for publishing personal writing in either English or Spanish.
The creator of Kidscribe wanted to provide an outlet that would hopefully build the young
authors' sense of confidence and pride in their own work, while also providing an opportunity for site users to see creative writing samples in two languages without the presence of
commercial advertisements. Although the site offers no writing supports per se, it is easy to
use and could be effectively used with teacher instruction on writing—especially for a
teacher that has limited resources (e.g., server space) for doing their own Web publishing of
student work.

Although certainly not an ad-free website, Scholastic.com also offers a potential
publication venue for poetry and other forms of writing.[1] But beyond simply providing
a potential publication venue, the Scholastic site also offers guided grade-level–specific
lessons on various aspects of writing poetry, memoirs, or short fiction. For instance,
the site offers an online tool called "story starters" for grades K–6 that is designed to
engage young writers in simple story writing with a colorful and animated graphical
user interface. Other writing tools include a "poetry idea engine" and a variety of structured individual student writing activities available under the "student activities/write
and publish" link. Activities often include simple practice exercises for the topic along
with feedback based on learners' responses. Such activities could easily be used for
whole-class discussion or for students working in small groups around a single computer. A variation on these lessons is the "Writing with Writers" section (Rowen, 2005)
of the website. A set of online workshops is designed by professional writers (of news,
myths, and poets for example), and each workshop provides a suggested process for
that particular type of writing. Each workshop ends with a mechanism for students to
submit their own work for publication. Scholastic does not publish all submissions.

Supporting Specific Writing Forms with Technology

Although Internet publishing provides many opportunities to support creating writing
with technology, there are a number of tools designed to support learners as they engage in
particular forms of writing (e.g., essays, poetry). Poetry Forge (www.poetryforge.org) was
developed by the University of Virginia's Center for Technology and Teacher Education
(www.curry.edschool.virginia.edu/teacherlink) and is an online site that offers tools to support creative writing—in this case focused on poetry.

Poetry Forge offers a set of open source writing tools for the English classroom.
Downloadable tools work on either a Windows or Mac platform and include a metaphor
generator, a tool for building new poems founded on existing poetry, and a tool that
explores the characteristics of "poetic text." The tools are designed to challenge student
understanding of simple parts of speech, complex phrases and what happens both seman-
tically and syntactically for language to effectively convey meaning in a poem. For

---

[1]At this writing, we found these resources under "teacher resources" and "tools."

Figure 7.10

Poetry Forge Online Metaphor Tool

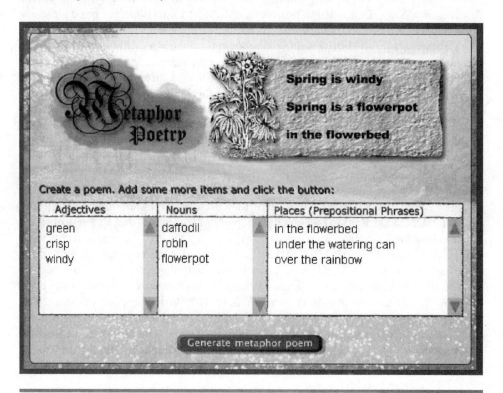

instance, Figure 7.10 shows the Poetry Forge online metaphor tool. Users enter their own adjectives, nouns, and prepositional phrases and the tool combines them into "poetic" phrases. According to the website, Poetry Forge tools are designed to be used with teachers working alongside students, coaching them and challenging their thinking. The site offers a good explanation of the technical requirements for the downloadable tools, as well as lesson plans and suggestions for teachers on how to use them in their classrooms.

Tools like Poetry Forge are not likely to create the next national poet laureate but they do help learners engage in poetry writing and practicing the application of literary structures that are essential and commonly used in poetry writing. The website authors directly acknowledge that the poetry that results from using Poetry Forge tools will be "unpredictable" (www.poetryforge.org/about.htm). They do however posit that even such results will provide the basis for editing, adjustment, and evaluation—all of which are critical and commonly acknowledged parts of the writing process—and often parts that are overlooked by novices.

Another example of this type of technology to support specific writing forms is Essay Punch (www.essaypunch.com). The tool walks writers through a series of preset writing prompts to help them to develop an idea into an essay of a descriptive, informative, or

Figure 7.11

Essay Punch Revisions Frame

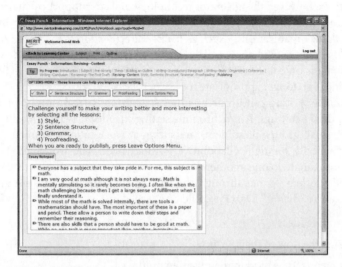

persuasive format. The tool structures the writing task into prewriting (e.g., brainstorming), developing a thesis, generating content, and revisions. Figure 7.11 pictures a screen designed to help writers revise their essay. Although not free, the software is relatively inexpensive; less than $100 for a single class of students. There are similar technologies offered by the same company for paragraph and book writing.

Supporting Collaborative Writing with Technology

Collaborative writing refers to written works that are created by multiple people together rather than individually. Ede and Lunsford (1983) described three general sets of collaborative writing activities: (1) intensive collaboration where authors create a text by working closely together; (2) significant writing is done separately but writers do work to a limited extent collaboratively; and (3) sequential group collaboration that occurs via a sequence of activities.

Just as in other collaborative processes, sometimes roles are assigned such as editor, reporter, or leader. Ethnographers of writing who have studied these roles in fact have described the complex interactions that can occur in collaborative reading and writing between "authors," "readers," and "texts" and posit that the roles are in fact constantly being renegotiated during collaborative writing (e.g., Flower, Long, & Higgins, 2000, as cited in Lunsford & Bruce, 2001). Potential benefits of having learners engage in collaborative writing include positive relationships among students, increased participation by students, opportunities for peer and self-assessment, more sources of input and ideas, varied points of view, and of course when writing with persons from other cultures, cross-cultural fertil-ization (Hernandez, Hoeksema, Kelm, Jefferies, Lawrence, Lee, & Miller, 2001).

Collaborative writing has been practiced for many years in business, educational and personal settings; however, the advent of technology tools to support collaborative writing has dramatically increased its popularity and its feasibility (Lunsford & Bruce, 2001). Further, standards organizations—such as ISTE—directly address the need for students to be able to "use digital media" to collaborate effectively (www.iste.org). Describing this increased emphasis on collaboration, some even go so far as to imply that to focus only on solitary writing is no longer appropriate for learners (Pasnik, 2007).

Collaborative writing can occur in either synchronous (real time) or asynchronous (with a time delay) settings. A synchronous setting may look as pictured in Figure 7.12. Individual or small groups of students are sitting at workstations running software that supports a (typically online) collaborative writing space. The workstations may or be immediately proximate to one another. If they are not, then users would need to be in con-tact with one another—either through the writing software itself, an instant messaging service or e-mail to "dialog." Learners could be engaged in:

- Brainstorming ideas
- Structuring the flow of their writing
- Generating text to be used in their written product
- Editing or commenting on text
- Negotiating meaning of any of the above tasks

Figure 7.12

Students at Different Workstations Writing Collaboratively

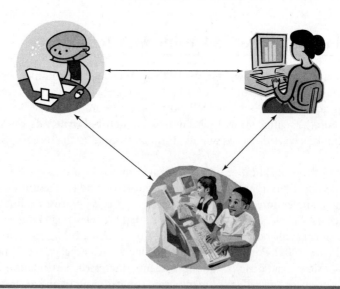

In an asynchronous setting, the activities could be similar; however, they would not necessarily occur in real time. Such a scenario and collaborative writing software makes nationwide and even global collaborative writing feasible.

Collaborative Writing Using Document Sharing Tools

Tools to support collaborative writing abound and offer many features. A recent Internet search on "collaborative writing online" produced thousands of results. Many tools that support collaborative writing fall into the classification of "cloud" computing tools—ones that reside on Internet servers—exist (e.g., Google Docs—formerly Writely) but others reside on one's individual computer or resident server. Readers may wish to refer to a "mini-guide" to collaborative writing tools from the independent organization Kolabora (www.kolabora .com) (Good, 2007). Tools are described by the features they offer such as RSS feeds for notification of changes to a collaborative document, the maximum number of editors, and price.

VanderMolen (2008) also offers a review of four free Web 2.0 collaborative writing tools. Among the four are Google Docs and Zoho writer (writer.zoho.com). Clearly, Google Docs (docs.google.com) is an extremely popular collaborative writing tool that offers features for K–12 learners. Google Docs offers many features that can facilitate collaborative writing. Here are a few of the most important (Godwin-Jones, 2008).

- *Importing documents.* Documents can be imported into Google Docs from Microsoft Word, HTML documents, text or image files or anything from which you paste and copy. Google Docs documents exist in an HTML format; however, you edit them in a what-you-see-is-what-you-get (WYSIWYG) method.

- *Sharing documents.* Once you create a document in Google Docs, you have the ability to immediately add up to 12 collaborators on that Google Docs document (see Figure 7.13). New collaborators are notified of their status via an e-mail that you compose.

Figure 7.13

Document Collaboration Using Google Docs

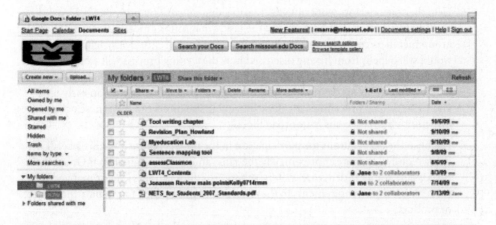

- *Revision history.* You can also view your document's revision history, compare versions, and roll back to any version.

- *Unlimited or generous storage space.* Documents can be up to 500K in size and each document can be shared with up to 50 people.

- *Levels of collaboration or sharing.* Google Docs allows you to specify that only specific users can also have edit and commenting privileges on your document. Other users can simply view the document. Google Docs calls this "publishing" the document.

- *Creating comments.* Any collaborator can insert comments. Anyone who can edit the document can see the comments that are inserted. Persons with "viewing only" privileges cannot.

- *Sharing documents.* Documents can be published for viewing (but not editing) by others via Google Docs by simply "publishing" it from the document window. Google Docs also offers publishing of documents to blogs.

Although word-processing software offers some of these features (such as commenting) the sharing attributes of software like Google Docs is what makes it well suited for collaboration. We also recognize that wikis may be used in similar ways to support collaborative writing as described in Sze (2008); we refer the reader to Chapter 6 in this book for more on wikis and how they can support community building in general.

Tips for Successful Collaborative Writing Even with the best software, we advise teachers to appropriately support not only the writing aspects but also the social aspects of the collaborative writing task. Students don't "just know" how to collaborate—they need help to be successful. The following guidelines can help students to successfully engage in collaborative writing as well as other collaborative activities (Herandez et al., 2001).

1. Structure activities at the beginning of the project to build cohesion among the collaborators and to establish positive interpersonal relationships. If students are working with other students at a distance, consider having them spend time engaging in Internet "chats" on nonacademic subjects (e.g., pets, family, afterschool jobs) before starting their writing projects.

2. Help the collaborators work out effective meeting or working procedures. Depending on the construction of the group and the task, synchronous meetings may not be how group members communicate, but even if students work entirely asynchronously they would still benefit from having discussed how the writing process will work. This may involve defining roles and timelines. Additionally, help students discuss how they will handle disagreements or conflicts within groups. Having this discussion early on and/or setting up procedures for these inevitable situations can turn these occurrences into minor bumps versus major road blocks.

3. Establish the expectations for participation in the project before it begins. Are all students required to write approximately the same amount of original text? Or are there roles where some students are writers, others are editors, others lead or manage the team? Align these requirements to the criteria that will be used to evaluate the project or product.

4. Pay attention to students who are more susceptible to marginalization, isolation—or in general, to being left out. Depending on the nature of the project and the group membership, the students in this category will vary. As the teacher you should be aware of students who are not being allowed to actively and meaningfully participate in the project. This requires frequent monitoring and can also be aided by periodic and preplanned team self-assessments.

5. Have students use the collaborative writing software for a "test" project before embarking on a major collaborative writing task. Packages such as Google Docs are fairly intuitive, but even so, taking the "new software package anxiety" variable out of the collaborative writing equation can help ensure success.

Collaborative Writing Examples Collaborative writing can be used meaningfully for a variety of tasks. Rogers and Horton (1992) suggest that teachers select topics for collaborative writing that encourage active participation, such as simulations of real-world job tasks, or have the potential for "conflict" between writers that needs to be resolved. And as we said previously, one advantage of collaborative writing is that it can support cross-disciplinary learning tasks.

The "Save the Turtles" nonprofit site exemplifies this cross-discipline collaboration. This site is a global initiative designed to promote collaborative writing via an environmentally oriented topic that is often appealing to students. The site exemplifies how collaborative writing can be structured and used even with young learners. It begins by clearly establishing the learning objectives of the site, which include to "learn about the global nature of sea turtle species, their behaviors and the marine eco-systems they inhabit," and "develop writing skills, including character development, plot and dialog" (www.costaricaturtles.org/costa_new_story.html). The site also includes specific lesson suggestions for structuring prewriting activities, and ideas for how to implement collaborative writing via poetry and story formats (see Figure 7.14).

Additionally, the following are examples of online collaborative projects that could easily include a writing task as well as potential cross-disciplinary collaborative writing tasks.

- Engage students in collaborative writing in the context of other Internet-based collaborative tasks. For instance, Telegarden (http://cwis.usc.edu/dept/garden) allows students to collaboratively tend a living garden over the Internet. In Telegarden, users control a robot arm that can plant seeds, water plants, and monitor growth. This type of environment clearly supports science learning outcomes; however, the activity could easily be combined with a collaborative writing task during which students from a single class in one school or multiple classes in multiple locations could collaborate on the experiments as well as report writing.

- Have students partner with others at a distance to engage in collaboratively writing a newspaper article. Choose to partner with a school district that has access to data sources that are not available to your students. For instance, students in Columbia, Missouri, might co-write news articles with students in Baton Rouge, Louisiana, about the aftermath of Hurricane Katrina. Students in Columbia have access to and can

Figure 7.14

"Save the Turtles" Story Prompts Exemplify Structuring Collaborative Writing

^ top

Ideas For Collaboration: Story Prompts and Poem

Two Story Prompts

1. Lost Sea Turtle Objectives:

- Learn about a sea turtle species, their behaviors such as diet, migration, nesting.
- Learn about threats to sea turtle survival such as pollution (oil spills, beach litter), fishing practices, predators, habitat destruction and degradation
- Learn the meaning and importance of "natal beach"
- Make a global connection! Learn cooperation, mutual support and problem solving

The Lost Sea Turtle

Each class will choose a different species of sea turtle and develop a dynamic character. The two sea turtles befriend one another during a journey across the ocean to find the natal beach they both share. During the journey they help each other avoid dangers of the land and sea. *Please note that different species of sea turtles nest in specific regions, so in order to have your story based on facts, please consider using the CCC or another resource to obtain the nesting areas of the species your class chooses.

Consider some of these sample questions for your students:

What species of sea turtle are you and what do you look like? Where does you turtle nest? How do you meet the other class's sea turtle character and share the journey home to your natal beach to lay eggs? What do you eat and how far did you migrate? What characters/marine life do you both meet at sea? How do the characters work together to help each other survive? What threats to your survival do you encounter in the ocean? Once you reach the shore, what threats do you encounter on the land? Perhaps you both become confused by bright lights and wander into a village or city. How do you both make it back to the beach to lay your eggs? What characters if any, help you to your nesting ground? How does the story end?

develop expertise with the Columbia-based Rescue One squad that did search-and-rescue operations after Katrina, while the Baton Rouge students can contribute the impact of Katrina on their community as refugees poured into the city and many now reside there permanently.

As teachers read these ideas, they may reasonably ask how they might find collaborative partners. The Global SchoolNet (www.globalschoolnet.org), described in Chapter 6, is a registry service that allows teachers to submit calls for collaboration, search ongoing collaborative projects, or add a project of their own. A recent visit to the site showed they currently have more than 3,000 online projects registered; projects are organized by topic grade and project date facilitating a variety of search strategies.

Supporting Peer Feedback on Writing

Writing instructors have come to realize the importance of multiple drafts in the writing process (Schriver, 1990). However, creating multiple drafts and the edit and reedit process is only effective when novice writers receive feedback. One reason writing instruction is difficult for teachers may be the time demands of providing the feedback necessary to help students both effectively revise their work or improve their writing in a next attempt. Teachers understandably have limited time to devote to such feedback, especially when they have many students and many subjects to teach. The result is often that students do not engage in many (if any) multiple draft writing projects. Further, even when instructors provide feedback, it is often focused on accuracy of content and clarity of writing (both of which are extremely valuable forms of feedback) but may completely ignore writing style (Ziv, 1981).

Implementing student peer feedback on writing may offer a solution to some of these problems. While having fellow students provide feedback to their peers on writing has been implemented, more recent research has shown that student-to-student feedback may be more effective in helping students improve in their writing than the "expert" feedback they may receive from teachers (Cho, Schunn, & Charney, 2006; Schriver, 1990). In addition to helping to reduce the burden on instructors of providing writing feedback, reciprocal peer assessment may help students to develop evaluation skills that can be applied in many settings, increase responsibility for their own learning, as well as improve writing skills.

SWoRD (Scaffolded Writing and Rewriting in the Discipline) (Cho, Schunn, & Charney, 2006) is a Web-based reciprocal peer review system that is designed to also provide mechanisms to ensure validity and reduce the potential of student bias in providing feedback. SWoRD enables teachers and students to manage the distribution of papers to reviewers and reviews back to authors, and addresses typical peer review concerns such as author and reviewer confidentiality. It also includes evaluation mechanisms that structure the "reviewer" students' tasks so that they can take the task seriously. For instance, SWoRD includes an evaluation rubric that reviewers must complete and requires that reviewers include written comments in their feedback. Then according to the draft, review, revision schedule the instructor has defined, SWoRD automatically distributes the completed reviews to the authors. Figure 7.15 shows the "reviews and back reviews" window an author would see for his or her draft.

SWoRD addresses another typically problematic part of high-quality writing: producing multiple drafts. To use SWoRD as an author, the student must submit first and revised drafts, and peers then evaluate both drafts. SWoRD is free to use for noncommercial purposes (www.lrdc.pitt.edu/schunn/sword/index.html). Note that to date, SWoRD has been used primarily in higher education.

Figure 7.15

SWoRD Reviews Screen

Reviews and Back-Reviews on Your 1st Draft		
Flows ★★★★★		
Reviewer	Comments	Back-Reviews
Reviewer 1 ★★★	**Average (4)** In order to certain writing can be regard as smooth flow, it is constructed locally and globally coherent. It means that each parts should written locally coherent, at the same time, they should be connected organizationally. For these connections, each paragraph has well associated with topic sentence or topic word, and subtitles also can play a role like that, I think. In this view point, if you present your writing procedure and revise each subtitle for global organization of paper, it will be definitely more coherent and flow smoothly.	★★★★★ Although this was certainly needed, I think maybe some specific suggestions would have helped me out more.
Reviewer 2 ★★★★★★★	**Average (4)** Prose Flow Your review and summary of Schunn and Dunbar's (1996) work under the heading of background was well written. However, it is not clear where the literature review ends and your argument begins. What exactly is your position? If this is the case, perhaps the paper would flow more smoothly if you provide more detailed descriptions of the concepts you are addressing. For example, defining learning, base-level activation and chunking may perhaps allow you to make smoother transitions. Additional comments: The author did not following the instructions regarding double spacing, running head and page margins.	★★★★★★★ I did not remember reading about instructions for spacing, running heads, and such, but after your comment I went back and saw that.

Conclusion

Even in today's technology-laden society, writing continues to be a skill critical to success in many in- and out-of-school endeavors. It also continues to be a task that is at best not pleasurable and at worst anxiety ridden for many—again both in and out of school. We might further argue that in today's text-message-focused society, teaching traditional writing skills is even more challenging. A faculty colleague recently described how one of his undergraduates submitted a paper entirely written in text-message abbreviations. That certainly wasn't what he had in mind when he assigned the task!

In this chapter we described tools available to help learners with different parts of the writing process (e.g., concept maps for planning and organizing), tools for different types of writing (e.g., Poetry Forge for poetry), and tools for supporting collaborative writing. The tools offer a variety of ways of making writing more fun for students (e.g., Poetry Forge's metaphor generator), experience the motivation of having their writing "published" (e.g., blogs), and providing supports and structure for different writing activities. Additionally, tools that support collaborative writing offer teachers and students opportunities to engage in meaningful writing tasks in cross-disciplinary settings with collaborators in almost any location. In nearly all cases however, writing remains a complex task that requires considerable supervision, encouragement, and, perhaps most of all, frequent and high-quality feedback from teachers.

NET Standards potentially engaged by writing activities described in this chapter:

1. **Creativity and Innovation**
   a. Apply existing knowledge to generate new ideas, products, or processes
   b. Create original works as a means of personal or group expression

2. **Communication and Collaboration**
   a. Interact, collaborate, and publish with peers, experts, or others employing a variety of digital environments and media
   b. Communicate information and ideas effectively to multiple audiences using a variety of media and formats
   d. Contribute to project teams to produce original works or solve problems

3. **Research and Information Fluency**
   a. Plan strategies to guide inquiry
   b. Locate, organize, analyze, evaluate, synthesize, and ethically use information from a variety of sources and media

4. **Critical Thinking, Problem Solving, and Decision Making**
   b. Plan and manage activities to develop a solution or complete a project
   c. Use multiple processes and diverse perspectives to explore alternative solutions

6. **Technology Operations and Concepts**
   a. Understand and use technology systems
   d. Transfer current knowledge to learning of new technologies

21st Century Skills potentially engaged by writing activities described in this chapter:

Think Creatively

- Use a wide range of idea-creation techniques (such as brainstorming)
- Create new and worthwhile ideas (both incremental and radical concepts)
- Elaborate, refine, analyze, and evaluate their own ideas in order to improve and maximize creative efforts

Work Creatively with Others

- Develop, implement, and communicate new ideas to others effectively
- Be open and responsive to new and diverse perspectives; incorporate group input and feedback into the work
- Demonstrate originality and inventiveness in work and understand the real-world limits to adopting new ideas

Communicate Clearly

- Articulate thoughts and ideas effectively using oral, written, and nonverbal communication skills in a variety of forms and contexts
- Use communication for a range of purposes (e.g., to inform, instruct, motivate, and persuade)

- Utilize multiple media and technologies, and know how to judge their effectiveness a priori as well as assess their impact
- Communicate effectively in diverse environments (including multi-lingual)

Collaborate with Others

- Demonstrate ability to work effectively and respectfully with diverse teams
- Exercise flexibility and willingness to be helpful in making necessary compromises to accomplish a common goal
- Assume shared responsibility for collaborative work, and value the individual contributions made by each team member

Access and Evaluate Information

- Access information efficiently (time) and effectively (sources)
- Evaluate information critically and competently

Create Media Products

- Understand and utilize the most appropriate media creation tools, characteristics, and conventions

Apply Technology Effectively

- Use technology as a tool to research, organize, evaluate, and communicate information

Things to Think About

We suggest that you can use the following questions to reflect on the ideas that we presented in this chapter.

1. What type or types of writing do your students struggle with the most? How can you use an understanding of the writing process to further diagnose students' writing difficulties?

2. What types of writing activities would make the best use of technology in your classrooms?

3. How can you increase the use of meaningful writing activities in cross-disciplinary projects? How can technology help with these cross-disciplinary writing tasks?

4. Would the act of "publishing" their written work (on the Internet for instance) be motivating to your students? How can you leverage this potential for motivation in your classroom?

5. Students' writing improves through multiple revisions and high-quality feedback. Recognizing that your teacher time is limited, how can you have students help each other during writing? How can you use technology tools to support peer feedback?

6. Collaborative activities have many potential benefits but students don't automatically know how to collaborate successfully. What strategies can you/have you put in place to make collaborative teams effective both in terms of completing the intended task as well as in helping students learn to be good collaborators?

References

Anderson-Inman, L., & Horney, M. (1996). Computer-based concept mapping: Enhancing literacy with tools for visual thinking. *Journal of Adolescent & Adult Literacy, 40*(4), 302. Retrieved from the Academic Search Premier database.

Bafile, C. (2009). The Concept-mapping classroom. *Education World*. Retrieved from http://69.43.199.47/a_tech/tech164.shtml

Cho, K., Schunn, C., & Charney, D. (2006). Commenting on writing: Typology and perceived helpfulness of comments from novice peer reviewers and subject matter experts. *Written Communication, 23*(3), 260–294.

Cook, A., & Schwier, R. (2008). *A review of K–12 virtual learning communities.* Retrieved from www.usask.ca/education/coursework/802papers/cook/cook.pdf

Ede, L. S., & Lunsford, A. A. (1983). Why write . . . together? *Rhetoric Review 5*(1), 150–158.

Eide Neurolearning Blog. (2005). *Brain of the blogger.* Retrieved from http://eideneurolearningblog .blogspot.com/2005/03/brain-of-blogger_03.html

Falloon, S. (2005, February/March). All the world's a stage. *Edutopia*, 16–18. Retrieved from www.edutopia.org/all-worlds-stage-teaching-through-online-journals

Feinberg, J. (2010). Wordle. In J. Steele & N. Iliinsky (Eds.), *Beautiful visualization looking at data through the eyes of experts* (pp. 37–58). Sebastopol, CA: O'Reilly Media.

Flower, L. S., Schriver, K. A., Carey, L., Haas, C., & Hayes, J. R. (1989). Planning in writing: The cognition of a constructive process. Technical Report, Centre for the Study of Writing, University of California, Berkeley.

Godwin-Jones, R. (2008). Emerging technologies Web writing 2.0: Enabling, documenting, and assessing writing online. *Language Learning and Technology, 12*(2), 7–13.

Good, R. (2007). Collaborative writing tools and technology: A mini-guide. Retrieved from www.kolabora.com/news/2007/03/01/collaborative_writing_tools_and_technology.htm

Hernandez, N., Hoeksema, A., Kelm, H., Jefferies, J., Lawrence, K., Lee, S., & Miller, P. (2001). *Collaborative writing in the classroom: A method to produce quality work.* Retrieved from http://scholar.google.com/scholar?hl=en&lr=&q=cache:QvZks0WKIGsJ:www.edb .utexas.edu/resta/itesm2001/topicpapers/s2paper.pdf+k-12+technology+OR+ software+%22collaborative+writing%22

Lenhart, A., Madden, M., Macgill, A., & Smith, A. (2007). *Teen content creators. Pew Internet & American Life Project.* Retrieved from http://pewresearch.org/pubs/670/teen-content-creators

Lunsford, K. J., & Bruce, B. C. (2001, September). Collaboratories: Working together on the Web. *Journal of Adolescent & Adult Literacy, 45*(1). Available: www.readingonline.org/ electronic/elec_index.asp?HREF=/electronic/jaal/9-01_Column/index.html

National Council of Teachers of English. (1996). *Standards for the English Language Arts.* Retrieved from http://cnets.iste.org/currstands/cstands-ela.html

n.a. (2003). Reading & writing tools. *T.H.E. Journal, 31*(5), 19.

n.a. (2008). Wordle: Thinking about time poems and calligrams. Retrieved from http://twowhizzy.blogspot.com/2008/06/wordle-thinking-about-time-poems-and.html

Pasnik, S. (2007). Bye-bye byline? What does it mean to be an author in today's Web 2.0 world? *Cable in the Classroom Magazine*, 12.

Partnership for 21st Century Skills. (2004). Partnership for 21st Century Skills. Retrieved from www.p21.org/index.php

Ramaswami, R. (2008). The prose of blogging (and a few cons, too). Retrieved from http://thejournal.com/articles/2008/11/01/the-prose-of-blogging-and-a-few-cons-too.aspx?sc_lang=en

Richardson, W. (2010). *Blogs wikis, podcasts, and other powerful Web tools for classrooms.* Thousand Oaks, CA: Corwin.

Riedel, C. (2010). Enhancing instruction with Web 2.0. Retrieved from http://thejournal.com/articles/2010/01/20/enhancing-instruction-with-web-2.0.aspx?sc_lang=en

Rogers, P. S., & Horton, M. S. (1992). Exploring the value of face-to-face collaborative writing. In J. Forman (Ed.), *New visions of collaborative writing* (pp. 120–146). Portsmouth, NH: Boynton/Cook.

Rowen, D. (2005, February). The write motivation. *Learning & Leading with Technology, 32*(5), 22.

Rushkoff, D. (2004). Renaissance prospects. IT Conversations. Retrieved from http://itc.conversationsnetwork.org/shows/detail243.html

Schriver, K. A. (1990). Evaluating text quality: The continuum from text-focused to reader-focused methods. *Technical Report No. 41.* National Center for the Study of Writing and Literacy.

Sze, P. (2008). Online collaborative writing using wikis. *The Internet TESL Journal*, Vol. XIV, No. 1. Retrieved from http://iteslj.org/Techniques/Sze-Wikis.html

VanderMolen, J. (2008). Four Web 2.0 collaborative-writing tools. Retrieved from www.techlearning.com/article/8906

Viégas, F. B., Wattenberg, M., & Feinberg, J. (2009). Participatory visualization with Wordle. *IEEE Transactions on Visualization and Computer Graphics 15*(6) 1137–1144.

Wetzel, D. (2010). 10 organization tools designed to ease the writing process. Retrieved from http://freelancewriting.suite101.com/article.cfm/10-organization-tools-designed-to-ease-the-writing-process

Ziv, Y. (1981). On some discourse uses of existentials in English, or, getting more mileage out of existentials in English. Presented at the LSA Annual Meeting, NY.

Modeling with Technologies

Liz Moore/Merrill

Chapter Objectives

1. Explain why modeling enhances conceptual understanding

2. Describe how concept maps, databases, and spreadsheets can be used to construct models of domain knowledge

3. Describe how modeling supports the development of NETS and 21st Century Skills

Learning by Building Models

"Scientific practice involves the construction, validation, and application of scientific models, so science instruction should be designed to engage students in making and using models" (Hestenes, 1996, p. 1). The same assumption applies to all disciplines. Constructing models of phenomena being studied is probably the most powerful strategy supporting meaningful learning. The assumption of this chapter is that if you cannot model it, you don't know it.

Building models using different computer-based modeling tools is perhaps the most conceptually engaging classroom activity possible that has the greatest potential for engaging and encouraging conceptual change processes (Jonassen, 2008; Nersessian, 1999). Building models externalizes the mental models that people construct. Another important reason for modeling is the evaluation of alternative models, that is, the comparison of two or more models for their relative fit to the world (Lehrer & Schauble, 2003). When students compare and contrast their own models, they are as conceptually engaged as possible. Why? Because comparing alternative models requires understanding that alternative models are possible and that the activity of modeling can be used for testing rival models.

What are models? Lesh and Doerr (2003) claim that models are conceptual systems consisting of elements, relations, operations, and rules that are used to construct, describe, or explain the behavior of systems. These models are in the minds of learners and may be represented in the equations, diagrams, computer programs and other media used by learners to represent their understanding. There are models in the mind (mental models) and there are models in the world. The relationship between internal and external models is not well understood. There is a dynamic and reciprocal relationship between internal mental models and the external models that students construct. The mental models provide the basis for external models. The external models in turn constrain and regulate internal models, providing the means for conceptual change. Here, we argue for the construction of models using different technology-based modeling tools, because each tool imposes a different set of structural or rhetorical constraints that enable students to tune their internal models.

If you talk to math and science educators about modeling, they like to represent phenomena in equations, which is the most succinct and exact form of modeling. They are using a quantitative representation of what they are studying. However, representing ideas in terms of equations is not enough for understanding. Qualitative models are just as important as quantitative. Qualitative modeling is a missing link in novice problem solving (Chi, Feltovich, & Glaser, 1981; Larkin, 1983). When students try to understand a problem only through equations that do not convey any conceptual information, students do not understand the nature of what they are studying. So, it is necessary to help learners construct a qualitative representation of the problem as well as a quantitative one.

Modeling is fundamental to human cognition. Humans are natural model builders. From a very early age, we construct mental models of everything that we encounter in the world. For example, toddlers construct theories about their environments, what they can get away with, and what they better not do. These models comprise their personal theories about the world that enable them to reason about the things that we encounter. Modeling helps learners express and externalize their thinking, visualize and test components of their theories, and make materials more interesting. We must first understand what is in the models that we build before we can ask questions about the system being represented.

Students may externalize their mental models using a variety of computer-based Mindtools (Jonassen, 2006), including databases, concept mapping, spreadsheets, microworlds, systems modeling tools, expert systems, hypermedia construction tools, constraint-based discussion boards, and visualization tools, for constructing models of the ideas that students are studying. When using computers as Mindtools to model phenomena, students are teaching the computer, rather than the computer teaching the student. Each tool requires that learners think in a different way about what they are studying. Mindtools function as intellectual partners with the students. The students make the computer smarter, and the computer makes the students smarter. Mindtools do not necessarily make learning easier. They are not "fingertip" tools (Perkins, 1993) that learners use naturally, effortlessly. In fact, learning *with* Mindtools requires learners to think harder about the subject-matter domain being studied than they would have to think without the Mindtool. Students cannot use Mindtools without thinking deeply about the content they are learning, and, if they choose to use these tools to help them learn, the tools will facilitate the learning and meaning-making processes.

In addition to using different Mindtools to engage different kinds of thinking, they can also be used to build models of different phenomena (Jonassen, 2006). Mindtools can be used to model domain knowledge, or the content that students are supposed to learn in schools. Building models of that content will help students better comprehend and remember what they are learning. Mindtools may also be used to build models of systems, which requires students to understand how domain knowledge is tied together. Systems are organizations of dynamic, interdependent parts that are oriented by a common purpose and controlled by feedback. Requiring learners to organize what they are learning into relevant systems that interact with each other provides learners with a much more integrated view of the world. Mindtools may also be used to build models of problems. In order to solve virtually any kind of problem, students must mentally construct a problem space that models the specific relations of the problem. Using modeling tools to create models externalizes learners' mental problem space. Some Mindtools, especially databases, can be used to collect, analyze, and organize stories of people's experiences. Stories are the oldest and most natural form of meaning making. Finally, Mindtools can also be used to model thinking processes. Rather than modeling content or systems, learners model the kind of thinking that they need to perform in order to solve a problem, make a decision, or complete some other task. Each different phenomenon on (content, systems, problems, stories, and reflective thinking) represents a different kind of knowledge. This is important because the more ways that learners can represent their conceptual understanding, the more they will understand. In the remainder of the chapter, we illustrate how some of the modeling tools have been used by students to construct models of different kinds of knowledge.

There are many reasons for constructing models to support meaningful learning and problem solving:

- Model building is a natural cognitive phenomenon. When encountering unknown phenomena, humans naturally begin to construct personal theories about those phenomena that are represented as informal models.

- Modeling is constructivist—constructing personal representations of experienced phenomena.

- Modeling supports hypothesis testing, conjecturing, inferring, and a host of other important cognitive skills.

- Modeling engages conceptual change.

- Modeling results in the construction of cognitive artifacts (externalized mental models).

- When students construct models, they own the knowledge. Student ownership is important to meaning making and knowledge construction.

Modeling Knowledge with Concept Maps

Concept maps are spatial representations of concepts and their interrelationships that simulate the knowledge structures that humans store in their minds (Jonassen, Beissner, & Yacci, 1993). These knowledge structures are also known as cognitive structures, conceptual knowledge, structural knowledge, and semantic networks. The semantic networks in memory (conceptual model in the mind) and the maps that represent them are composed of nodes (concepts or ideas) that are connected by links (statements of relationships). In computer-based semantic networks, nodes are represented as information blocks and the links are labeled lines. Figure 8.1 illustrates one screen of a complex concept map of domain knowledge related to water, produced with Semantica (www.semanticresearch.com), the most powerful concept-mapping program available. Double-clicking any concept on the map puts that concept in the middle of the screen and shows all of the other concepts that are associated with it. Most semantic networking programs also provide the capability of adding text and pictures to each node in order to elaborate that concept.

Figure 8.2 (on page 196) illustrates a concept map of the human body and how it functions. It was produced using Inspiration (www.inspiration.com). This map describes many of the major concepts and their relationships about how the human body processes food. Understanding those relationships is essential to understanding how the human body functions. Many readers will probably react to the very crowded nature of concepts in Figure 8.2. Inspiration, like most concept-mapping programs including the popular C-Map, presents concepts on a single map (although it is possible to create submaps in Inspiration). This is a pity, because the larger a map is, the more it helps to integrate domain ideas. The most effective use of concept-mapping tools for representing domain knowledge is for students to spend the entire year constructing a concept map that models content from textbooks, lectures, or other information sources. Such a map may include a few thousand concepts, helping students to better comprehend the integrated nature of the domain. As with all other modeling tools, comparing students' semantic networks with others often results in conceptual change as students see how other models represent and structure the same ideas. When students compare their concept maps with others, they are thinking deeply.

The articulation of one's own ideas through concept mapping can be magnified by considering others' conceptual representations. Working collaboratively to build a concept map can provide opportunities for cognitive dissonance, causing students to pause and reflect upon their current conceptual knowledge in conjunction with new ideas presented by others. Online tools such as MindMeister (www.mindmeister.com) provide an environment for creating, collaborating, and sharing semantic networks.

The most important intellectual requirement, we believe, is the ability to describe or type the links between concepts. Note the link names in Figures 8.1 and Figures 8.2. The more exact and descriptive these links are, the better the map is. Many concept-mapping

Figure 8.1

Concept Map of Water Using Semantica

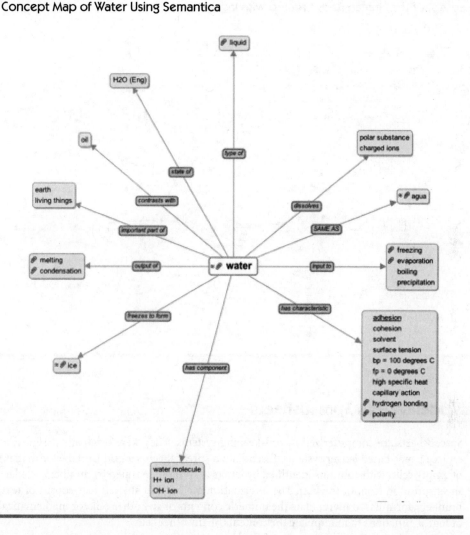

programs do not support describing links. We argue that they are not worth using in classrooms. Linking is challenging, but absolutely necessary for constructing anything similar to an internal semantic network.

Some concept-mapping programs, like Inspiration, provide a graphics library to illustrate each concept. Too often, when this feature is available, students (even adult, graduate students) limit their concepts to illustrations available in the library, completely ignoring the semantic nature of the maps. We urge care in using those libraries. Note that the map in Figure 8.2 is devoid of illustrations, focusing on the semantic relationships among concepts.

Figure 8.2

Concept Map About the Human Body Created with Inspiration

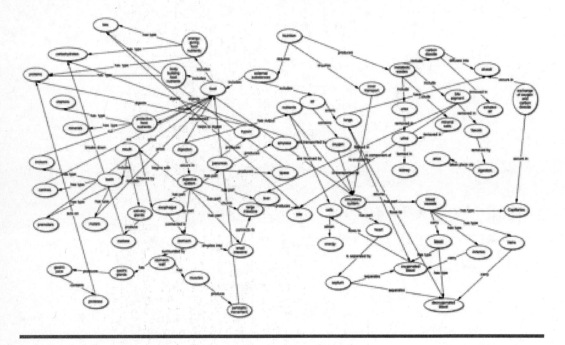

Modeling with Spreadsheets

Spreadsheets are computerized record-keeping systems. They were originally designed to replace paper-based ledger systems. Essentially, a spreadsheet is a grid (or table or matrix) of empty cells, with columns identified by letters and rows identified by numbers, a ledger sheet spread in front of the user. The information included in any cell may consist of text, numbers, formulas to manipulate the numeric contents of any other cells, or mathematical or logical functions to manipulate the contents of any other cells.

Spreadsheets have three primary functions: storing, calculating, and presenting information. First, information, usually numerical, can be stored in a particular cell, from which it can be readily accessed and retrieved. Second, and most important, spreadsheets support calculation functions, such that the numerical contents of any combination of cells can be mathematically related in just about any way the user wishes. Finally, spreadsheets present information in a variety of graphs and charts, as well as graphics.

Spreadsheets are an example of a Mindtool that amplifies and reorganizes mental functioning. Building spreadsheet models engages a variety of mental processes that require learners to use existing rules, generate new rules describing relationships, and organize information. The emphasis in a spreadsheet is on identifying relationships and describing those relationships in terms of higher order rules (generally numerical), so it is probable that if users learn to develop spreadsheets to describe content domains, they will be thinking more deeply. So, spreadsheets are rule-using tools that require that users become rule makers (Vockell & Van Deusen, 1989). Defining the arithmetic operations that calculate values in a spreadsheet requires users to identify relationships and patterns among the data they want to represent in the spreadsheet. Next, those relationships must be modeled mathematically using rules to describe the relationships in the model. Building spreadsheets requires abstract reasoning by the user.

Spreadsheets can help learners in a number of ways. One of the most obvious ways is to help students better comprehend mathematics. For instance, spreadsheets were used by Hoeffner, Kendall, Stellenwerf, Thames, and Williams (1993) to help students develop a conceptual understanding of relationships between variables while solving problems such as planning a party, holiday shopping, and calculating interest. Spreadsheets are also used by students to analyze, summarize, and report data that they have collected from experiments or other activities. For example, Figure 8.3 illustrates spreadsheet charts that students created to represent relative intake of different food groups.

Figure 8.3

Spreadsheet Analysis of Food Intake

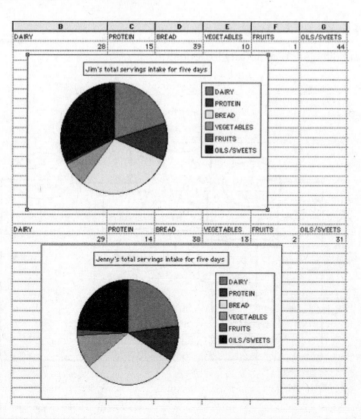

The underlying assumption of this chapter is that spreadsheets, like other tools, are used most effectively to construct simulations models of ideas and problems. For example, Figure 8.4 shows a simulation of a problem involving Ohm's Law. The simulation presents a series of batteries and allows a user to manipulate the values of the impedance (ohms) or voltage. Simulating phenomena using spreadsheets provides a "direct and effective means of understanding the role of various parameters and of testing different means of optimizing their values" (Sundheim, 1992, p. 654). Having students construct simulations engages them more than simply using simulations that teachers develop.

Spreadsheet models may be constructed to represent any quantitative information that students are studying, such as

- Planetary motion in science class

- Demographic variables among populations or amounts of money spent on welfare, defense, and other variables in different countries in social studies class

- Levels of affection, jealousy, or revenge in a story, play, or novel for English class

The possibilities are endless.

Figure 8.4

Spreadsheet Simulation of Battery Experiment

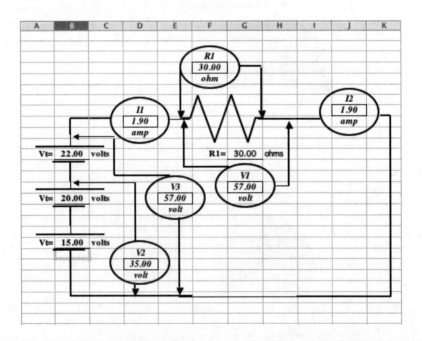

Modeling Experiences with Databases

Database management systems (DBMSs) are computerized record-keeping systems. They were originally designed to replace paper-based information retrieval systems (such as patient medical records). DBMSs are, in effect, electronic filing cabinets that allow users to store information in an organized filing system and later retrieve that information, just as a secretary stores documents in organized filing drawers. Database management systems store, retrieve, and manipulate information in databases. Databases consist of one or more files, each of which contains information in the form of collections of records that are related to a content domain, event, or set of objects (e.g., an individual's account information). Each record in the database is divided into fields that describe the class or type of information contained therein. The same type of information for each record is stored in each field. These records are systematically broken down into fields (subunits of each record) that define a common pattern of information. The content and arrangement of each field are standardized within the records, enabling the computer to locate a particular kind of information more quickly.

Databases are everywhere in our society. Records containing information about each of us are maintained by schools, utilities, doctor and dentist offices, libraries, merchandising companies and so on. Whenever we check out a book, buy something online, pay our bills, or perform just about any other activity, someone looks up our record or creates a new one in a database.

When students model phenomena with DBMSs, they are required to integrate and interrelate content ideas into one or more matrices. Databases convey information in matrix form. Matrices are an effective way to represent information that supports comparison-contrast reasoning. Rather than comparing and contrasting ideas, students may also build databases that collect, compare, and contrast stories of people's experiences. For example, Figure 8.5 shows a database of vocabulary words that students are learning. By representing and comparing the structural elements of words, students learn how to use new vocabulary words more effectively. Figure 8.6 illustrates a database of different kinds of cells. As students study each new cell, they add its description to the database, which functions as a structured note-taking tool because students organize what they are learning. If information is not organized, students will not be able to retrieve it. Such databases also enable students and teachers to evaluate the quality of their databases. For instance, by sorting the database by shape, students may examine whether there is a relationship between the shape of a cell and its functions. Those kinds of questions engage meaningful learning.

Although schools often do not regard stories highly, stories are a primary means for negotiating meanings (Bruner, 1990), and they assist us in understanding human action, intentionality, and temporality. Stories can function as a substitute for direct experience. For instance, we have included "stories" of how teachers have used and can use technology in their classrooms throughout this book in order to increase the relevance of the content. If, as most people do, we assume that we learn more from our experiences, then we should also be able to learn from stories of other people's experiences. Many of our decisions are based on the experiences of other people. Rather than studying content, students might analyze the stories and experiences of others for what they have to teach us. If you replay and analyze almost any conversation, it is probably comprised of a series of stories. One person tells a story to make a point, which reminds other conversants of related events, so they tell stories that

Figure 8.5

Database of Vocabulary Words

Vocabulary Chart

word	related words	synonym	antonym	origin	part of speech	suffix	prefix	baseword part	baseword
admiration	admirer,	respect		french	noun	ation		verb	admire
contentedly	contentment,	complacently	disappointedly	french	adverb	ly		adjective	content
cordially	cordiality	genially	coldly	mediev	adverb	ly		adjective	cordial
description	descriptive,	explanation		latin	noun	tion		verb	describe
digestion	digestbility,	devouring		latin	noun	ion		verb	digest
explanation	explanatory,	clarification		latin	noun	ation		verb	explain
freedom		liberty		old	noun	dom		noun	free
illegible	legibly	unclear	distinct	latin	adjective		il	adjective	legible
illiterate	illiteracy,	uneducated	learned	latin	adjective		il	adjective	literate
illustration	illustrator,	depiction			noun	ion		verb	illustrate
immobilized	immobilization	disabled	capable		adjective	ize	im	adjective	mobile
impatient	impatiently	eager	reluctant		adjective		im	adjective	patient
inhuman	inhumanity,	nasty	nice		adjective		in	adjective	human
invisibility	visor, vision	obscurity	discernible		noun	ity	in	adjective	visible
irresponsible	responses,	careless	careful		adjective	ible	ir	noun	response
irresponsible	responsibly,	careless	careful		adjective	ible	ir	noun	response
kingdom		realm			noun	dom		noun	king
leadership	leadability,	dominance			noun	ship		noun	leader
motherhood	motherly,				noun	hood		noun	mother
neighborhood	unneighborly,	area			noun	hood		noun	neighbor
ominously		threateningly	promisingly		adverb	ly		adjective	ominous
partnership		alliance			noun	ship		noun	partner
permission	permisability,	approval			noun	sion		verb	permit
population	depopulate,	community			noun	ion		verb	populate
suspension	suspend,	delay	continuance		noun	sion		verb	suspend
tension		anxiety			noun	ion		adjective	tense
unabridged	abridging,	complete	shortened		adjective		un	verb	abridge

Figure 8.6

Database of Cells

cell type	location	function	shape	related cells	specialization	tissue system	associated pr	related disease
Astocyte	CNS	Supply	Radiating	Neurons,	Half of Neural	Nervous		Neuroglia
Basal	Stratum	Produce New	Cube,	Epithelial	Mitotic	Epithelial		Cancer
Basophils	Blood	Bind Imm E	Lobed	Neutrophil,	Basic Possibl	Connective,	Histamine,	
Cardiac Muscle	Heat	Pump Blood	Branched	Endomysium	Intercalated	Muscle	Actin,	Athrosclerosis,
Chondroblast	Cartilage	Produce	Round			Connective	Collagen	Chondrocyte
Eosinophil	Blood	Protazoans,	Two	Basophil,	Acid,	Connective,		
Ependymal	Line CNS	Form	Cube		Cilia	Nervous		Neuroglia
Erythrocytes	Blood	Transport O2,	Disc	Hemocytobla	Transport	Connective	Hemoglobi	Sickle Cell
Fibroblast	Connectiv	Fiber	Flat		Mitotic	Connective	Collagen,	Cancer?
Goblet	Columnar	Secretion	Columnar	Columnar	Mucus	Epithelial		
Keratinocytes	Stratum	Strengthen	Round	Melanocytes		Epithelial	Keratin	
Melanocytes	Stratum	U.V. Protection	Branched	Keratinocyte	Produce	Epithelial	Melanin	Skin Cancer
Microglia	CNS	Protect	Ovoid	Neurons,	Macrophage	Nervous		Neuroglia
Motor Neuron	CNS(Cell	Impulse Away	Long, Thin	Sensory	Multipolar,Ne	Nervous		
Neutrophil	Blood	Inflammation,	Lobed	Basophils,	Phagocytos,	Connective,	Lysozyme	
Oligodendrocyte	CNS	Insulate	Long	Neurons	Produce	Nervous		Multiple Sclerosis
Osteoblast	Bone	Produce	Spider	Osteoclasts	Bone Salts	Connective	Collagen	Osteoporosis,
Osteoclast	Bone	Bone	Ruffled	Osteoblasts	Destroy	Connective	Lysosomal	Osteoporosis,
Pseudostratified	Gland	Secretion	Varies	Goblet	Cilia	Epithelial		
Satellite	PNS	Control	Cube	Schwann,	Chemical	Nervous		
Schwann	PNS	Insulate	Cube	Neurons,	Form Myelin	Nervous		Multiple Sclerosis
Sensory Neurons	PNS(Cell	Impulse to	Long, Thin	Motor	Unipolar,	Nervous	Neurotran	
Simple Columnar	Digestive	Secretion,	Columnar		Cilia	Epithelial		
Simple Cuboidal	Kidney	Secretion,	Cube		Microvilli	Epithelial		
Simple Squamous	Lungs,	Diffusion of	Flat	Basal,		Epithelial		
Skeletal Muscle	Bone,	Movement,	Long	Neurons	Neuromuscul	Muscle	Actin,	
Smooth Muscle	Organ	Movement	Disc	Endomysium	Gap	Muscle	Actin,	
Stratified Columnar	Epithelial	Protection	Columnar	Simple	Cilia	Epithelial		
Stratified Cuboidal	Sweat,	Protection	Cube	Simple		Epithelial		
Stratified	Lining	Protection	Layered	Basal		Epithelial	Keratin	
T Lymphocytes	Lymphoid	Cell Mediated	Round	B,T Cells	Antigen	Immune	Lymphokin	Autoimmune
T-Lymphocytes	Lymphoid	Cell Mediated	Round	Helper T	Graft	Immune	Antigen,Pe	Autoimmune
T-Lymphocytes	Lymphoid	Cell Mediated	Round	Killer T, B	Stimulates	Immune	Lymphokin	Aids.
Transitional	Uterus,	Stretches	Surface		Expansion	Epithelial		

they were reminded of, which in turn reminds other conversants of stories they were reminded of, and so on. Why do we use stories to support conversation? Because we remember so much of what we know in the form of stories. Stories are rich and powerful formalisms for storing and describing memories. So, one way of understanding what people know is to analyze their stories. Databases are the primary tool for doing that.

Students can build models of people's experiences, which is a form of ethnography. The model building is accomplished by collecting stories about people's experiences, indexing them, and storing them. Having collected stories, we must decide what the stories teach us. We tell stories with some point in mind, so the indexing process tries to elucidate what that point is, given a situation. Each index becomes a field in a database. Having determined the indexes (fields) for the stories, students next find excerpts in the stories that represent each index and include those excerpts in records, the fields of which represent the themes, goals, plans, results, and lessons or whatever indexes the students believe are appropriate. The database in Figure 8.7 recounts one of many stories that were collected by students

Figure 8.7

Record from a Database of Stories About Northern Ireland

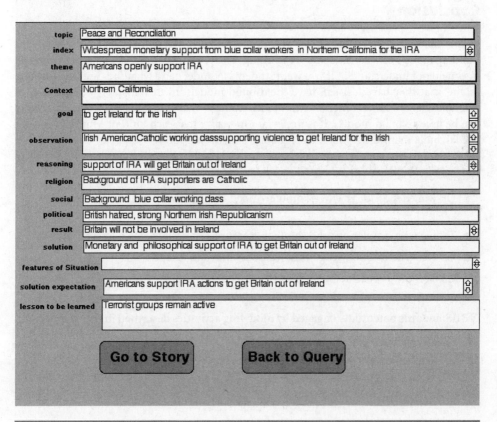

topic	Peace and Reconciliation
index	Widespread monetary support from blue collar workers in Northern California for the IRA
theme	Americans openly support IRA
Context	Northern California
goal	to get Ireland for the Irish
observation	Irish American Catholic working class supporting violence to get Ireland for the Irish
reasoning	support of IRA will get Britain out of Ireland
religion	Background of IRA supporters are Catholic
social	Background blue collar working class
political	British hatred, strong Northern Irish Republicanism
result	Britain will not be involved in Ireland
solution	Monetary and philosophical support of IRA to get Britain out of Ireland
features of Situation	
solution expectation	Americans support IRA actions to get Britain out of Ireland
lesson to be learned	Terrorist groups remain active

Go to Story   **Back to Query**

studying the conflict in Northern Ireland. The database contains many stories that have been indexed by topic, theme, context, goal, reasoning, religion, and so on. When students analyze stories in order to understand the issues, they better understand the underlying complexity of any phenomenon in terms of the diverse social, cultural, political, and personal perspectives reflected in the stories.

You may also be interested in a case library of technology integration stories that we created, Knowledge Innovation for Technology in Education (kite.missouri.edu), which was funded by a PT3 (Preparing Tomorrow's Teachers to Use Technology) grant from the U.S. Department of Education (Jonassen, Wang, Strobel, & Cernusca, 2003). We interviewed more than 1,000 teachers, asking them to share with us a story about a successful use of technology in their classroom. After each story is submitted, we had to decide what the stories taught us, so the stories were indexed. These indexes became the fields in an Oracle database. You may retrieve relevant stories about how to use technologies in the classroom by searching the database based on characteristics that are defined by the fields. Although this was not a student-constructed database, it provides an additional example of how databases may be use to collect and retrieve stories.

Conclusion

In this chapter, we have introduced you to the idea of using computers as Mindtools for building models of what students are learning. The premise is simple: if you cannot model it, you do not understand it. If you want students to understand what they are studying and retain what they have learned, have them build models. In this chapter, we have shown examples of how three different Mindtools (concept maps, spreadsheets, and databases) can be used to build models. It is important to realize that each kind of Mindtool may be used to build many different kinds of models (Jonassen, 2006).

Student construction of models using different kinds of technologies is described throughout this book, including:

- Drawing design ideas with Computer-Aided Design (CAD) software, described in Chapter 4
- Testing with simulations and simulation software, described in Chapters 3 and 4
- Co-constructing knowledge with wikis, described in Chapter 6
- Collaborative construction of hypermedia, described in previous editions

NET Standards potentially engaged by modeling activities described in this chapter:

1. **Creativity and Innovation**
   a. Apply existing knowledge to generate new ideas, products, or processes
   b. Create original works as a means of personal or group expression
   c. Use models and simulations to explore complex systems and issues

2. **Communication and Collaboration**

   a. Interact, collaborate, and publish with peers, experts, or others employing a variety of digital environments and media

   b. Communicate information and ideas effectively to multiple audiences using a variety of media and formats

   d. Contribute to project teams to produce original works or solve problems

3. **Research and Information Fluency**

   b. Locate, organize, analyze, evaluate, synthesize, and ethically use information from a variety of sources and media

   c. Evaluate and select information sources and digital tools based on the appropriateness to specific tasks

4. **Critical Thinking, Problem Solving, and Decision Making**

   a. Identify and define authentic problems and significant questions for investigation

   b. Plan and manage activities to develop a solution or complete a project

   c. Collect and analyze data to identify solutions and/or make informed decisions

   d. Use multiple processes and diverse perspectives to explore alternative solutions

21st Century Skills potentially engaged by modeling activities described in this chapter:

Think Creatively

- Elaborate, refine, analyze, and evaluate their own ideas in order to improve and maximize creative efforts

Work Creatively with Others

- Develop, implement, and communicate new ideas to others effectively

Reason Effectively

- Use various types of reasoning (inductive, deductive, etc.) as appropriate to the situation

Use Systems Thinking

- Analyze how parts of a whole interact with each other to produce overall outcomes in complex systems

Make Judgments and Decisions

- Effectively analyze and evaluate evidence, arguments, claims and beliefs
- Analyze and evaluate major alternative points of view
- Synthesize and make connections between information and arguments
- Interpret information and draw conclusions based on the best analysis

Communicate Clearly

- Articulate thoughts and ideas effectively using oral, written, and nonverbal communication skills in a variety of forms and contexts

- Utilize multiple media and technologies, and know how to judge their effectiveness a priori as well as assess their impact

Collaborate with Others

- Demonstrate ability to work effectively and respectfully with diverse teams

Access and Evaluate Information

- Access information efficiently (time) and effectively (sources)
- Evaluate information critically and competently

Use and Manage Information

- Use information accurately and creatively for the issue or problem at hand
- Manage the flow of information from a wide variety of sources

Apply Technology Effectively

- Use technology as a tool to research, organize, evaluate, and communicate information
- Use digital technologies (computers, PDAs, media players, GPS, etc.), communication/networking tools and social networks appropriately to access, manage, integrate, evaluate and create information to successfully function in a knowledge economy

Things to Think About

To reflect on the ideas that we presented in this chapter, articulate your responses to the following questions and compare them with others' responses.

1. Can you as a teacher really teach students what you know? Is it possible for them construct the same kind of models that you do?

2. Do carpenters learn *from* their hammers, saws, levels, and other tools? Can they learn anything about them without using them? Do they learn about carpentry *with* their tools?

3. If mindful thinking is active, constructive, intentional, authentic, and cooperative (as we have claimed), then what is mindless thinking? Can you describe what students do if they are mindless? Is mindless thinking even possible?

4. Recall the first time that you had to teach a new topic or skill. How well did you know the topic before you taught it? Did you know it better after you taught it? Should learners become teachers without using technology? Recall that we have argued that learners should be teaching the technology.

5. Can a modeling tool be intelligent? What is the smartest tool that you know of? What makes it smart?

6. We claim that the goal of Mindtools is to help students to build external models of their internal, mental models. How can you know that the models that students build are their own and not what you taught them?

7. We argue that language and software applications like databases are formalisms for representing what you know. Can you think of other formalisms for representing what you know? How is the syntax of that formalism different from language?

8. Databases and concept maps focus on the semantics of a knowledge domain. That is, they engage learners in describing the organization of meanings in a domain. Can you think of any other semantic formalisms?

9. Concept maps are like the frame and foundation of a house. If you accept that analogy, how would you describe the rest of the house (plumbing, trim, decorations, walls, etc.)?

10. We have claimed that building models with Mindtools reflects the learner's internal mental models. Is there knowledge in the external models? Does knowledge reside only in the head, or can it reside in the computer as well?

11. Mindtools represent an intellectual toolbox that can help students learn. However, we do not believe that these are the only kinds of intellectual tools that students should use. What other nontechnological intellectual tools should students have or develop to help them learn?

References

Bruner, J. (1990). *Acts of meaning*. Cambridge: Harvard University Press.

Chi, M.T.H., Feltovich, P.J., & Glaser, R. (1981). Categorization and representation of physics problems by experts and novices. *Cognitive Science*, 5, 121–152.

Hestenes, D. (1996). Modeling methodology for physics teachers: Proceedings of the International Conference on Undergraduate Physics Education. http://modeling.asu.edu/modeling/ModMeth.html

Hoeffner, K., Kendall, M., Stellenwerf, C., Thames, P., & Williams, P. (1993, November). Problem solving with a spreadsheet. *Arithmetic Teacher*, 52–56.

Jonassen, D. H. (2006). *Modeling with technology: Mindtools for conceptual change*. Columbus, OH: Merrill/Prentice-Hall.

Jonassen, D. H. (2008). Model building for conceptual change. In S. Vosniadou (Ed.), *International handbook of research on conceptual change* (pp. 676–693) New York: Routledge.

Jonassen, D. H., Beissner, K., & Yacci, M. A. (1993). *Structural knowledge: Techniques for representing, conveying, and acquiring structural knowledge.* Hillsdale, NJ: Lawrence Erlbaum Associates.

Jonassen, D. H., Wang, F. K., Strobel, J., & Cernusca, D. (2003). Application of a case library of technology integration stories for teachers. *Journal of Technology and Teacher Education, 11*(4), 547–566.

Larkin, J. H. (1983). The role of problem representation in physics. In D. Gentner & A.L. Stevens (Eds.), *Mental models* (pp. 75–98). Hillsdale, NJ: Lawrence Erlbaum Associates.

Lehrer, R., & Schauble, L. (2003). Origins and evolution of model-based reasoning in mathematics and science. In R. Lesh & H. M. Doerr (Eds.), *Beyond constructivism: Models and modeling perspectives on mathematics problem solving, teaching, and learning* (pp. 59–70). Mahwah, NJ: Lawrence Erlbaum Associates.

Lesh, R., & Doerr, H. M. (2003). Foundations of a models and modeling perspective on mathematics teaching, learning, and problem solving. In R. Lesh & H. M. Doerr (Eds.), *Beyond constructivism: Models and modeling perspectives on mathematics problem solving, teaching, and learning* (pp. 3–33). Mahwah, NJ: Lawrence Erlbaum Associates.

Nersessian, N. J. (1999). Model-based reasoning in conceptual change. In L. Magnani, N. J. Nersessian, & P. Thagard (Eds.), *Models are used to represent reality.* New York: Kluwer Academic/Plenum Publishers.

Perkins, D. N. (1993). Person-plus: A distributed view of thinking and learning. In G. Salomon (Ed.), *Distributed cognitions: Psychological and educational considerations.* Cambridge: Cambridge University Press.

Schank, R. C. (1990). *Tell me a story: Narrative and intelligence.* Evanston, IL: Northwestern University Press.

Sundheim, B. R. (1992). Modeling a thermostated water bath with a spreadsheet. *Journal of Chemical Education, 69*(8), 650–654.

Vockell, E., & Van Deusen, R. M. (1989). *The computer and higher-order thinking skills.* Watsonville, CA: Mitchell Publishing.

Visualizing with Technologies

Scott Cunningham/Merrill

Chapter Objectives

1. Describe how paint/draw programs, digital photography, and video support personal visualization skills

2. Compare the utility of different visualization tools for learning domain knowledge

3. Create new ways that GIS can be used in the classroom

4. Create lesson plans for implementing digital photography and video

5. Describe how visualization tools support the development of NETS and 21st Century Skills

What Are Visualization Tools?

Humans are complex organisms that possess well-balanced sensorimotor systems, with counterbalanced receptor and effector systems that enable them to sense psychomotor data and act on it using complex motor systems. Likewise, humans have reasonably keen aural perception, allowing them to hear a large range of sounds. Those sounds can be replicated or at least responded to orally by forcing air through the diaphragm, palette, and lips to create an infinite variety of sounds. However, our most sophisticated sensory system, vision, where the largest amount and variety of data are received by humans, has no counterbalancing effector system. We receive massive amounts of visual input, but we have no output mechanism for visually representing ideas, except in mental images and dreams, which cannot be easily shared with others. Visual images are powerful mediators of meaning making. Many of us often have to visualize something before we can make sense of it, but sharing those images is difficult. In order to visualize ideas and to share those images with others, humans need visualization tools. However, tools that help us to visualize ideas can also help us to learn many difficult concepts.

Some individuals prefer to process information by seeing, through the use of graphics, diagrams, or illustrations, while others prefer to process information in words, through reading or listening. The former are visualizers; the latter are verbalizers. Visualizers tend to think more concretely, use imagery, and personalize information. When learning, they prefer graphs, diagrams, or pictures added to text-based material. Verbalizers prefer to process information from words, either by reading or listening, rather than through images (Kirby, Moore, & Shofield, 1988). So, it is for the visualizers that this chapter is written, although we suspect that verbalizers will also benefit from using some of the technologies described in this chapter.

This chapter describes a rapidly growing class of technologies that allow visualizers and verbalizers to reason and represent ideas visually without the artistic skills required to produce original illustrations. These tools help us to interpret and represent visual ideas and to automate some of the manual processes for creating images. Visualization tools can have two major uses, interpretive and expressive (Gordin, Edelson, & Gomez, 1996). Interpretive tools help learners view and manipulate visuals, extracting meaning from the information being visualized. Interpretive illustrations help to clarify difficult-to-understand text and abstract concepts, making them more comprehensible (Levin, Anglin, & Carney, 1987). Expressive visualization helps learners to visually convey meaning in order to communicate a set of beliefs. Crayons, paints, and paper or paint and draw programs are powerful expressive tools that gifted learners may use to express themselves visually. However, they rely on graphical talent. Visualization tools go beyond paint and draw programs by scaffolding or supporting some form of expression. They help learners to visualize ideas in ways that make them more easily interpretable by themselves and other viewers.

In this chapter, we present a variety of visualization tools: draw and paint programs, scientific visualization tools, mathematical visualization tools, GIS tools, sketching tools, digital cameras and mobile phones, video productions, and video modeling and feedback.

Draw/Paint Programs

The most obvious visualization tools are draw and paint programs that enable us to create drawings and paintings electronically. There are literally hundreds of paint and draw programs, many of which are free. These programs enable users to make free-hand drawings or paintings or manipulate photos taken with cell phones or digital cameras. These tools provide a palette of tools (left side of Figure 9.1) with which the users can draw, paint, write text, add figures, and create sophisticated graphics effects. More expensive programs assist users in constructing animations. However, in order to represent our mental images using paint/draw programs, we have to translate those images into a series of motor operations and apply a lot of rules for using the software, because it is not yet possible to dump our mental images directly from our brains into a computer. Skilled artists commonly use these tools to visualize ideas, which can help others to interpret ideas.

Visualizing with Sketchcast

A tool to help the least artistic among us is Sketchcast. It makes a movie of what one draws and says while drawing, using a simple palette of tools. First-grade students in Mrs. Cassidy's class used Sketchcast to create pictures of their mothers for Mother's Day (see Figure 9.2, http://classblogmeister. com/blog.php?blog_id= 1151927&mode=comment&blogger_id=1337).

Visualizing Scientific Ideas with Computers

So much of the scientific world is not easily visible to humans. The scale of scientific phenomena is too often so large or so small that we cannot observe those phenomena. From astronomy to atomic structures, science requires understanding dynamic visual relationships among things that are impossible to see. We briefly describe a couple of tools for visualizing atomic structures.

Imaging Molecules with Chemistry Visualization Tools A number of visualization tools have been developed for the sciences, most especially chemistry. Figure 9.3 (on page 211) illustrates a molecule of androsterone. Not only does the Spartan (www.wavefun.com) program enable the learners to visualize molecules using five different representations (wire, ball and wire, tube, ball and spoke, and space filling) but it also enables the student to test different bonds and create ions and new molecules (see Figure 9.4 on page 211). Notice the phosphorus

Figure 9.1

Palette of Tools Available in Draw and Paint Software

Figure 9.2

First Grader's Drawing Made with Sketchcast

ion added to the molecule on the left. Understanding molecular chemistry is greatly facilitated by visualizing these complex processes. There has been a bit of research on these tools. High school students used eChem to build molecular models and view multiple representations of molecules. Students using the visualization tool were able to generate better mental images of chemicals that aided their understanding (Wu, Krajcik, & Soloway, 2001). Students who engaged in discussions while building models benefited the most. Providing extra visualization including colored drawings of experiments and ionic representations of reactions facilitated concept acquisition in chemistry (Brandt, Elen, Hellemans, Heerman, Couwenberg, Volckaert, & Morisse, 2001).

The Molecular Workbench is a free, open-source tool that delivers visual, interactive simulations for teaching and learning science and engineering (www.concord.org). The Molecular Workbench is a software package that supports student learning through experimentation and collaboration across a broad range of science fields and grades. It is an open-source learning environment that allows middle school, high school, and college students to explore the physical origins of phenomena such as gas laws, fluid mechanics, properties of materials, states of matter, phase change, heat transfer, chemical bonding, chemical reactions, structure-function relationships, the genetic code, protein synthesis, light-matter interactions, electron-matter interactions, and quantum phenomena. For example, Figure 9.5 (on page 212) illustrates a still version of a dynamic image along with related explanations and questions to form a powerful lesson on cellular respiration in biology and chemistry.

Visualizing Mathematical Ideas with Technologies

Because of the abstractness of mathematics, visualization is an important strategy that helps learners to understand mathematical concepts. Such visualization tools are not always computer-mediated. For example, Cotter (2000) showed that using Asian forms of visualization (abacus, tally sticks, and place cards) advanced understanding of place value, addition, and subtraction. Mathematics educators have promoted the use of manipulatives and similar visual comparative devices for many years. Snir (1995) argues that computers can make a unique contribution to the clarification and correction of commonly held misconceptions of phenomena by visualizing those ideas. For example, the computer can be used

Figure 9.3

Visualization of a Molecule of Androsterone

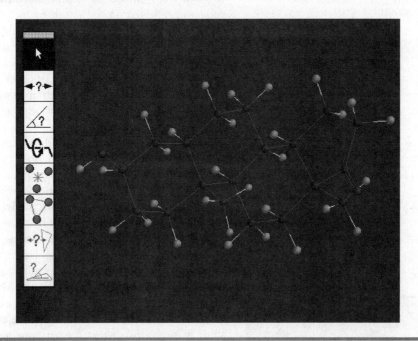

Figure 9.4

Manipulating Molecules in Spartan

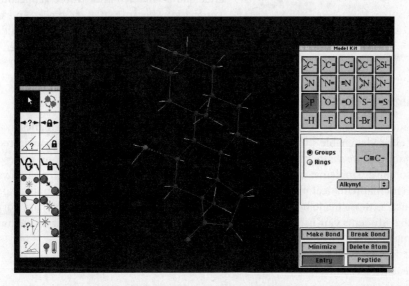

Figure 9.5

Lesson in Biology and Chemistry from Molecular Workbench

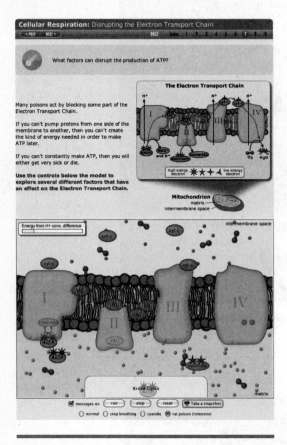

to form a representation for the phenomenon in which all the relational and mathematical wave equations are embedded within the program code and reflected on the screen by the use of graphics and visuals. This makes the computer an efficient tool to clarify scientific understanding of waves. By using computer graphics, one can shift attention back and forth from the local to the global properties of the phenomenon and train the mind to integrate the two aspects into one coherent picture (Snir, 1995).

Visualization tools have been developed primarily for mathematics and the sciences. Understanding equations in algebra, trigonometry, calculus, and virtually all other fields of math is aided by seeing their plots. Understanding the dynamics of mathematics is aided by being able to manipulate formulas and equations and observe the effects of that manipulation. Programs such as Mathematica (www.wolfram.com/products/mathematica/index.html) and Matlab (www.mathworks.com), and even Excel are often used to visually represent mathematical relationships in problems so that learners can *see* the effects of any problem manipulation. Being able to interrelate numeric and symbolic representations with their graphical output helps learners understand mathematics more conceptually. Those tools, because of their power and complexity, are seldom used with K–12 students. Most of the research on these tools has been conducted in universities.

Visualizing Formulas with Graphing Calculators*

The National Council of Teachers of Mathematics recommends that mathematics instruction at all grades enable students to: (1) create and use representations to organize, record, and communicate mathematical ideas; (2) select, apply, and translate among representations to solve problems; and (3) use representations to model and interpret physical, social, and mathematical phenomena (NCTM, 2000, p. 360). Handheld graphing calculators (such as those made by Casio, Hewlett-Packard, and Texas Instruments) are portable tools that students can use in the classroom or at home to support their mathematical sense making.

*Section written by Fran Arbaugh.

Figure 9.6

Four Different Representations of Linear Relationships

Text Representation

Cell phone company A charges a flat rate of $.75 per call plus $.05 per minute. Cell phone company B has no flat rate, but charges $.08 per minute. What cell phone Company would you use?

Symbolic Representation

y : total cost
x : number of minutes

Company A : y = .75 + .05x

Company B : y = .08x

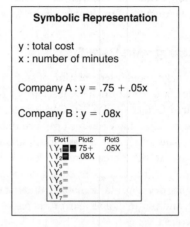

Graphical Representation

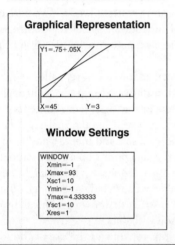

Window Settings

```
WINDOW
 Xmin=−1
 Xmax=93
 Xsc1=10
 Ymin=−1
 Ymax=4.333333
 Ysc1=10
 Xres=1
```

Numeric Representation

X	Y₁	Y₂
0	.75	0
1	.8	.08
2	.85	.16
3	.9	.24
4	.95	.32
5	1	.4
6	1.05	.48

X=2

Students often have difficulty distinguishing important features of functional relationships. For example, to build understanding of linear relationships, students can use different representations, generated by the graphing calculator, to make connections between what is happening contextually, numerically, graphically, and symbolically for a particular mathematical relationship. Figure 9.6 contains four different representations of the same linear relationship.

Students using a graphing calculator can easily move between the symbolic, graphical, and numeric representations of the two functions. They can trace along both functions to find (x, y) values graphically. They can then compare those values to the (x, y) pairs in the table. Students can find x and y intercepts on the graph and table, and discuss how to manipulate the symbolic representation to find the same information.

Research indicates that the use of graphing calculators has a positive influence on students' understanding of mathematics (Ruthven, 1990). In addition, Dunham and Dick

(1994) report that students who use graphing calculators are more flexible problem solvers, are more persistent when faced with a new problem situation, and are highly engaged in the act of problem solving. As more and more mathematics textbooks incorporate the use of a graphing calculator in learning and teaching high school mathematics, more research needs to be conducted on the impact of this technology on student understanding.

Tinkering with Data Sets

Data analysis and interpretation of statistics are key skills, according to standards published by the National Council of Teachers of Mathematics (NCTM). The Technical Education Research Center (TERC) in Cambridge, Massachusetts, created a simple-to-use database program called TableTop to support database construction and analysis by school-age children (Hancock, Kaput, & Goldsmith, 1992). Tabletop works with existing databases or with databases students create themselves. Data are visually represented by mobile icons that can be arranged into box plots, cross tabulations, histograms, scatter plots, and Venn diagrams. Students develop mathematical understanding of attributes, logical relationships, place value, and plotting, and learn to perceive the stories and patterns that lie within the data they collect.

TableTop has been replaced by new data visualization software, called TinkerPlots (www.keypress.com). TinkerPlots is data visualization software for grades 4 through 8 that enables students to see different patterns and clusters in statistical data. Students begin by asking a question that requires a prediction or inference (see Chapter 3). They collect data (e.g., shoe size and height), assign units to the data (e.g., size and inches), and then represent the data graphically in many ways. With all of the data points on a graph, students can group them in clusters, sort them by amount or other sequence, and display them in a seemingly infinite variety of formats. Students are able to use rich data sets or generate their own data sets based on problems they invent and construct their own graphical displays to help them solve the problem. Students learn to reason with data.

Cliff Konold (2006), the designer of TinkerPlots, introduces the use of the software by asking the class whether they think students in higher grades carry heavier backpacks than do students in lower grades. He has them explore a data set to see whether it supports their expectations. In order to help them answer the question, students can separate the cases into four bins according to the weight of the backpacks (see Figure 9.7). In order to view the data in different representations, the icons representing each case can be stacked, then separated completely until the case icons appear over their actual values on a number line (see Figure 9.8). By selecting the attribute Grade, the grade-five students were separated vertically from the other grades. By pulling out each of the three other grades one by one, students could then see the distributions of PackWeight for each of the four grades in this data set (grades one, three, five, and seven). These different views enable students with different cognitive styles to find a mathematical representation that makes sense to them. By the way, TinkerPlots can also import Microsoft Excel spreadsheet files to enable students to visualize data in more ways than those afforded by Excel. Students can assign different icons to the data points and generate numerous comparative plots that Excel cannot. Here is what one teacher had to say about the use of these programs.

Figure 9.7

Separating Cases into Bins in TinkerPlots

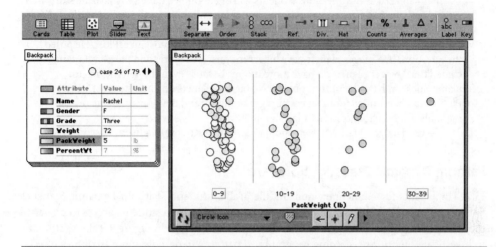

The students in my multiage fourth- and fifth-grade classroom love TinkerPlots. I start off each year with a short demo of the software. Then I pose some questions about a data set that the students might find interesting and have them create plots that will answer their questions. That is all it takes. I find that any time we are working with a data set, the kids will ask if they can enter it into TinkerPlots.

Figure 9.8

Stacked Cases with Grade 5 Students Separated Out

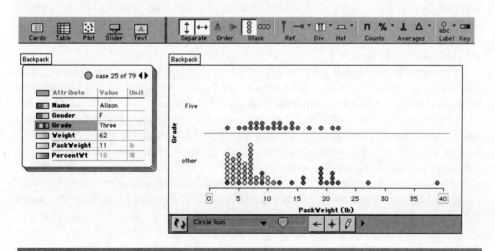

It is so powerful when a student can quickly try dragging a variety of variables to the axis and explore the data set without the frustration of having to draw and redraw the graph.

I am amazed at the questions students will ask about a data set. My favorite story is the day that we had free time in the computer lab and many of the students asked if they could use TinkerPlots. One student looked up the size of each of the planets and the number of moons each planet has and entered the data into TinkerPlots. He posed the question, "Do bigger planets have bigger moons?" After creating the plot he concluded that "bigger planets do have more moons because even though the biggest planet does not have the most moons, the 4 biggest planets do have the most." TinkerPlots is an open-ended tool that encourages creativity and develops students reasoning skills. Every school computer lab should have it!

—Teri Hedges, Madison Metropolitan School District in Madison, Wisconsin

Fathom Dynamic Statistics Software*

Like TinkerPlots for elementary and middle grades students, Fathom Dynamic Statistics Software (Finzer, Erickson, & Binker, 2001) allows high school students access to powerful tools for making sense of large data sets. The data set displayed in Figure 9.9 allows students to investigate questions regarding geographical patterns in demographic attributes of each state in the United States.

Visual Geometry with Geometer Sketchpad

One of the best-known visualization tools is Geometer's Sketchpad (www.keypress.com), a tool for making and testing conjectures in geometry through the process of constructing and manipulating geometric objects and exploring the relationships within and between these objects (Schwartz & Yerushalmy, 1987). Geometer Sketchpad allows students to construct shapes, such as a cone, and analyze them geometrically and algebraically (see Figure 9.10 page 218). Sketchpad also animates the images. The program plots and remembers each manipulation and can apply it to similar figures. Students may make conjectures about mathematical functions and test them immediately using Sketchpad. Constructing these test examples manually would require more effort than students are likely to generate, but the computational power of the computer makes this testing very easy.

Geometry instruction is traditionally based on the application of theorems to prove that certain relationships exist among objects. This top-down approach requires analytic reasoning, which a majority of students find difficult. Geometer's Sketchpad supports the learning of geometry by enabling the student to inductively prove these relationships by manipulating the components of geometric objects and observing the results. Rather than having the student apply someone else's logic, Geometer's Sketchpad makes explicit the relationships between visual properties and the numerical properties of the objects (Yerushalmy, 1990). Rather than using the computer to provide conclusive results, the computer calculates the results of students' experiments. The research results with Geometer's Sketchpad have been consistently positive.

*Section written by Fran Arbaugh.

Figure 9.9

Screenshot from Fathom Software

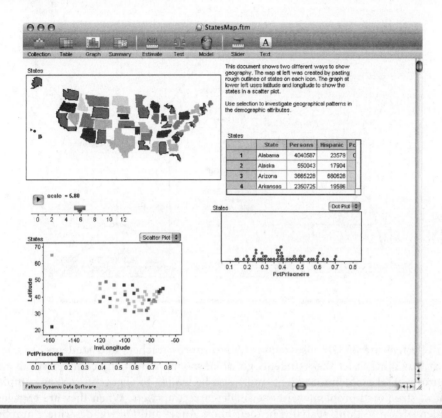

Visualizing Geography with GIS

Richard Audet and Gail Ludwig (2000) have written a wonderful book, *GIS in Schools*, in which they describe how geography information systems (GIS) can be used to engage students in authentic problem solving. GIS is a system for storing, retrieving, displaying, analyzing, and manipulating geographic data. It is an excellent way to support students' spatial thinking, and geospatial data is widely available. ESRI (www.esri.com) is a major designer and developer of geographic information system (GIS) technology. Using GIS requires a relatively fast computer with lots of available storage that can connect to large geographic databases that contain vast amounts of spatial databases related to population, land use, precipitation, vegetation and other physical geography. GIS software enables students to query those databases in order to construct maps, create charts and tables to summarize data, and formulate specialized searches. Additionally, schools may purchase ready-made maps from companies or acquire them from local, regional, or state authorities (e.g., http://education.usgs.gov).

Figure 9.10

Investigating Triangle with Geomoter Sketchpad

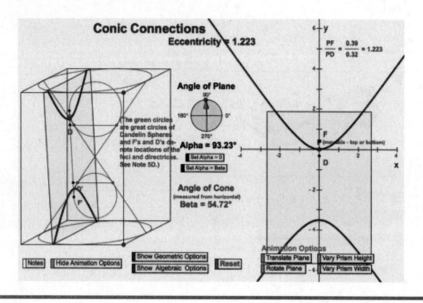

Effective use of GIS also requires adventurous teachers and students. Teachers must be willing to let their students go while solving potentially complex social and environmental problems. Students must also be willing to engage in solving complex and ill-structured problems without single correct answers. When they are engaged, students learn to think spatially. In their book, Audet and Ludwig describe a number of classrooms in which students have used GIS to solve some fascinating problems, such as:

- High school students in Chelsea, Massachusetts, worked with the local fire department and the Environmental Protection Agency to design and react to a simulated toxic chemical spill, by tracking the spill, rerouting traffic, and warning the public.

- Students in Perham, Minnesota, used GIS and global positioning systems (GPS) to help track newly reintroduced wolves into the Minnesota wilderness.

- Students in Raleigh, North Carolina, created a culturally anthropological view of the history of Raleigh by tracing annexations. They also created individual "life maps" showing the geographical progressions of individuals as they moved around the city. These students developed a new understanding of history.

- Students in Columbia, Missouri, investigated the economic impacts related to the concentration of businesses in the downtown area (see Figure 9.11).

Among the many websites that offer maps and database information that could be used in classrooms are:

- Map Maker from Nationalatlas.gov: http://nationalatlas.gov/mapmaker

- American FactFinder from the U.S. Census Bureau: http://factfinder.census.gov/home/saff/main.html?_lang=en

- National Geographic Map Machine: http://maps.nationalgeographic.com/map-machine

- ArcGIS: www.arcgis.com/home/

- Geodata.gov: http://gos2.geodata.gov/wps/portal/gos

- Seamless Data Distribution Delivery from U.S. Geological Survey (USGS): http:// seamless.usgs.gov/website/seamless/viewer.php

- Terraserver: www.terraserver.com

Students may also search for different types of maps at Find A Map! USGS Map Databases, http://education.usgs.gov/common/map_databases.htm.

Figure 9.11

GIS Graphic from Gail Ludwig

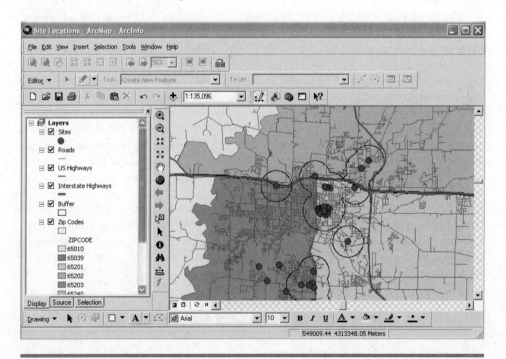

Figure 9.12

Google Earth's Interface

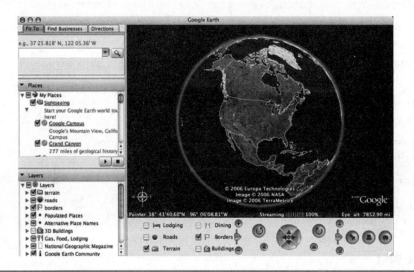

Google plays a major role in providing mapping information and tools to a broad segment of the population. Google Earth (see Figure 9.12) is a free 3-D interface to the planet that combines satellite imagery and maps with Google Search. Clicking the Earth begins a slow zoom in until distinct features can be viewed. Layers allow many types of information to be displayed. Categories such as transportation, terrain, and borders allow users to view and interact with the map in multiple ways; users can also import GPS data from select GPS devices.

Other Google tools include SketchUp, a free, easy-to-learn 3-D modeling program (see Chapter 4) that enables users to create 3-D models of buildings, which can then be placed in Google Earth. Google Maps combines directions, maps, and satellite imagery for searching locations. For example, when 10 Market St., San Francisco is entered and the zoom feature used, the exact building at that location is visible. A mobile version of Google Maps works with cell phones that have a data plan.

While GISs are primarily used in conjunction with a computer, including a laptop computer or other mobile device in a field equipment kit gives students the means to apply GPS data to maps as it is being collected. GISs are progressively being integrated more into mobile technologies (e.g., cell phones), permitting students new opportunities to utilize global positioning data.

Visualizing with Digital Cameras and Mobile Phones

In the past decade, photography has been revolutionized by the use of digital cameras and mobile telephones. Each new generation of digital camera (Figure 9.13) provides higher

Figure 9.13

Modern Digital Cameras

resolutions (up to 10 million screen pixels per picture) for less money. Excellent digital cameras can be purchased for $100. These cameras feature light weight, multiple megapixels for high resolution pictures, zoom lenses with image steadying functions, selectable color modes (black and white, natural, rich, sepia), image storage on memory sticks, compact flash, secure digital cards, automatic focusing, movie mode with up to 60 frames per second, image processors, built-in flashes, self-timers, and a host of other technical features. After taking high-resolution pictures, the pictures can be quickly and easily downloaded onto any computer, where the images may be pasted into any other kind of document (word processing, PowerPoint, multimedia, etc.). They can also be printed, or they can be manipulated in an infinite variety of ways using photo manipulation software, such as PhotoShop, or many of the draw and paint programs described earlier. Novice photographers with photo manipulation software can now create visuals that only ten years ago were the domain of graphics artists.

Most modern mobile phones (Figure 9.14) also enable users to take pictures with their telephone. Although these images do not possess the picture resolution available from digital cameras, they can be immediately sent to other people who have phones with similar capabilities. The mobile phones are much lighter and more portable than digital cameras, however, the picture quality is not as good.

Digital Documentaries

Digital cameras and mobile phones have become the tool of choice among modern reporters, storytellers and ethnographers, those social scientists who study cultures using observation, interviews, and other qualitative methods. These people create documentaries that are usu-

Figure 9.14

Modern Mobile Phones with Picture-Taking Capabilities

ally accompanied by visuals. Pick up any newspaper or magazine, and you can easily see the importance of visuals to the stories being told. Students can create documentaries that examine local issues or controversies. In doing so, they observe and document real-world phenomena as well as become more concerned and productive members of society.

An good way to get students warmed up to the process of creating documentaries is to create personal documentaries. That is, they produce a documentary about themselves. They decide the most appropriate setting, the perceptions about themselves that they want viewers to have, and the format of the personal description. Personal documentaries have taken many forms. Some students create a personal diary. Others have taken viewers on a tour of their room, while others have played musical instruments, recited poetry, or acted out different personae. The self is the most interesting topic for most kids, so this can be an engaging activity.

An extension of the personal documentary is to conduct it in a foreign language. Pelletier (1990) recommends sending students in foreign language classes out with a camera to tape a short (3–5 minute) tour of their room, home, classroom, library, or a video synopsis of some activity, such as a family supper, miniature golf, or bowling, or any other activity, requiring them to conduct the tour in the language they are studying. Personalizing the use of language, rather than treating it as an object to be studied, is an important component in language acquisition. So students combine new words with previously learned vocabulary in order to express more meaningful ideas. Have the students be as verbally expressive in their narrations as possible.

A really neat tool for piecing together still shots into videos is Animoto (http://animoto.com/education). Photos are uploaded and then combined using a variety of special effects to enhance the presentation. Kindergarten students in Mrs. Cassidy's class (mentioned earlier in the chapter) have used Animoto to demonstrate how they are reading (http://classblogmeister.com/blog.php?blog_id=1145297&mode=comment&blogger_id=1337). Students love to use this type of software, and their parents are usually impressed with the outcome.

Visualizing with Video

Today's children cannot imagine a world without television. The average child spends several hours per day parked in front of the television, inactively absorbing image after image. The results of excessive television viewing (e.g., lethargy, hyperactivity, social isolation, obesity) have been well documented.

The premise of this book is that any technology, including television, can become a powerful learning tool when students are critical users and producers, rather than consumers. Producing videos requires learners to be active, constructive, intentional, and cooperative—to solve numerous decision-making problems while solving design problems associated with production. Video production requires the application of a variety of research, organization, visualization, and interpretation skills. Producing videos engages critical and creative thinking in order to plan and produce programs. Additionally, there are a variety of social values gained from producing videos in schools (Valmont, 1994):

- Improving students' self-confidence by planning, producing, and sharing video productions in class
- Producing feelings of self-satisfaction
- Providing valuable feedback to students about how others perceive them
- Fostering cooperative learning while sharing ideas, planning and producing programs, and evaluating outcomes
- Providing great public relations at open houses and other school functions

In this chapter, we describe a number of learning activities where television can provide meaningful learning contexts that can engage learners when they identify a purpose for viewing the program in order to find information and solve problems. However, most of the activities described in this chapter make students television producers. As producers, teachers and students need to understand a little about video production hardware, which we describe next.

Using video to engage meaningful learning requires three things: imaginative students willing to take chances, ideas for how to engage them, and some equipment. The equipment may be the easiest part, so let's briefly describe some of the hardware that you will need first. Following that, we will provide numerous ideas for engaging learners. You will have to provide the students with the following technologies.

Video Cameras

Video cameras are portable electronic recording systems that are capable of recording live motion video and audio for later replay on video monitors or computers. Many models are also capable of taking still images (see Figure 9.15). When they first arrived, camcorders recorded in analogue format (VHS and Beta) onto reel-to-reel tape and later videocassettes for replay from VCRs. These camcorders produced less than ideal quality images and the large video cameras had to be rested on the shoulder. As technology improved, other smaller analogue formats became available such as S-VHS, Hi-8, and 8 mm. These formats produced better quality images, were a fraction of the size of the original camcorders, and enabled longer recording times than previously. In order to transfer the images from an analogue camera to a computer, the computer had to be equipped with a video board that would convert the analogue signals into digital.

Video cameras today record images digitally. Rather than scanning line-by-line, light values for each pixel on the screen are registered digitally in memory. Re-creating the image is a matter of lighting up each pixel on the screen. Most digital camcorders feature the following:

- Zoom lenses with electronic zoom controls (up to 500 times magnification) and optical zoom (up to 25 times magnification) for sharp and clear images
- LCD video screen for viewing the subject while recording, as well as playback and the editing of previously recorded material
- Videocassette recorder with record, playback, fast forward, and rewind controls, and playback through the viewfinder
- High video resolution range (200k–500k pixels per frame)

Figure 9.15

Digital Video Cameras

- Built-in microphone, CD-quality sound (PCM stereo digital audio recording), and external microphone input jack. Some cameras have low base filters to eliminate the roar of the wind

- Various shooting features, including time lapse (setting specific time intervals), slow motion, remote control, self timer, still image capture, and many others

- Automatic and manual video controls for adjusting exposure (how light or dark the video will be), shutter speed (number of images per second), white balance (for different sources of light, such as daylight, incandescent light, fluorescent light)

- Separate connection jacks for inputting and outputting audio, video, or for playback through regular TV

- Character generators, known as titlers, for adding titles or other text on your video, date and time stamp that records the date and time on the video, special effects (fade, dissolves, and wipes)

- *Autofocus* (allowing you to concentrate on the subject being recorded without having to worry about the quality) and *image stabilization* (minimizing the minute tremors of videoing by hand)

Recording with different camcorders will vary slightly, so we will not attempt to show you how to do these things. You should consult the manual that accompanies your digital video camera and experiment extensively with your equipment before trying to use it for learning. We also recommend that for every camcorder you acquire, you purchase a tripod to hold the video camera steady while it is being used. The tripod also permits individuals to create videos of themselves.

A variety of video editing software, such as iMovie, is available for piecing together video scenes into a final edit. Digital video editing is fast and convenient. Our experience has shown that kids easily learn how to perform sophisticated editing.

When your masterpiece is completed you may want to export it so that you can share it with others. You can export your video to YouTube (www.youtube.com) or other more serious sites for video sharing, such as Vimeo (http://vimeo.com). Many classrooms shoot video of their activities, convert them into QuickTime files, and post them on the Web. Next, we describe one teacher's experience with using video in the classroom.

Digital Storytelling*

In digital storytelling, technology is not the focus of the activity but rather a tool used to create the story. With digital storytelling, students use their creative skills to create a storyboard on a paper, use a camera to shoot their video, and finally edit their video on a computer using some type of software. Through the combination of working with visual images, text, and sound, students develop their critical-thinking skills in a number of different ways that are not necessarily dependent on computer hardware. In order to create digital stories students must create a desktop movie.

---

* Section written by Kate Kemker.

Figure 9.16

Video Storyboard

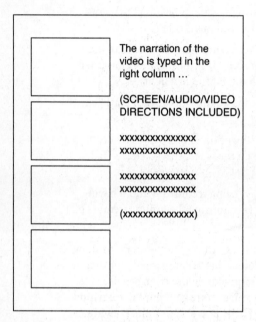

The narration of the video is typed in the right column ...

(SCREEN/AUDIO/VIDEO DIRECTIONS INCLUDED)

xxxxxxxxxxxxxxx
xxxxxxxxxxxxxxx

xxxxxxxxxxxxxxx
xxxxxxxxxxxxxxx

(xxxxxxxxxxxxxx)

In the first part of the activity (preproduction), students plan the story they will be telling. In preproduction, students research, write, and organize information about the structure of their story. It is during this portion of the activity that the majority of the work takes place, providing students with the opportunity to generate their ideas on paper before using the camera. The preproduction portion of the activity allows students to optimize their time when actually using the camcorder. An essential part of preproduction is storyboarding. The storyboard (Figure 9.16) is a document that provides students the opportunity to create a plan for their story from which they can begin filming. Storyboards can take on a number of formats combining verbal and/or graphic descriptions of screen shots. The storyboard includes specific information and the logistics for shooting the footage for the digital story.

Students should also create a checklist that includes the basic elements of a story: exposition, rising action, climax, and falling action. Students should use the checklist to evaluate their project to ensure that their story is communicating to the viewer their intended message. Sample questions could be: What is the plot? Who are the characters? Does there appear to be conflict between the characters? Is there some kind of resolution?

During the production portion of the activity, students begin to shoot their video. Before students shoot their video, it is important to prepare them with a basic knowledge of how this digital medium works. Fundamentals that the students should understand include types of camera shots, camera angles, and camera movement. Some issues in digital filming that should be addressed include: the difference between a close-up shot, a medium range shot, and a long shot; framing a subject in the shot; camera angles not from the human eye–level perspective; and creating action with the camera movement.

A digital storytelling activity provides students the opportunity to work collaboratively in a variety of roles, such as the director, actor, videographer, and editor. When shooting video, each student should be involved in the process. As one student uses the camera, another student should be directing the shots, other students acting, and another student should be logging the video to remember the shots taken. This type of project should lead to an understanding that each role in the production plays an important part in completing the project, and no role is more important than another. The director has the plan for how the video should be done; however, she must communicate that idea effectively to the actor, the videographer, and the editor. It is a true team process.

The final stage, postproduction, is when students edit their video (described before). In this process, it is the role of the editor to bring to fruition what the director had envisioned for the project. In the postproduction process, students act as editors using nonlinear editing

Figure 9.17

Students in Postproduction Editing of a Digital Story

Kate Kemker

software to create the final product (see Figure 9.17). We have used Apple iMovie as well as more powerful products like Final Cut Pro or Adobe Premiere.

At the conclusion of this activity, students should review their digital stories, as well as those done by other students. At the movie premiere, all the movies' students not only take on the roles of stars, but also of critics to review the digital stories. A video production rubric can be used to assess students' progress based on guidelines set out for the given project. Students then write a critique for each movie, evaluating the structure, the fundamentals of digital media, and the editing.

Digital storytelling provides students with the opportunity to establish a connection between the creator and the viewer. Well-told stories can have a powerful effect on an audience, but the secret of their success is the structure of the story: how it is put together and the order in which events appear. A digital story involves the same structural components of any good story: a beginning, middle, and end. As with other types of narrative, digital storytelling also involves a sequence of events that follows characters in a particular context. Through the digital storytelling activity, student will begin to understand how all of the elements work together, and how you can manipulate video to create the effect you want for your story. Such an activity allows students to critically understand that the information they see and hear influences many of their thoughts and decisions as critical thinkers.

Video Modeling and Feedback

One of the most productive ways to use video for teaching is to model specific performances. Video models are used frequently in teaching athletics, where skilled performers show you how to improve your golf or tennis swing. However, video modeling is useful for more than just psychomotor tasks. Any kind of performance can be modeled by the teacher or other skilled performer, such as public speaking or acting for theatrical performers, empathic behavior for counselors or social workers, interpersonal communication skills for personnel workers or librarians, even thinking and research behaviors.

Teachers and students together might think about developing a study strategies video by acting out what a skilled learner would do in order to write a term paper or study for a test. Shoot the video from the point of view of the student—reading a book, looking in a catalog, searching the library stacks, turning off the television. After shooting the video, dub in the voice, using an echo chamber to make it seem like the person in the video is talking to himself or herself. Find out what skills students possess, and videotape them performing what they do best. Not only will you have a series of useful videos, but students will gain self-confidence, as well. Getting students to articulate what they should be doing is usually a good idea.

When modeling performances for students, it is important to model not only the actual performance but also the mental processes (decision making, questioning, resolving) involved with the performance. This think-aloud process can be very informative for the learners while watching the video performance, especially if the teacher conveys his or her uncertainties as well as solutions while thinking aloud. Although providing video models of any desired performance is one of the most powerful video teaching methods available, it is maximally successful if used in conjunction with video feedback (described later). Essentially, providing video models and then videotaping the learners' performances and using those tapes as feedback is probably the most powerful use of video possible.

Learning through Video Feedback

Video can help learners reflect on their own performance primarily through video feedback—that is, the process of videotaping a performance and then viewing that performance, with or without a teacher or expert accompanying you. For instance, Orban and McLean (1990) used video cameras for self-evaluations and teacher evaluations of French-speaking ability. "Video is like a mirror in which a magician practices his tricks, a way to evaluate his performance over and over" (Taylor 1979, p. 28). You can use video to engage constructive (articulative/reflective) learning with the following activities.

Video feedback is perhaps the most constructivist use of video. Select virtually any meaningful performance task in schools (theatrics, foreign language usage, public speaking, performing a chemistry experiment, anything but test-taking) and assess the learners' performance by videotaping them while performing the activity. That performance can then be evaluated, and feedback about their performance can be provided to the student. Video feedback is one of the deepest, most incisive learning experiences possible. Having learners watch themselves perform provides them with an unfiltered, unbiased view of themselves. Caution needs to be exercised. Teachers should prepare students for using such feedback constructively, because video feedback can be intimidating and demotivating if not used correctly. This method is often (though not often enough) used to help prepare preservice teachers for teaching. Teachers are videotaped teaching lessons to students. Reviewing the videotape, with or without a supervisory teacher to provide feedback, teaches new teachers more about teaching than all of the textbooks they have read.

Visualizing Your Self with Video

In addition to providing performance feedback, video feedback can also be used to provide insights into the self. When people see themselves on a video, it often affects their self-perceptions (Jonassen 1978, 1979). The video provides an unfiltered mirror into the self. Viewers become more evaluative and less role-oriented in their perceptions of themselves. This experience is very powerful and should not be used with troubled individuals without proper care.

NET Standards potentially engaged by visualization activities described in this chapter:

1. **Creativity and Innovation**
   a. Apply existing knowledge to generate new ideas, products, or processes
   b. Create original works as a means of personal or group expression

2. **Communication and Collaboration**
   a. Interact, collaborate, and publish with peers, experts, or others employing a variety of digital environments and media
   b. Communicate information and ideas effectively to multiple audiences using a variety of media and formats
   c. Develop cultural understanding and global awareness by engaging with learners of other cultures
   d. Contribute to project teams to produce original works or solve problems

3. **Research and Information Fluency**
   a. Plan strategies to guide inquiry
   b. Locate, organize, analyze, evaluate, synthesize, and ethically use information from a variety of sources and media
   c. Evaluate and select information sources and digital tools based on the appropriateness to specific tasks

4. **Critical Thinking, Problem Solving, and Decision Making**
   b. Plan and manage activities to develop a solution or complete a project
   c. Collect and analyze data to identify solutions and/or make informed decisions
   d. Use multiple processes and diverse perspectives to explore alternative solutions

5. **Digital Citizenship**
   a. Advocate and practice safe, legal, and responsible use of information and technology
   b. Exhibit a positive attitude toward using technology that supports collaboration, learning, and productivity
   c. Demonstrate personal responsibility for lifelong learning

21st Century Skills potentially engaged by visualization activities described in this chapter:

Think Creatively

- Use a wide range of idea creation techniques
- Create new and worthwhile ideas (both incremental and radical concepts)
- Elaborate, refine, analyze and evaluate their own ideas in order to improve and maximize creative efforts

Work Creatively with Others

- Develop, implement and communicate new ideas to others effectively
- Be open and responsive to new and diverse perspectives; incorporate group input and feedback into the work
- Demonstrate originality and inventiveness in work and understand the real world limits to adopting new ideas

Implement Innovations

- Act on creative ideas to make a tangible and useful contribution to the field in which the innovation will occur

Solve Problems

- Solve different kinds of non-familiar problems in both conventional and innovative ways
- Identify and ask significant questions that clarify various points of view and lead to better solutions

Communicate Clearly

- Articulate thoughts and ideas effectively using oral, written and nonverbal communication skills in a variety of forms and contexts
- Use communication for a range of purposes (e.g., to inform, instruct, motivate and persuade)
- Utilize multiple media and technologies, and know how to judge their effectiveness a priori as well as assess their impact
- Communicate effectively in diverse environments (including multi-lingual)

Collaborate with Others

- Demonstrate ability to work effectively and respectfully with diverse teams
- Assume shared responsibility for collaborative work, and value the individual contributions made by each team member

Access and Evaluate Information

- Access information efficiently (time) and effectively (sources)
- Evaluate information critically and competently

Analyze Media

- Understand both how and why media messages are constructed, and for what purposes

- Examine how individuals interpret messages differently, how values and points of view are included or excluded, and how media can influence beliefs and behaviors

Create Media Products

- Understand and utilize the most appropriate media creation tools, characteristics and conventions
- Understand and effectively utilize the most appropriate expressions and interpretations in diverse, multi-cultural environments

Apply Technology Effectively

- Use technology as a tool to research, organize, evaluate and communicate information

Things to Think About

If you would like to reflect on the ideas that we presented in this chapter, then articulate your responses to the following questions and compare them with others' responses.

1. In this chapter, we have described various technologies that can function as visual aids. Can you think of other ways that technologies can help us "see things" in a new way? Are there scientific concepts that you had a hard time imagining in school?

2. Google Earth goes a long way toward mapping the world. How will that affect our perceptions of the world?

3. Mathematics is one of the most, if not the most, abstract subject matter domains. Helping students visualize mathematical concepts is very useful in helping students to make math real. What other methods suggested in this book will also help make math more real to students?

4. What kinds of reasoning/thinking are students performing when they think mathematically?

5. Is it ever possible to learn from television alone—that is, learn how to do something merely from watching television instruction? What meaning will it have after only watching the show? What meaning will it have after you try it yourself?

6. "Public television exists to enrich people's lives." What does that mean? In order to be enriched, what does the individual viewer have to contribute?

7. Video production is a constructivist activity; that is, students are learning by constructing an artifact. What other kinds of constructionist activities can you think of (using technologies or not)?

8. After the Watergate investigation that brought down Nixon's presidency, investigative journalism increased dramatically. What kinds of issues (personal, local, regional, national) would be most likely to attract students to investigative reporting? How can you support that in your school?

9. Video feedback has been called a "mirror with a memory." Why is seeing yourself on television such a compelling and incisive experience? How do you see yourself? Why is that so powerful?

References

Dunham, P., & Dick, T. (1994). Research on graphing calculators. *Mathematics Teacher, 87*, 440–445.

Finzer, W., Erickson, T., & Binker, J. (2001). Fathom Dynamic Statistics Software [Computer software]. Emeryville, CA: Key Curriculum Press.

Gordin, D. N., Edelson, D. C., & Gomez, L. (July, 1996). Scientific visualization as an interpretive and expressive medium. In D. Edelson & E. Domeshek (Eds.), Proceedings of the Second International Conference on the learning sciences (pp. 409–414). Charlottesville, VA: Association for the Advancement of Computers in Education.

Jonassen, D. H. (1978). Video as a mediator of human behavior. *Media Message, 7*(2): 5–6.

Jonassen, D. H. (1979). Video-mediated objective self-awareness, self-perception, and locus of control. *Perceptual and Motor Skills, 48*, 255–265.

Kirby, J., Moore, P., & Shofield, N. (1988). Verbal and visual learning styles. *Contemporary Educational Psychology, 13*, 169–184.

Konold, C. (2006). Designing a data analysis tool for learners. In M. Lovett & P. Shah (Eds.), *Thinking with data: The 33rd Annual Carnegie Symposium on Cognition*. Hillside, NJ: Lawrence Erlbaum Associates.

Levin, J. R., Anglin, G. J., & Carney, R. N. (1987). On empirically validating functions of pictures in prose. In D. M. Willows & H. A. Houghton (Eds.), *The psychology of illustration, Vol. 1, Basic research*. New York: Springer-Verlag.

Orban, C., & McLean, A. M. (1990). A working model for videocamera use in the foreign language classroom. *The French Review, 63*(4): 652–663.

Pelletier, R. J. (1990). Prompting spontaneity by means of the video camera in the beginning foreign language class. *Foreign Language Annals, 22*(3): 227–232.

Ruthven, K. (1990). The influence of graphic calculator use on translation from graphic to symbolic forms. *Educational Studies in Mathematics, 21*, 431–450.

Taylor, C. B. (1979, January). Video to teach poetry writing. *Audiovisual Instruction*, 27–29.

Valmont, W. J. (1994). Making videos with reluctant learners. *Reading and Writing Quarterly: Overcoming Learning Difficulties, 10*(4): 369–377.

Assessing Meaningful Learning and Teaching with Technologies

Debbie Moda/The Modesto Bee/Zuma/Newscom

Chapter Objectives

1. Introduce readers to technology tools that can help assess meaningful learning outcomes

2. Define rubrics and describe their significance to assessing meaningful learning outcomes

3. Provide guidelines on how to construct an effective rubric for assessing student work

4. Describe the uses of rubric generators and rubric banks and provide examples of these tools

5. Define e-portfolios, describe the software packages used to support them and describe how e-portfolios can be used to meaningfully assess student learning, including how they can be used to address state and national standards

6. Describe "student response systems" (AKA "clickers") and how they can be used to effectively assess (both formatively and summatively) student learning

7. Review the different types of technology-based tests, quizzes, and survey tools

8. Describe how the technology-based assessment tools may support the development of NETS and 21st Century Skills

This entire book has provided examples of how technology can support different types of complex learning outcomes. But technology can also be used to support another key aspect of learning—assessment. This chapter describes technology-based means of conducting learner assessment. As we will see, the line between an assessment activity and a learning activity can often be blurred when assessing meaningful learning with technology.

Assessing Meaningful Learning: Authentic and Performance Assessment

We have argued throughout this book that technology-supported meaningful learning should be authentic and therefore complex. Just as the learning activities we have described engage learners in meaningful experiences, so must our assessments. Educators are finally beginning to understand that in order to evaluate authentic learning, we must use *authentic assessments*. In the last decade, calls for authentic assessment have encouraged educators to discard outdated evaluative methods designed to *sort* students, in favor of *assessment systems* designed to provide important information required to *improve performance*. Similarly, for our assessments to be "congruent" or in alignment with the activities we have described, we must adopt authentic and/or performance assessment practices.

Performance assessment refers to the process of assessing a student's skills by asking the student to perform tasks that require those skills. Performances in science might examine the ability to design a device to perform a particular function or to mount an argument supported by experimental evidence.

One source (ERIC, 2002) defines performance assessment as having these elements:

- Students must construct a response or a product, rather than simply select from a set of predefined alternatives or answers. So, in Chapter 9 we saw that students can create or "construct" a news broadcast rather than completing a multiple-choice test on current events.

- Assessment then consists of direct observation or assessment of student behavior on tasks or on the product that they produced, and further, the tasks or products are designed to resemble activities commonly required for functioning in the world outside school.

In essence, the performance of the learning task and the assessment tasks are interwoven and inseparable. Rather than assessing an activity that is completely separate from the activity that learners engage in, we assess the product of that very same learning activity; we assess the learners' performance.

Other terms—authentic assessment, alternative assessment—are sometimes used for performance assessment. These terms, however, are not interchangeable. *Alternative assessment* generally refers to assessments that are in opposition to standardized achievement tests (e.g., the SAT or ACT exam) and to objective test item formats. On the other hand, *authentic assessment* is a term that is closely related to performance assessment and means that learners engage in educational tasks that are meaningful and directly related to real tasks that they may need to perform in the future. For example, having social studies students engage in an activity to poll public opinion on a local issue would be an authentic assessment task as compared to having these same social studies students taking a closed book exam on principles of democracy.

Many of the technology-supported activities described in this book can become performance assessment activities when accompanied with a set of performance criteria and a scoring rubric. In all cases the students should be aware of the scoring system and the criteria used to determine the scores for the assessment of the activity.

Technology-Based Assessments

Assessment is the process of gathering data and analyzing it to determine if intended learning outcomes have been achieved (Gagne, Bridges, & Wagne, 1998). As described in this book, it makes sense to harness technology for assessment particularly because at least one aspect of assessment is the management of data—potentially large amounts of data. Because of this, educators have begun to harness technology to make assessment more feasible and more effective. Beyond the simple fact that technology can make assessment data easier to manage, it may also allow teachers to assess more frequently—and provide more and better feedback to learners in order to improve their performance. Before you dismiss this idea because it means more data for you to manage, more grades to record and more student anxiety, consider that an easy-to-use, technology-based assessment can allow a teacher to *formatively* assess—that is gather assessment data quickly and easily *only* to determine if learners are "getting it" (not to record a "grade"), potentially revise instruction and then move on.

Technology-based assessment could also address another need presented by implementation of learning environments to support complex learning outcomes. Such outcomes cannot effectively be assessed by any *single* means of assessment. Using technology-based assessments may provide teachers with the ability to assess these outcomes in multiple ways thus providing a more complete and arguably valid assessment picture.

Although most readers are familiar with computer-based testing, quizzes or surveys, the use of technology to support assessment has developed beyond simply placing traditional forms of assessment in a digital format. This chapter describes applications of technology to the assessing of higher-order learning outcomes.

Assessing Performance with Technology-Based Rubrics

By definition, a *rubric* is a code, or a set of codes, designed to govern action. In educational settings, the term has evolved to mean a tool represented as a set of *scales* to be used for assessing a complex performance. In recent years many technology-based rubric creation, implementation and management tools have become available. We begin this section with an overview of rubrics that includes fairly detailed guidelines on characteristics of effective rubrics and how to construct them. We then describe the functions, benefits, and applications of technology-based rubric tools.

Rubrics and Meaningful Learning

Many terms are used to name the documents or methods we use to assess learner performance. These include scoring grids (because they are often in grid form), scoring schemes, rating scales and, perhaps the most commonly used term—*rubrics*. In schools, rubrics often take the form of a scale or set of scales. Applying a rubric to a complex learning process or product (such as an e-portfolio) provides a means for systematically assessing the degree that certain criteria are demonstrated in the product or process. In essence, a rubric helps the scorer consistently apply a set of valid criteria to the product. The process of developing and applying a rubric addresses the problem that both teachers and learners often face when it comes to grading complex learning products.

For instance, in a typical classroom, oral reports are mysteriously *graded* (neither students nor teachers can really tell you where the grades come from) and a few comments generally accompany the grade. Little substantive feedback about the performance is made available to the student, who cares only about the grade received. On the other hand, using a rubric, perhaps jointly developed by students and teachers, can promote intentional learning by identifying important aspects of the performance, gathering information about the learner's performance, and using the information to improve learner performance.

The "Anatomy" of a Rubric

A rubric is generally represented as a set of *scales* that are used to assess a complex performance and to provide rich information regarding improving performance. For example, consider the task of effectively working in groups. There are several *elements* (components) that combine to form effective group participation, including (but certainly not limited to) extent of group participation, and content of group discussions. So, a simplified, but useful, rubric used to assess this task might include scales similar to those shown in Figure 10.1.

Figure 10.1

Portion of a Group Work Rubric

Student Participation in Group Discussions

Inadequately		Adequately		Exceptionally
Never participates; quiet/passive	...	Participates as much as other group members	...	Participates more than any other group member

Comments Related to Topic under Discussion

Inadequately		Adequately		Exceptionally
Comments ramble, distracted from topic	...	Comments usually pertinent, occasionally wanders from topic	...	Comments are always related to topic

This rubric is clearer and more informative than simply assigning a letter grade, but there are several ways to enhance the value of this rubric. First, let's establish a common vocabulary to use when discussing rubrics: A rubric is a set of *scales*, one for each element that is considered important. The scale for each element consists of several *ratings* that describe the different levels of performance that might be expected.

Heuristics for Developing an Effective Rubric

Developing rubrics is a complex task. As is the case in most complex tasks, there's no single "right answer." For most activities for which a rubric might be an appropriate assessment device, it is quite likely that different people would develop different rubrics, each with its own set of advantages and shortcomings. Although there is not a single right way to go about developing a rubric, the following set of heuristics will help to provide some direction to your initial rubric development activities. As you become more proficient, you will no doubt refine these heuristics to meet your own needs. We've presented the heuristics as a sequential list, but it is likely you will need to revisit steps as needed.

1. Start by writing a few sentences that define the importance of the topic of the rubric. Why should learners perform this activity? This will help as you move through the rest of the rubric development process.

2. Make a list of the major "elements" of the activity or topic. An *element* is essentially an important component of the overall task or activity. You should create elements for every aspect of the activity that you wish to assess. Additionally, as described in the section Characteristics of a Good Rubric (page 242), your elements should be *unidimensional*. That means each element should be a single item that can't be reduced to a set of other items. When your elements are not unidimensional, you will have a hard time defining the actual performance activities that define the element. A general rule of thumb would be that you should have somewhere between three and seven elements. If you feel you need more than that, you may need to consider separate rubrics. For example, for a rubric for multimedia presentations, we might define three elements: organization, content, and delivery.

3. For each element, you then have several activities to develop your rubric:
   - *Define the element.* What activities define that element? What is it you wish to see in the students' performance relative to that element? For instance for a multimedia presentation, we might define organization as "the thoughtful structuring of the elements of the presentation in order to achieve the stated objectives."
   - *Define the rating scale for each element.* Remember, you shouldn't necessarily use the same rating scale for all elements. Refer to the Characteristics of a Good Rubric on page 242 for more hints on defining a rating scale. You'll want to make sure that the scale is descriptive of the element in question. For the organization of the multimedia presentation, the scale might be: inadequate, adequate, and excellent.
   - *Define the meanings of each scale item.* Each scale item must be defined in very action- or behavior-oriented terms. This is probably the hardest work involved in rubric creation. It isn't very difficult to decide that you will have a rating scale of three levels—but very clearly defining what each level of the scale means can be

hard work. It is in many senses like writing a good instructional objective—and if, in fact, you have already specified very clear objectives for the performance task, you'll definitely want to refer to those objectives for guidance on the content of your rubrics.

Here's a definition in specific action and product-oriented terms of an *inadequate organization* for a multimedia presentation. Descriptors:

- The presentation was untitled
- The objective was not stated
- The objective was unclear
- The outline or storyboard was not provided
- The outline or storyboard provided did not match the content of the presentation
- The speaker notes were not prepared
- The speaker notes were present, but were not well enough prepared to allow for a smooth polished speaking role

On the other end of the spectrum, here's a description of *excellent*:

- All the descriptors of an effective organization were presented
- The sequencing of events built a compelling, even artistic expression of the idea, opinion, or argument being presented

All aspects of a rubric should be focused on providing useful feedback to students that will help them to improve performance. As you develop the definitions of each scale item, it is also useful to develop recommendations that are appropriate for students when they achieve that particular rating. Returning to our organization element for the "inadequate" performance, the recommendations might include:

- Select a title after writing the objective and make choices about content and organization
- Rewrite the objective after a rough draft of the presentation
- Utilize peer editing to get feedback concerning the sequence of storyboard elements
- Rewrite speaker notes in a way that effectively prompts the speaker to deliver a smooth performance

Creating these recommendations up front will help you to provide students with consistent feedback based on the rubric definition.

Once you've followed these guidelines, revisit the rubric you've created. In the next sections, we address technology-based rubrics and describe ways to ascertain whether the rubrics you have created, found, or modified are effective for assessing meaningful learning.

Technology-Based Rubric Tools

There are a variety of technology tools for creating and supporting the use of rubrics. They fall into two basic categories: rubric banks and rubric generation tools (Dornisch & Sabatini McLoughlin, 2006). Online rubric banks offer already-created rubrics for a wide array of learning tasks. One impediment to using rubrics is that the task of creating a high-quality rubric—as described in the prior sections of this chapter—is not trivial in any circumstances and even less so when one is creating a rubric for a complex learning task.

So creating such a rubric may be a time-consuming task—although we would argue that it is a beneficial one because it requires that teachers clearly and precisely articulate the characteristics of a high-quality learning activity (e.g., what characteristics does a really good multimedia presentation have?) which in turn can help them design their instructional activities to help support the development of those characteristics. Nonetheless, teachers are undoubtedly short on time, so banks of existing rubrics certainly have potential. Figure 10.2 shows a sampling of rubric banks available at this writing. These are general banks; however, it has become common practice for school districts to post rubrics that are aligned to their curricular standards. For instance the Greece Central School district in New York provides a list of standards-based rubrics on writing, speaking, and class participation (www.greece.k12.ny.us/instruction/ela/6-12/Rubrics/Index.htm).

We caution users of rubric banks for several reasons. First, before using any rubric the user needs to evaluate it for appropriateness for your intended learning task. Just because you are in need of a rubric for a group discussion—and you find one (or a dozen)—none of these rubrics may align with the learning outcomes you had intended for *your* classroom group discussion. We perused several rubrics on class discussions and found that they addressed a broad range of activities including: consensus building, speaking and listening, conflict resolution, facilitation skills, summarization skills, keeping track of time, and so on. Which of these (if any) are you interested in? Our point is that finding a rubric that fits your learning outcomes even if the "task" is the same, is quite unlikely. Be prepared to both examine many rubrics that match your task, and then modify them to meet your needs (perhaps by combining several of them).

In many cases, the rubrics you find may not clearly state the intended outcomes they are to assess, so you will need to glean these outcomes from the content of the rubric—which may or may not be feasible depending on the rubric's clarity. We suggest that the better rubrics will in fact clearly state the outcomes they intend to assess and teachers can use this as a way of sorting through the many rubrics they may find.

Lastly, there are a lot of rubric banks out there (Figure 10.2 shows only a sampling). The main argument for using them is that they could save teachers time. You may, however,

Figure 10.2

A Selection of Online Rubric Banks

Discovery School:

http://school.discovery.com/schrockguide/assess.html

Provides a fairly comprehensive set of domain-specific and general rubrics.

Rubrician:

www.rubrician.com

Offers a collection of rubrics by subject matter area, plus under the "general" category offers links to other rubric banks. It is not clear how the quality of submitted rubrics is maintained on this site.

wish to consider that by the time you search all these banks, find a rubric and then almost certainly modify it to fit your learning outcomes to create an effective rubric, you may have had time to create your own rubric that can avoid some of the problems of using someone else's conception of your learning task.

The other category of technology-based rubric tools is rubric generators. As the name implies, a rubric generator helps the user to actually create a rubric. With rubric generators, you create a rubric that is customized to your desired learning objectives, and can avoid some of the issues discussed pertaining to the use of rubric banks. But, what do rubric generators offer over sitting down with a word processor?

Rubric generators can scaffold or support the user through the rubric generation process. A good rubric generator will force you to address the critical components of a high-quality rubric (see Figure 10.3).

For instance, the Rubric Processor (http://ide.ed.psu.edu/ITSC/RubrProc/) takes users through a series of screens that each represent a critical step in creating a rubric. In addition to asking you for a rubric title, the tool requires you to define up to seven "elements" you wish to assess in your rubric, and then for each element you are prompted to define the different performance levels or "ratings" for that element. Keeping with our "group discussion" activity example, one "element" might be "activity level." As prompted by the rubric processor, we would define "activity level" as the amount of participation an individual

Figure 10.3

Sample Rubric Generators

ClassMon

www.foliosinternational.com/content2.php?contentid=21

Commercial rubric-based observation product that includes a rubric builder, rubric importer and the ability to include student work samples as evidence of learning.

The Rubric Processor

http://ide.ed.psu.edu/ITSC/RubrProc/

Provides step-by-step screens for creating rubrics as well as built-in tools for completing them and distributing feedback to students.

Rubistar

http://rubistar.4teachers.org/index.php

Users do not create a rubric from scratch but rather customize rubric templates that are available in a variety of subject area domains.

Tech4Learning Tools RubricMaker

http://myt4l.com/index.php?v=pl&page_ac=view&type=tools

Provides scaffolded interface for creating rubrics. Features include pull down menus for types of learning outcomes, and four definable levels of performance for each criterion/component defined.

Figure 10.4

Performance-Level Descriptions for a Group Discussion

Performance Level	Definition
Inadequately:	Never participates; quiet/passive
Adequately:	Participates as much as other group members
Exceptionally:	Participates more than any other group member

contributes to the discussion during one class period. Then the processor prompts us to define the different performance levels and their definitions (see Figure 10.4). A person using the rubric generator would continue this process, defining each element and their associated performance levels. Once completed, your rubric is stored for later use.

The Rubric Processor is an example of a technology-based rubric tool that also provides support for using rubrics with students. As you define the performance levels for each element, you create the stem of a sentence which, used in combination with your performance level definition, can be used in creating a feedback report for a student as you apply the rubric to his or her product. So student Juan—who demonstrated adequate activity level during the discussion—would see on his report "Juan participates as much as other group members." This focus on creating qualitative feedback for students is a positive aspect of this particular tool.

While the Rubric Processor is a good example of a free product that supports rubric creation, the commercial ClassMon product, developed in Australia, includes a rubric "builder" within a broader tool that can help teachers manage and implement the process of conducting performance assessments with their classes. ClassMon includes tools and features that teachers can use to build rubrics, modify, and further customize the rubrics that come with the tool (see Figure 10.5), import rubrics, associate different rubrics with different students, generate reports and checklists, keep track of which students have been rated with different rubrics or checklists, and load student work samples to support their observations.

The tool uses slightly different terminology than we have defined concerning rubrics here. For instance, it refers to *phases of learning*, which are akin to what we have called *performance levels* (see Figure 10.4). These are applied to different *learning areas* (e.g., the LA social learning—sustaining relationships shown in Figure 10.5), which are broad overarching areas where teachers may wish to assess student skills. Within these, it defines *learning statements* and these appear to be akin to what we have called *elements*—although we note that they are not unidimensional and are much broader. We also note that because ClassMon is predominantly set up for supporting observation of learner performances, many of the learning statements included in the product are geared toward observable outcomes (such as how learners work in groups).

Figure 10.5

ClassMon Rubric Builder Screen

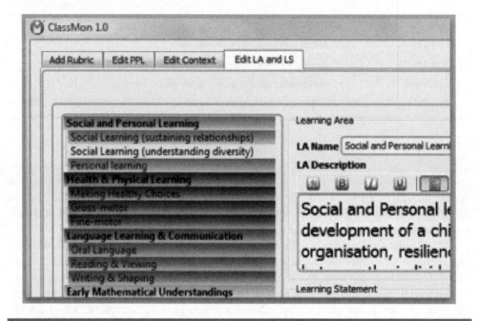

Characteristics of a Good Rubric

Whether you are trying to decide if the rubric you found online is high quality, or whether you are using an online rubric generator to create your own, you need to know the characteristics of a good rubric. The most effective and useful rubrics tend to display certain important characteristics. We will discuss these characteristics briefly, along with the most common pitfalls experienced by novices.

In an effective rubric, all important elements are included. If something is important enough to assess, consider it an element and develop a scale with ratings that describe it. By definition, the rubric identifies (both for the assessor and the student) the aspects of the performance that are considered important. Consider the rubric a sort of contract between educator and student, and resist the temptation to assess anything not included in the rubric. If you forgot an important element, then renegotiate the rubric.

In an effective rubric, each element is unidimensional. Avoid using elements that are really *molecules*. In chemistry, an *element* is irreducible. Water is a molecule; composed of both hydrogen and oxygen—it can be separated into these elements, which cannot be further separated. For instance, an "element" called Voice Qualities for an oral presentation rubric is not elemental and should be broken down into the separate elements of Volume and Intonation. The penalty for attempting to assess molecules rather than elements is that assigning ratings is more difficult, as is deriving specific feedback on which to base attempts to improve performance. Just what was it about the voice quality that was not adequate?

In an effective rubric, ratings are distinct, comprehensive, and descriptive. The ratings should cover the range of expected performances. Some elements are best assessed in a simple, two-rating scale—a yes/no distinction—while others might require as many as seven distinct ratings. For example, the Volume element in an oral report might simply be assessed as "too quiet" or "loud enough," while an element like Social Interaction might justifiably involve five or more ratings.

A common problem in rubric design involves an attempt to use a similar scale for all elements; for example, using a standard five-point scale:

Weak	Poor	Acceptable	Good	Excellent

Although it might seem simpler and cleaner to use such a scale for each element, can you really describe the difference between ratings of Weak and Poor, or between Good and Excellent, say, for example, for the pace of an oral presentation? Would these assessments be defensible or too subjective? Also, when a standard scale is used for multiple elements, you lose a lot of information that is better transmitted by descriptive ratings rather than generic labels. For example, a student might learn more about his or her presentation performance if an element titled Motivation was rated as Boring rather than being rated as Weak. Use labels that make sense and describe the behaviors, and use just enough of them to cover the range of possibilities.

An effective rubric communicates clearly with both students and parents. The ultimate purpose of a rubric is to improve performance. This is accomplished by clarifying expectations and by providing important information about progress toward the desired goal states. Rubrics convey the complexity of the task and focus intentional learning. The feedback their use provides serves as an important baseline for reflection by both learners and educators. For these purposes to be realized, the rubric must communicate clearly with those it is to serve. Make sure that all who use the rubric (learners, parents, and educators) share a common understanding of all of the terms used. This common understanding is often achieved as the educators and students develop the rubric collaboratively, after which students explain it to their parents. This is a great way to develop metacognition (understanding of cognitive processes used), and it helps students regulate their learning as they proceed through the complex tasks offered by meaningful learning environments. Avoid educational jargon and words with weak or several meanings. Consider developing, preferably with students, descriptions of each element and each rating, or using elaborate, full-sentence rating labels instead of single terms.

An effective rubric provides rich information about the multiple aspects of the performance and avoids the temptation to create a contrived summary score. Despite the fact that the real value of a rubric lies in its ability to provide information on the separate elements that comprise a complex task, novice users (especially teachers in the public schools) seem compelled to turn the ratings given on individual *elements* into *scores* for each element, and then to combine these scores to form a total score and then, worse yet, a *grade*. When individual elements are combined, information that could improve performance is lost. When ratings are treated as numeric scores and combined, elements of more and less importance are generally treated as if they were of equal value, and an inaccurate picture of the performance is created. For example, suppose that ratings for Organization and Intonation are combined after using a rubric to assess an oral presentation. Generally, the scores are added in a way that makes the two appear equally important. Even when the different elements are combined using some sort of weighting system that assigns different numbers of points based on the importance of the element, when scores are combined, attention is paid to the total at the expense of the information about how to improve performance on each element.

A Rubric for Assessing the Effectiveness of a Rubric

Even when you follow the heuristics previously described, developing rubrics is still a difficult task. Thus, regardless of whether you develop your own rubric or consult a bank of rubrics for a starting point, you need to be able to evaluate a rubric to see if it will be effective for the task you have in mind.

A rubric is effective to the extent that it helps learners focus on the important elements of a performance and provides information on which they can reflect and base strategies for growth. Most rubrics can be improved by a sincere attempt to assess them against the criteria just discussed.

For example, although the rubric for the oral presentation provided in Figure 10.1 was a step in the right direction and would be useful to learners, it was not fully developed (important elements were missing and ratings were undefined) and it included an element, "Voice Qualities," that was really a *molecule*—a combination of components that should have been addressed separately. That rubric can be improved. Other rubrics have serious flaws as well. For this reason, we offer a rubric that you can apply to *your own* rubrics (see Figure 10.6).

Using Rubrics

In order to gain the maximum benefits that rubrics offer, innovative educators creating meaningful learning environments should consider the following tips:

- Develop rubrics collaboratively with learners. This is an outstanding opportunity to get students thinking about what expert performance looks like, and to help students learn how to learn.

- Encourage learners to use the rubrics to guide them during the learning process. Throughout this book, we have promoted the idea of intentional learning. When rubrics are made public before the learning activity begins, students can use the content of rubrics to focus their activities.

- Encourage students to explain the rubrics to parents and other interested individuals, perhaps in the context of student-led conferences during which they describe the progress they're making and the lessons they have learned.

Figure 10.6

Rubric for Assessing and Improving Rubrics

Elements

Comprehensiveness: *Are all of the important elements of the performance identified?*

Important elements are missing (attach list of missing elements).	All important elements are identified.

Unidimensionality: *Are the elements irreducible, or do they represent factors that are better addressed separately?*

More than one element should be broken down (attach list). _____	One element should be broken down.	All elements are unidimensional.

Ratings

Distinctiveness: *Do the ratings represent clearly different categories, or is there overlap or ambiguity?*

Ratings for one or more elements seem to overlap. (attach list of elements)	Ratings for each element are distinct from one another.

Comprehensiveness: *Do the ratings cover the full range of expected performances?*

Ratings are missing (attach list of suggested additions).	All important ratings are identified.

Descriptiveness: *Do the ratings provide meaningful input for reflection?*

Several ratings have generic or minimally useful labels (attach list).	Few ratings have generic or minimal useful labels (attach list).	All ratings communicate clearly.

Clarity

(the extent to which key stakeholders will understand)

Among Students

Few students will understand all of the terms used in elements and ratings (attach list of suggestions).	Few students will understand all of the terms used in elements and ratings (attach list of suggestions).	All students will understand.

Among Parents

Few parents will understand all of the terms used in elements and ratings (attach list of suggestions).	Few parents will understand all of the terms used in elements and ratings (attach list of suggestions).	All parents will understand.

Quality of Information Provided

Richness

Misses many opportunities to communicate clearly about the quality of the performance.	Adequate information is provided to serve as the basis for growth.	Lots of specific information is provided to facilitate development.

(continued)

Figure 10.6 (*continued*)

Rubric for Assessing and Improving Rubrics

Resists Temptation of Generic Scales

"Generic" scales seem to compromise the value of the rubric (attach list of offending elements).

The scale for each element reflects a sincere effort to identify distinctive ratings.

Resists Temptation to Summarize

Information of value may be over-looked because a summary collapsing categories is used (attach list of sug-gested additions).

No attempt to create an overall score or grade is evident.

- View rubrics as providing important information that educators and learners can use to select learning activities, rather than as evaluative devices with which to label, sort, or grade students. Gaps between what is reported and what is desired on a single element should be viewed as opportunities for growth.

- View rubrics as powerful tools in your own professional development. Consider designing a rubric that will help you become a more effective educator in promoting meaningful learning. Ask peers to develop it with you, and perhaps to use it to assess your progress from time to time. These assessments, combined with your own, can be the most important factor in your development as an innovative educator.

- Use rubrics to help you assess the quality and power of the learning environments you create, as well as the progress of individuals. Using such a process, you are likely to identify additional ways to enhance the educational experience you provide for your students.

Assessing Growth over Time with Electronic Portfolios

As more and more teachers are having students create digital artifacts of their learning (e.g., presentations, word processing documents, blogs, websites) they are then also asking them to put these artifacts together in a coherent way to represent a body of work that addresses defined learning outcomes. These are often called electronic portfolios, or *e-portfolios*. For instance, a visual/performing arts high school teacher had students keep digital portfolios of their artwork for later use in other projects such as theatre backdrops, calendars and so on. The purpose of the portfolio was to have students work with multimedia programs, learn to organize information coherently, and collaborate with one another. Digital pictures of tradi-tionally created pieces were mixed with digitally created artifacts. Students used a variety of technologies including digital cameras, graphics programs, and web page programming tools (KITE, 2001).

E-portfolios are a collection of digitized artifacts that may include video clips, graph-ics, sound, writing samples, art work, and multimedia presentations, to name a few. Taken together they can represent the accomplishments of an individual or group of learners (Lorenzo & Ittelson, 2005). E-portfolios are meant to be more than simply a collection of student work stored in an electronic format. Rather, they are intended to purposefully exhibit students' efforts, progress and achievements (Paulson, Paulson, & Meyer, 1991).

Portfolios (either e-portfolios or in hardcopy form) are part of the move toward performance assessment and a move away from teacher-centered forms of assessment, as portfolios can provide more autonomy to students as they make their own choices on which artifacts to include and how to present them (McAlpine, 2000; Tombari & Borich, 1999). Generally portfolios can be used to demonstrate students' ability to create a certain type of product (e.g., a newspaper article that describes a recent PTA meeting), demonstrate their ability to follow a process (e.g., reconcile income and expenses in an accounting ledger), or, by using a variety of products over a period of time, demonstrate student growth in a learning domain.

Portfolios have traditionally been classified in three types associated with the intended purpose of the portfolio—and any of these can be implemented as e-portfolios. Notice that an important distinction between the types of portfolios is how much control students have over choosing portfolio content.

- *Working portfolios.* This type of portfolio shows a student's best performance or performance over time in specified learning areas. Such portfolios tend to be more formative in nature, and students would have the chance to get feedback and improve their portfolio over time.

- *Standards-based portfolios.* In this type of portfolio, teachers are likely to define the content based on meeting certain curricular requirements. In Missouri, a fifth-grade teacher might ask students to put together a portfolio that demonstrates the "grade-level expectations" for the understanding of the water cycle.

- *External evaluation portfolio.* This type of portfolio is generally summative and is used for an *external* audience such as an accrediting body to demonstrate that your school or grade has met this external body's requirements.

Why Use Them?

There are many reasons to use e-portfolios. From a logistical perspective, the electronic nature of portfolios makes them searchable, transportable, and more easily modifiable (Batson, 2002). This is an advantage both for teachers and students. But more substantively, e-portfolios can be useful for assessing many types of learning outcomes.

In fact, the range of learning outcomes one can assess is essentially limitless, is defined by the portfolio designer, and will vary based on the types of products included in the e-portfolio. For instance, e-portfolios that include documents containing narratives might demonstrate writing or literacy skills. A video clip of a student-generated news editorial might demonstrate the learner's ability to develop a persuasive argument as well as oral presentation and technology literacy skills. Or a spreadsheet containing data collected at a local stream might be used to demonstrate an ability to perform simple descriptive statistics, as well as to draw and present conclusions from data. This list could be endless; the key is in defining what the goal of the e-portfolio is—we'll discuss that soon.

So, how do e-portfolios offer teachers flexibility in terms of how they are implemented?

- E-portfolios can be developed over varying periods of time (e.g., a three-week earth science unit on streams or an entire fifteen-week semester of earth science content). A longer duration format offers students the opportunity to get peer or teacher feedback, make modifications and create an improved product, and demonstrate student growth on learning outcomes. E-portfolios can also be developed by individual students or student groups. When done in groups, different group members can contribute different artifacts to meet portfolio requirements. Having group members negotiate which artifacts best fit the portfolio task can be another means for helping students to engage in deep or evaluative thinking about artifacts.

- E-portfolios can also be a combination of both student work and teacher annotations and additions to that work. For instance a *working portfolio*, or one that is used as a basis for ongoing student feedback, might include a reading/writing log, writing samples, work samples from many disciplines (e.g., a social studies project), plus teacher additions such as teacher anecdotes and observations, or teacher notes from student conferences (Miller, 1996).

- E-portfolios can provide a tangible, structured way for teachers, schools, and districts to show how they are meeting state and national standards. For instance, the page excerpt shown in Figure 10.7 describes the state and NETS standards that can be met by an exploratory class portfolio project on owls. Another example

Figure 10.7

State and National Standards Met by Portfolio Project

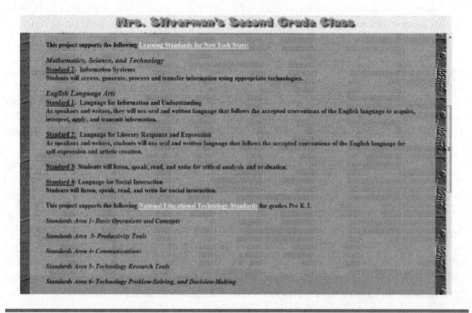

Figure 10.8

Portfolios Mapped to 21st Century Skills

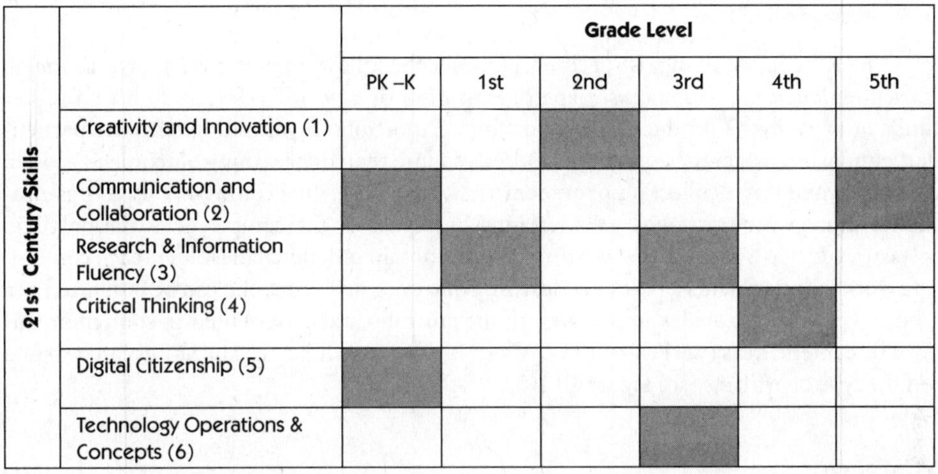

		Grade Level					
		PK –K	1st	2nd	3rd	4th	5th
21st Century Skills	Creativity and Innovation (1)			▓			
	Communication and Collaboration (2)	▓					▓
	Research & Information Fluency (3)		▓		▓		
	Critical Thinking (4)					▓	
	Digital Citizenship (5)	▓					
	Technology Operations & Concepts (6)				▓		

(see Figure 10.8) is from a presentation from a New Hampshire statewide effort that maps their portfolio activities to the 21st Century Learning Skills (Boisvert, Schneiderheinze, & Rubega, 2009).

E-portfolios offer a way to encourage meaningful learning outcomes. As previously described, e-portfolios can be used to demonstrate an endless set of learning outcomes. An additional benefit is that the task of assembling an e-portfolio can offer students a chance to reflect on their work (e.g., What did I learn from this activity? What does this product demonstrate? What would I do differently next time?). The act of reflection on one's work can contribute to modifying one's thinking based on comparisons of one's own work with that of experts and peers (Lin, Hmelo, Kinzer, & Secules, 1999). It is important to specifically include such reflective components in portfolio guidelines and to offer students chances to practice self-reflection in order for this task to be meaningful. Lastly, but certainly not insignificantly, e-portfolios can be compelling from a student's point of view as students can take pride in their assembled products and, in certain types of portfolios, may have some autonomy in their choices about what to include.

How Do I Define an E-Portfolio Task for Students?

The components of an e-portfolio task will vary depending on what your goals are for the students as they complete the e-portfolio. To help you define your e-portfolio, here are some questions you should consider (Tombari & Borich, 1999):

■ What is the purpose of the portfolio? Do you want the portfolio to show growth over time? Exemplify students' best work? Is the portfolio intended to show students that have achieved a particular set of standards?

- What learning outcomes should the portfolio demonstrate? Then for each outcome, what tasks or artifacts from your students will you require or suggest?

- What audience is intended for the portfolio (teachers only, other students, parents or other stakeholders)?

Once the initial design is specified, consider the following point: *What organizational structure should the portfolio use?* The organization of e-portfolios refers to how a reader finds or accesses the products in the portfolio. E-portfolio organization becomes particularly important when the e-portfolio addresses more than one learning outcome as is often the case when it is a collection of student work over time. One commonly used organizational strategy for portfolios is by learning outcomes or the competencies the portfolio measures. Just as a paper-based portfolio might contain individual file folders each containing work that represents a particular learning outcome, an e-portfolio can be organized as a "home" page that provides an overview of the portfolio and a list of links to content organized by content areas (see Figure 10.9). Alternatively, a portfolio's organization can be based on the type of artifacts (see Figure 10.10).

Figure 10.9

Student Portfolio Home Page Organized by Content Area

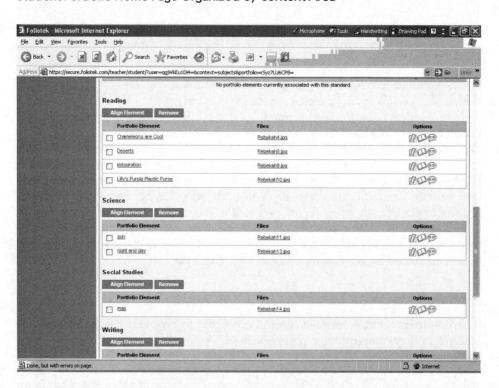

Figure 10.10

Portfolio Page Organized by Artifact Type

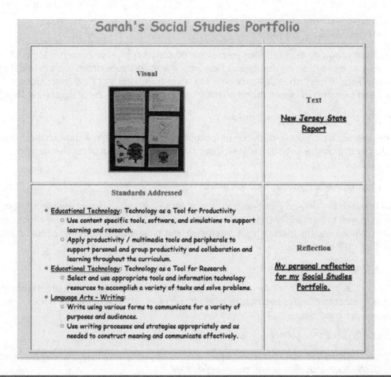

Of course using an electronic format means that there can be multiple paths to individual portfolio products—perhaps not only by learning outcome, but also by content domain or the timeframe in which the product was produced (e.g., first attempt at designing a science experiment, third attempt). Other e-portfolio organizations are possible; it is important to consider portfolio organization and either define the organization for your students or work with them to negotiate an organization that is appropriate for the portfolio's purpose.

What Sorts of Synthesizing Documentation or Reflection Will You Require from Students in the Portfolio?

An e-portfolio is intended to be more than simply a collection of digital artifacts. It must be a cohesive body of work that represents students' ability for a defined set of learning outcomes. In some cases it may be self-evident how a particular product meets a portfolio requirement, but in others, students may need to annotate or reflect on their work to explain what aspects of the product meet a learning outcome, their understanding of the strengths and weaknesses of the work, or how they might improve a similar product in the

Figure 10.11

Sample Student Portfolio Reflections

Give a brief description of the piece.

This portion of my portfolio provides an example of a final project completed in Social Studies. It contains a written report on the state of New Jersey, a Bibliography of the sources used in the report, a "Facts in Brief" sheet, a Political/Physical map constructed of New Jersey done in Claris-Works, and examples of clip art found on the Internet that relate to the State of New Jersey.

Why was this piece included in the portfolio?

The New Jersey report was included in my portfolio because I felt that it showed that I knew how to use technology as both a research and productivity tool and because it demonstrates my writing skills.

What did you learn when you created this piece?

When I created this project I learned many things. I learned how to download clip art from the Internet as well as from a CD-ROM. I learned how use search engines when doing research on the Internet. Writing was the most difficult part for me, but I was able to learn that I could complete it if I worked on it after school.

Why is this piece important to you?

This project is important to me because it was the first time that I was able to use the computer and the Internet to do a research project. Usually we have had to look only at books. I am proud of the way it turned out.

What does this piece show about you as a learner?

This project shows that I can persevere as a learner. It also shows that I know how to do research and communicate that information to other people.

How will what you learned creating this piece help you in the future?

Now that I was able to complete this research project, I will be able to use these skills when I go to intermediate school and high school. I would like have a career in technology.

Source: www.k12.hi.us/~cmin/tethree/learning/portfoliosample.htm

future. Researchers in the field of student writing report that having students annotate their own writing can increase a student's autonomy in initiating feedback and lead to improvements in student performance (Cresswell, 2000).

A sixth-grade student's annotations or reflections on the social studies portion of her portfolio can be seen in Figure 10.11. This student's teacher structured the reflections or annotations by a series of questions. Such structuring may be necessary to help students learn to reflect on portfolio products.

The portfolio page in Figure 10.12 exemplifies another form of reflection from a high school student completing this portfolio for her photography class. Students chose photos to exemplify different characteristics—this photo chosen for "color." The text from the

Figure 10.12

Photography Portfolio Justification Statement

> "This photo is meant to exemplify color. I picked a color that would really pop when standing alone, rather than something that blended everything together. . . . I chose this particular photograph for the way it exemplified almost all the different shades of orange. Although it is a photograph of something very simple, it stood out to me as something with depth. It is something we see everyday but do not seem to look at very closely. . . . The oranges seem to have a glowing effect. They are orange and the area around them seem to be glowing orange also. Because of this I chose to keep part of the background in, rather than cropping it all around. . . ."

Source: http://campus.digication.com/samallen/Work_Samples/published

figure was accompanied by a vividly detailed close-up photo of several oranges grouped together. The photo magnifies the "orangeness" of the oranges and showcases the texture of their rind. While the picture exemplifies the orange color, we learn even more about the student's thought processes that undergirded this selection because of the justification statement that the teacher required for each photo.

Another important aspect of e-portfolio design is assessment criteria. As with all the meaningful learning tasks described in this book, students should be aware of the criteria that will be used to assess their work. Thus, establishing assessment criteria for the e-portfolio should be considered *before* students begin the portfolio task. We refer readers to our discussion of creating criterion-based rubrics in this chapter's section on electronic rubrics; however, Figure 10.13 lists a few criteria that one would often consider in a rubric for electronic portfolios (Vandervelde, 2006). Applying an e-portfolio rubric will allow teachers to create a score for the portfolio; however, even if creating a numeric score is not necessary for a particular portfolio (e.g., a portfolio that is simply intended to show students' best work), providing students with criteria will guide their portfolio construction.

What Technology Do I Need to Implement E-Portfolios?

Although the fact that e-portfolios are technology-based offers many advantages (e.g., reduced physical storage requirements, flexibility of editing and updates), one may be unfamiliar with the actual software used to create e-portfolios. And that landscape of tools is changing! As one author describes it, "Systems that were once little more than digital filing cabinets have evolved into sophisticated multimedia environments that can integrate with a range of e-learning technologies" (Waters, 2009).

Developing an e-portfolio can be as simple as using HTML editors or commonly available tools like Microsoft's Front Page or Adobe Dreamweaver to develop simple Web-based portfolio sites (simple websites). However, e-portfolio specific software packages such as Digication (www.digication.com/k-12) have also been created. Such packages provide features such as the ability to accept a full range of file types and content: text, graphics, video, audio, photos, and animation (Batson, 2002), as well as secure storage and portfolio management.

Figure 10.13

Sample E-Portfolio Rubric Criteria and Performance Ranges

Criteria	Performance Ranges				
Selection of artifacts	Artifacts meet defined portfolio purpose.				Artifacts do not meet defined purpose (or artifacts are missing).
	X	X	X	X	X
Student annotations	Describe clearly reason for artifact inclusion.				Annotations are missing or do not describe reason for artifact inclusion.
	X	X	X	X	X
Student reflections	Illustrate ability to self-evaluate artifacts.				Reflections are missing or do not demonstrate ability to self-evaluate artifacts.
	X	X	X	X	X
Navigation	Portfolio is easy to navigate; finding artifacts is easy.				Site navigation is confusing or does not work.
	X	X	X	X	X
Text design (use of white space, font size, etc.)	Text layout is clear and easy to read enhances portfolio's goals.				Text layout is sloppy or misleading; detracts from portfolio purpose.
	X	X	X	X	X
Use of multimedia	Demonstrates appropriate use of multimedia that enhances how the artifacts and portfolio show student competencies.				Multimedia are distracting or do not work; detract from overall portfolio purpose.
	X	X	X	X	X
Writing mechanics	Writing is correct grammatically; clearly communicates to reader; no spelling errors.				Writing contains many grammatical errors, misspellings, or incorrect punctuation.
	X	X	X	X	X
Audience	Contains materials and is presented in manner appropriate for specified audience.				Materials, design, and/or content are inappropriate for specified audience.
	X	X	X	X	X

More recently, e-portfolio packages have also begun to integrate Web 2.0 interactive social networking features such as blogging and wikis, as well as providing seamless interfaces to online learning management systems (Waters, 2009). Readers may wish to refer to some reviews of e-portfolio systems. For instance, educator Helen Barrett (2010) has done a fairly extensive review of e-portfolio software evaluating them on functionality and cost, and a recent article from *T.H.E. Journal* (Waters, 2009) also provides a short overview of portfolio tools. Your choice of e-portfolio software will invariably depend on the resources available at your institution.

Clicker Assessment Tools

Clicker technology, AKA "student response," "audience response," or "classroom response" systems, have small wireless alphanumeric keypads that are linked to a computer (Bruff, 2009; Duncan, 2005; Hafner, 2004). Clickers are being used in elementary- through college-level classes to support assessment, and promote student engagement via interactive question and response activities.

A clicker looks a lot like a TV remote control (see Figure 10.14). They have several buttons labeled with letters or numbers. You use them with your class by distributing them to your students to allow them to respond to questions—not by raising their hands, but by selecting their answer choice through one of the clickers' buttons—and the results can appear on a screen in the front of the class.

Student responses are transmitted to a receiver connected to a computer at the front of the classroom. The computer tabulates, analyzes, and can display the results—if the machine is hooked to a projector. Results can also be posted to a website or loaded into a spreadsheet. Students can't tell from the results how their peers "voted," but

Figure 10.14

Clicker Student Remote

Source: Quizdom, www.qwizdom.com/education/q6.php

the teacher can link responses to students through the clicker serial numbers (which are associated with the answers transmitted). When using these systems, students should understand that teachers can identify their responses, but that their peers cannot.

One may wonder how these TV remote-like devices can be beneficial to learning, but those who have used them report that clickers do offer legitimate ways to support assessment (and other practical applications) in the classroom. Clicker systems are being widely adopted in university settings where class sizes are often large (Bruff, 2010); however, the use of these systems is also growing in K–12 classrooms. Here are some strategies.

- Use them as a quick preassessment at the beginning of a class or unit. Design a few items that contain distracters that represent common misconceptions to find out what students do and do not know. Because the responses are anonymous (and quick) you can get a more accurate picture of what misconceptions students have and directly address them.

- After instruction, use them to gauge whether you are getting your points across; you get immediate feedback about what misconceptions students still have.

- Have students predict the outcome of a class demonstration or experiment you are about to perform (Duncan, 2005). Create an item(s) that includes common misconceptions about the phenomenon you are investigating and ask students to predict the outcome (see Figure 10.15 for instance). You can hold a peer-to-peer discussion before and/or after to have students provide an argument for their predictions.

- To develop distracter responses that represent student misconceptions, use past student work (e.g., papers, exams, quizzes) as a resource; they are likely to represent common student misconceptions and provide you with a good discussion basis (Bruff, 2010).

- If you have easy and constant access to the clicker systems, you can use them for simple logistic tasks such as taking attendance, conducting a quick poll on student preferences ("How shall we spend our indoor recess today?"), or signing up for lunch preferences.

- Assess conceptual knowledge and other higher-order learning outcomes. Clickers can be used to respond only to "forced response" type items (e.g., true/false, multiple choice). We often think such items can only assess recall and recognition knowledge, but with some thought these items can also be used to assess conceptual understanding and other higher-order learning outcomes. For example, the item in Figure 10.15 assesses a learner's conceptual understanding of gravity and mass.

Beyond their ability to support assessment—gathering data about students' performance or knowledge—clickers are described as having the potential (when used in moderation) to be intrinsically motivating, increasing student interaction (among themselves and teachers) and actively engaging students (Crouch & Mazur, 2001; Roschelle, Penuel, & Abrahamson, 2004). Research has shown that engaging students actively in learning can increase retention and performance on various measures. The following clicker strategies can facilitate active learning. We note that most of these strategies are only effective when used in combination with a clicker question that involves more than simply recall and recognition.

Figure 10.15

Sample "Prediction" Question

We will drop feather and a marble from the exact same height and at the exact same time. Which one will hit the floor first?

a. the marble

b. the feather

c. at the same time

- *Using clickers can "even the playing field" allowing (and expecting) all students to respond to the posed question.* Systems enable teachers to see a count of responses so they can encourage all students to respond. This allows those learners that need more time to respond—and the reflection needed to generate the answer—to have that time and thus participate in the answer-giving activity.

- *I'm not the only one who got it wrong.* Students who don't normally actively participate may be reticent for fear of getting a wrong answer. Well, that student may or may not answer a posed question correctly, but it is unlikely that he or she is the only one who didn't get it right. By displaying the class distribution of responses such learners see they are not alone and teachers can reinforce this with their comments. This could eventually lead to a more confident student.

- *Use clickers to provide a learner-centered, active component in a class with a large number of students.* Technology can be used in effective and ineffective ways. In Chapter 1 we argued that we should take advantage of what each component of the learning system (e.g., human learners, teachers versus technology) does best. Using technology in large classroom settings often has the potential to be effective because the technology enables a large number of students to all participate in a complex or meaningful learning task in the same way.

  In the case of clickers, it allows all students to respond *and* the teacher to keep track of responses and trends. Even in a classroom with many students, this activity enables teachers to have students discuss or defend their choices. Teachers don't have to be involved in each of these paired or small-group discussions; the discussions don't have to be very long—in fact you will probably maintain more engagement and energy if you make them stop before they are actually finished; and teachers can still quickly debrief with a sampling of students to find out what they discussed. Better yet, the teacher can design a follow-up clicker question that asks them to choose which justification they used for their answer. So the follow-up question to the one in Figure 10.15 might be as shown in Figure 10.16. We don't argue that such a technology is the *only* way to actively engage a large number of students, but they do facilitate such engagement.

Figure 10.16

Question That Requires Students to Explain Reasoning

Which justification did you use for your response about the marble and the feather?

a. the marble weighs more so it would fall faster

b. gravity works the same way regardless of weight

c. neither

Clicker System "How-Tos" and Technologies

There are numerous clicker systems available and as with most technologies, the cost is dropping (making them increasingly feasible for K–12 use) and the features are growing. Although configurations will vary by system, a typical one is shown in Figure 10.17 and the elements are described in the bullet list.

> To locate potential vendors, type "clicker" or "classroom response system", or "audience response system" into your favorite Internet search engine.

To use a clicker system, the teacher projects the question to the class. Teachers can compose questions using their preferred word processing or presentation software. Students then select their answers using their clickers. The response system software includes a status screen that indicates when each registered clicker's response has been recorded (see Figure 10.18). Students are aware of their registration number. When their number shows up on the screen they know that their response has been recorded.

When the responses are collected, the teachers can see the results using the clicker system software and display them if they wish—generally in the form of a bar chart showing percentages of the class that responded with each possible answer.

Figure 10.17

Hardware Components as Described by Qwizdom Student Response Systems

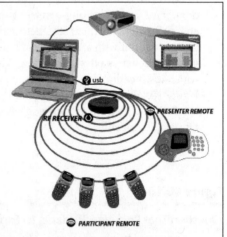

• A computer to run the clicker data collection software preferably running a spreadsheet and presentation software packages. One does not need a particularly powerful PC to run the software and the software is generally free when other clicker system components are purchased.

• An LCD projector to display the clicker question, and the class's response results. Two projectors can be useful as one can be used to continue to display the question while the other provides an updated read out of student responses.

• Clicker remotes for students to respond to questions. Each clicker has a unique ID or registration number associated with it. Students look for their ID number on the response display to ensure that their response has been received and recorded by the system. Clickers range in price from $6 to $60 each, depending on the system and the features incorporated (Gilbert, 2005). Discounts may be available when purchasing large numbers of clickers or when purchased in association with specific textbooks.

• A receiver in the classroom to receive students' response transmissions. The receiver is part of the clicker packages available from vendors. Depending on the technology your system uses, you will need about one receiver for every 25–40 students; otherwise, students may experience a "jam" where their responses are not initially detected.

Source: www.qwizdom.com

Figure 10.18

Clicker Status Screen Showing Responding Clicker IDs

Question 3	Time: 09:43			
000		002		004
005	006	007		
010		012	013	014
	016	017		019
020	021		023	024

Clicker systems are becoming cheaper as manufacturers replace infrared technology with radio frequency. They are also easier for students to use as they don't have to aim the remote at anything in particular. Beyond the basic functionality described, new features are being incorporated into clicker systems. Here are a few you may wish to consider or seek out.

- *Two-way receivers.* Systems have traditionally included receivers that can only "receive" input from the students. With two-way receivers, students' clickers receive a transmission from the receiver indicating that their response has been received and recorded.

- *Confidence levels.* Some systems are now incorporating a confidence level feature where students not only indicate their response, but also how confident they are that their response is correct. Such data can show teachers if students are primarily guessing the correct answer. Of course constructing high-quality questions can help alleviate this from consistently occurring.

- *Seamless interfaces between presentation and clicker software.* Some manufacturers are creating built-in interfaces between their clicker software and commonly used presentation packages such as PowerPoint. This allows teachers to easily create and display questions in PowerPoint and then associate the created questions with the results in the clicker software.

Clicker Closing Comments

Clickers are a relatively new phenomenon and are, in general, being positively received by teachers (see Duncan, 2005). Additionally, there is a growing body of research conducted mostly in higher education settings that indicates that they may be effective when combined with higher order questions, discussion and feedback (Penuel, Boscardin, Masyn, & Crawford, 2007). Good sense and prior experience indicates, however, that effective use of clickers—particularly if one hopes clickers to have the "engaging" effect on students that we discussed—requires that teachers set the stage for their use, and use them in moderation.

Students must understand that, in general, you are *not* "grading" their responses bur rather using their responses to find out what they do or don't understand so that you can modify your instruction to be most beneficial. For younger students, teachers might present the use of clickers as a game—something fun to do.

Further, clickers rely on the use of well-written questions. We've argued that some of the most effective uses of clickers are in diagnosing student learning and in the process creating an activity around which teachers can build student-to-student interaction and discussion. Such applications require that clicker questions engage students in more than simply recall and recognition. After all, how much discussion can you really have about the definition of an isosceles triangle? Further, writing forced response questions that assess more than recall and recognition can be hard work. So, teachers should be prepared to put a bit of preparation into clicker lessons in order to reap the potential benefits discussed.

Assessing Learning with Technology-Based Tests, Surveys, and Assessment Items

No chapter on assessment would be complete without addressing the increased focus schools have had on testing during the last decade or so. The No Child Left Behind Act has been a major force behind this increase, and some research shows that it has—among other impacts—increased the time students spend taking tests (Jennings & Renter, 2006) and, by extension, the time teachers are preparing students to take tests. Whether we agree with it, it appears this increased focus on testing as a means of achieving "accountability" in education may be with us for the duration. Technology definitely has a role in this aspect of assessment.

The types of technology tools that can be used to support assessment are varied in many ways. A few of these characteristics are: who they are intended for (e.g., students or teachers), types of outcomes they assess, and the amount of interactivity they provide. Table 10.1 provides one potential organizing framework for technology-based or assisted assessments based on the degree of student interactivity the tool provides. The most interactive tools are shown at the top.

At the lower end of interactivity we find computerized tests or surveys that are completed by students directly on a computer. With computer-scored tests, students record their responses on a "bubble" or scan sheet that can be scanned and scored by a computer. This type of testing has been used to simplify the testing process for teachers and administrators, and to enable a faster turn around on scoring students' work. Unlike many of the other technology applications we address in this book, a student's experience of a computer-based test or quiz is not terribly engaging or motivating. Other than selecting a response to the posed item, students are passive recipients of what is being shown on the computer screen. Clearly this use of technology does not embody the student-centered nature that the technology applications throughout this book promote.

Test item repositories have become more popular with the increased focus on standardized tests. Sites such as the one listed provide access to "released" test items—that is, items that have been used in the past on state and federal tests but are no longer in the active item pools. Teachers who tend to be spending a lot more time on preparing students to take standardized tests can refer to these sites for finding practice items. Other tools provide more possibilities for both interactivity and student feedback. We address several of these technologies in the following sections.

Table 10.1 Types of Online Assessment Resources

Degree of Student Interactivity	Type	Description	Audience	Sample Site(s)/Tools
Most ↑	Complete online learning environments	Learning environments that include embedded assessments	Students	Calipers http://calipers.sri.com/assessments.html Virtual Science Club www.discoverchampions.com/main/do/Virtual_Club_Highlights
	CATs	Computerized adaptive testing	Students	Assessment Systems Corporation www.assess.com
	Internet-based tests, quizzes, games	Student interactions included but types of problems can be low level (e.g., recall)	Students	MyPyramid Blast Off Game http://teamnutrition.usda.gov/Resources/game/BlastOff_Game.html Quiz Hub http://quizhub.com/quiz/quizhub.cfm ASSISTment System** www.assistments.org
	Online survey builders*	Build and deliver surveys online for assessing attitudes, or gathering self-report data	T, Ad, Students	SurveyMonkey www.surveymonkey.com Zoomerang www.zoomerang.com
	Online test builders*	Create customized tests for academic outcomes from often validated item banks. Deliver and score tests online.	T, Ad	Galileo K–12 www.ati-online.com/GalileoK12/K12Features Online. html Assistment System** www.assistments.org
	Test item repositories	Provides online access to released state test items and samples from standardized tests	T, Ad	EDinformatics www.edinformatics.com/testing/
↓ Least	Computer-scored tests	Bubble sheets	Students	N/A—provides easy, automated scoring

*Approximately same level of student interactivity.

**Includes both test building function as well as ability to do individual administration with students.

T = Teachers; Ad = Administrators

Online Environments with Embedded Assessments

This category of online assessment tool—from our perspective—has the possibility for the most student interactivity. These tools are not simply assessment tools, but complete learning environments that include authentic assessment activities. So, as we described earlier in this chapter, the assessment is really embedded in the learning activities rather than something separate.

One such example of an environment comes from the Calipers project. Calipers are a set of simulations-based assessments developed for areas in middle and high school science: forces and motion (physical science) and populations and ecosystems (life science) (SRI International, 2007). Students work with the online simulations to "investigate" a phenomenon that is set up in a scenario and then accomplish assessments that are embedded in the investigation tasks. Results are saved to create reports for both teachers and learners.

The screenshot shown in Figure 10.19 is from the WestEd SimScientists program (http://simscientists.org). These excerpts are from a lake simulation scenario designed to assess middle school life sciences learning outcomes (Quellmalz, Timms, & Buckley, in press). Students are told that a pristine mountain lake is slated for development. Students are to learn about the lake ecosystem to provide information for a new visitor center. Assessment tasks engage students in observing animations of the lake organisms to determine their

Figure 10.19

Calipers Lake Simulation Screens

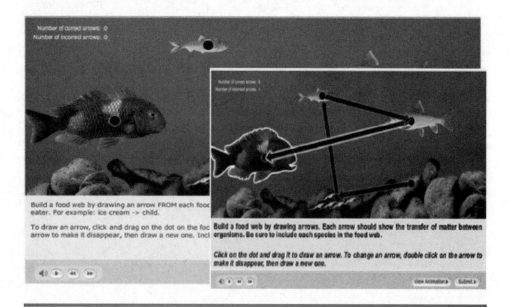

Source: http://calipers.sri.com/assessments.html

roles (e.g., producer, consumer) and to represent their interactions, by drawing a food web. Then students use simulations to conduct investigations about how changes in the numbers of organisms might affect the size of their populations. One version of the assessments is designed to be embedded in a unit and provides feedback and coaching for formative uses. The summative end-of-unit benchmark assessment provides no feedback. The assessments have been pilot tested in three states with 55 teachers, 28 districts, and 5,500 students. Ongoing analyses indicate the formative assessments are engaging and of value to teachers to adjust their instruction (Quellmalz et al., in press).

DIAGNOSER is another tool that falls into this category. Its creators describe it as an Internet tool designed for both instruction as well as delivering "formative assessment and feedback." DIAGNOSER is designed for high school physics instruction (Thissen-Roe, Hunt, & Minstrell, 2004). As the name of the tool communicates, there is a diagnostic element to this tool—so it is doing much more than simply presenting static instruction and assessment items. As students complete online lessons, they also answer questions on content. Questions are mostly multiple choice but often require higher-order thinking, which requires the students to predict what will happen in the new situation (see Figure 10.20).

Figure 10.20

DIAGNOSER Question Example

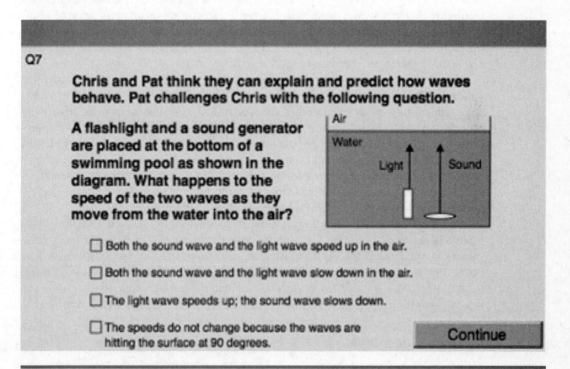

Source: Thissen-Roe, Hunt, & Minstrell, 2004

Some questions may also require entering a number or a text-based explanation. The uniqueness and intelligence in terms of design of the system comes with a follow-up question that students must answer; this question requires that students choose a response to explain their reasoning for their response to the first question. If the student provides an explanation that is not in alignment with the answer to the first question, she receives a message from the system informing her of the inconsistency along with an explanation. This type of questioning strategy can diagnose when a student has an underlying misconception about the physics content—such as confusing velocity with acceleration.

The fundamental downside to these types of tools is that they are costly to develop and require programming expertise. Both of the examples shown were developed via external funding. Even so, we felt it important to include these types of tools as high quality environments containing high-quality assessments and further note that such projects are almost always in need of schools, teachers, and classrooms to partner with them and use the materials they have created.

CATs

Computerized adaptive testing (CAT) is a form of computer-based testing that adapts what items are presented to learners based on their past responses; thus it attempts to adapt to the learner's ability level (Clark, 2004). CAT relies on educators creating a pool of potential items of varying difficulty level; difficulty levels could be based on the types of thinking required to correctly answer the item (e.g., recall or recognition versus application or analysis), or the degree of transfer required (see Wainer & Dornas, 2000). Learners are presented with differing items based on their prior answers or on an ability level that is determined before they begin to use the test.

The potential to adapt the sequence of items answers a difficulty long expressed about standardized tests—that they test those who are of "average" ability level quite well but do not work well for learners at either end of the spectrum. A CAT that adapts can answer this concern and also increase learner engagement and persistence, as the level of items is appropriate for the learner to be challenged but not overly frustrated. Software that creates adaptive tests is relatively sophisticated (and consequently expensive) because of the need to support item banks and the underlying item response theories. However the Assessment Systems Corporation (http://assess.com/xcart/product.php?productid=273&cat=1&page=1#Downloads) does offer a free 30-day trial of their software as well as a comparison of CAT tools.

Although they are called tests, such software does not have to be used for testing in the traditional sense (e.g., take a test, record the grade that impacts your overall school performance). Districts such as the Meridian district in Idaho report that they are using them as diagnostic tools to help assess learner skills and adapt instruction to better meet learner needs (Clark, 2004). We argue that any use of an assessment process—computerized or not—that is used to modify instruction to improve learner performance is a good use of assessment!

Internet-Based Tests

Many of the online tests and quizzes that are readily available on the Internet are more like games that assess simple knowledge (e.g., recall). The U.S. Department of Agriculture's site,

Figure 10.21

"Blast Off" Game Screen is an Example of Internet-Based Game

MyPyramid Blast Off game is an example of such a tool. In this game designed to teach younger kids about nutrition and exercise, players "drag" food and exercise choices into their "rocket ship" to fuel their journey (see Figure 10.21). They also have the option of displaying facts about their food and activity choices as they play.

Although these types of Internet-ready games and simple assessments do not generally assess higher-order thinking skills, they can have the advantage of being—even if briefly—motivating for students. Such tools could be used to help introduce students to a new topic, used as collaborative tools where more than one student must negotiate a response or strategy, or used in conjunction with classroom discussion on why students chose they way they did. Used in these types of ways, these tools that assess introductory level knowledge may be useful for teachers.

Other online testing tools are more sophisticated both in terms of the types of knowledge they assess and in the ways they provide feedback and, in some cases, scaffolding to learners. The "ASSISTments" site (www.assistments.org) is a good example of this type of tool. A teacher can create his or her own login on ASSISTments and then create item sets for one's students that are available to them online. You also have access to items—focusing predominantly on math and science—that have been created by others. These features are

Figure 10.22

"ASSISTments" Problems and Student Scaffolds

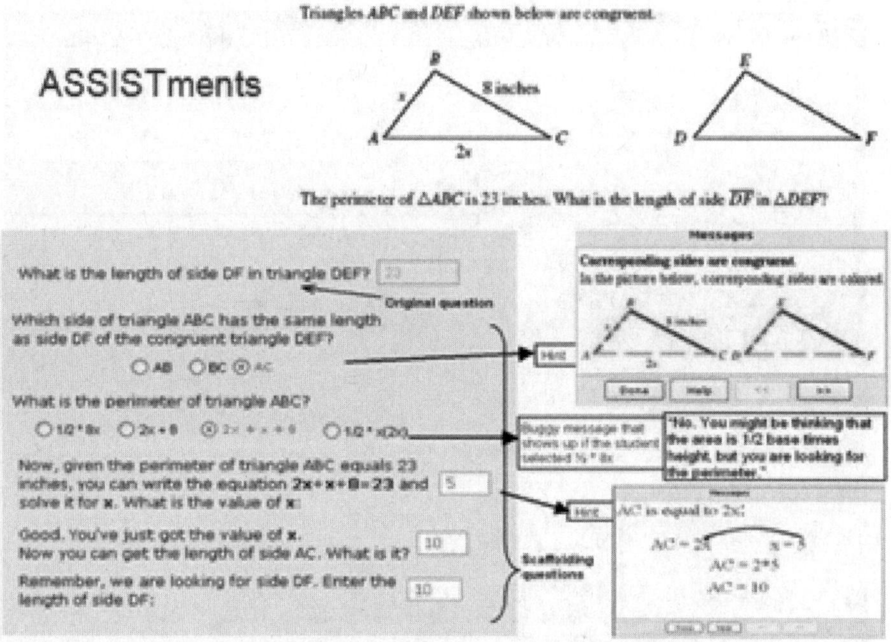

Razzaq, Feng, & Nuzzo-Jones (2005). Reprinted with permission. http://nth.wpi.edu/pubs_and_grants/papers/2005/RAZZAQ-0555.pdf

not that unique, but what ASSISTments also supports is building coaching, or tutoring to go along with the items that one creates. These prompts (or "assistments") that are available to students as they work on their assessment items are best designed to both unpack the problem into its component parts, and also recognize consistent misconceptions that students might bring to such problems.

Figure 10.22 shows the originally stated problem on triangles, and then the guiding prompts (lower portion of figure) designed to help students solve the problem. Teacher-users—with a fully functioning login—can view templates to help them to create these learner scaffolds.

Online Test and Survey Builders

Less sophisticated than the adaptive CATS, online testing, and surveying tools have also found a home on the Internet. Any Internet search for "online test" or "online survey" will literally produce hundreds if not thousands of hits. Although these tools vary significantly both in features and in price (from free to several thousand dollars), one major distinction among tools is those that are stand-alone test or survey tools versus tools that are embedded within an overall online course management system (e.g., Blackboard).

Online instrument development tools allow users to easily create an online test or survey that is hosted on the Internet. Respondents complete tests or surveys at a computer and their responses are stored by the tool provider. Then, test givers can download the results for their own records, or for providing feedback and/or scores to the respondents. Features of these systems vary; however, the following is a set of features that are generally available in these tools.

- Support of a variety of formats of forced response items (see Figure 10.23)

- Ability to implement "logic" or branching in the instrument based on responses to prior items

- Inclusion of graphics, and in some applications, animation within test or survey items

- Ability to identify an instrument URL that can be included in other course materials, or in an e-mail message

- Tracking of respondents (who has completed this test or quiz and who has not?) in some packages

Figure 10.23

SurveyMonkey Screen Showing Question Type Supported

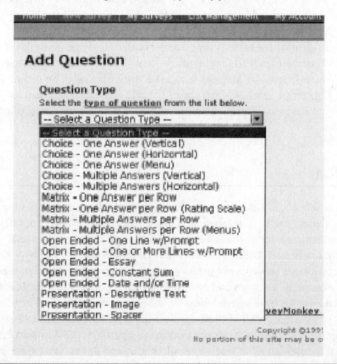

Users may also wish to consider price-based features such as the number of questions, responses, and/or participants that are allowed (Leland, 2008). Fee-based tools are more likely to allow unlimited instruments, customizing options, and data analysis tools that filter results to help users find patterns in the data. Other features include sharing of results, downloadable files for export to spreadsheets, randomizing the order of answer choices to reduce bias, and requiring responses to questions the instrument creator specifies.

We normally assume that such item types can only assess lower level learning outcomes such as recall and recognition. While this is often how such items are *used*, in the spirit of maintaining our focus on assessing meaningful learning, we want to remind readers that a well-structured forced response item paired with well-crafted response choices can indeed assess complex learning outcomes such as knowledge of concepts, analysis, and application. For instance, an item such as the one shown in Figure 10.15 could easily be implemented in these online packages.

Online testing tools are prevalent and we felt we should include them in this chapter. We don't see their main value in being able to generate lots of extra testing of students— although one can use them in that way—but rather that they can be used for collecting formative feedback on student progress. Free tools such as SurveyMonkey (SurveyMonkey .com, Portland, Oregon) allow teachers to easily gather data on student progress and use it for monitoring and adapting instruction as indicated by the results. Such tools can also make it possible for teachers to gather data from parents that may impact student activities. For instance, a quick survey could be constructed to determine how parents feel about the possibility of a planned field trip, or parents' observations of how much time students spend doing homework each evening.

The downside of these tools is that teachers can quickly generate *poorly* constructed items; the tools make it easy to create online items but nothing can change the fact that writing good assessment (or survey) items is a difficult task. The online nature of the tool should not tempt teachers into short changing good item creation practices that include creating items in alignment with desired learning outcomes, pilot testing, and revising items.

Conclusion

Assessment in schools is a necessity. Assessing students' learning takes time and in some cases creates anxiety for both teachers and students. Lately, certain types of assessment— generally standardized tests—have been mandated by state and national governments. Consequently, teachers and administrators may be scrambling to "teach to the test" for fear of the repercussions of students not performing up to the standards. All of these factors culminate in "assessment" getting a bad rap these days in schools. But, it is necessary!

In this chapter, we have offered ideas for assessing what students know using different applications of technology. All of these applications have the potential to assess meaningful learning (e.g., more than recall and recognition) and perhaps, most important, to provide a window into discovering what learners really know, and at the same time providing rich information that can be organized into meaningful feedback that can improve learners' performance. We argue that such assessment applications help us know more about what students know and whenever we can attain that knowledge, we can, in turn help students to learn more and better.

NET Standards potentially engaged by technology-based assessments described in this chapter:

3. **Research and Information Fluency**
    a. Plan strategies to guide inquiry
    b. Locate, organize, analyze, evaluate, synthesize, and ethically use information from a variety of sources and media
    c. Evaluate and select information sources and digital tools based on the appropriateness to specific tasks
    d. Process data and report results

4. **Critical Thinking, Problem Solving, and Decision Making**
    b. Plan and manage activities to develop a solution or complete a project
    c. Collect and analyze data to identify solutions and/or make informed decisions
    d. Use multiple processes and diverse perspectives to explore alternative solutions

21st Century Skills potentially engaged by technology-based assessments described in this chapter:

Reason Effectively

- Use various types of reasoning (inductive, deductive, etc.) as appropriate to the situation

Use Systems Thinking

- Analyze how parts of a whole interact with each other to produce overall outcomes in complex systems

Make Judgments and Decisions

- Effectively analyze and evaluate evidence, arguments, claims and beliefs
- Analyze and evaluate major alternative points of view
- Synthesize and make connections between information and arguments
- Interpret information and draw conclusions based on the best analysis
- Reflect critically on learning experiences and processes

Solve Problems

- Solve different kinds of unfamiliar problems in both conventional and innovative ways
- Identify and ask significant questions that clarify various points of view and lead to better solutions

Access and Evaluate Information

- Access information efficiently (time) and effectively (sources)
- Evaluate information critically and competently

Things to Think About

We suggest that you can use the following questions to reflect on the ideas that we presented in this chapter.

1. Is assessment really a separate activity from learning? What circumstances may impact whether it is or isn't?

2. How do you use assessment activities as a way to generate feedback that can improve learner performance? After reading this chapter, are there ways you can see how technology can contribute to this?

3. How can you use technology to make assessment activities less threatening to learners, or maybe even a positive experience?

4. What processes do you use to generate your assessment items and activities? Are there other teachers you can collaborate with to (a) pilot test your assessments; (b) help develop forced response items that assess higher-level thinking; or (c) share the development of technology-based assessments?

5. Does the use of technology-based assessments impact validity and reliability? Does technology help address these? Does it make any difference at all?

References

Batson, T. (2002). The electronic portfolio boom: What's it all about? *Syllabus: Technology for Higher Education*. Retrieved May 17, 2004 from www.syllabus.com/article.asp?id=6984

Barrett, H. (2010). *My online portfolio adventure*. Retrieved from http://electronicportfolios.org/myportfolio/versions.html

Boisvert, D., Schneiderheinze, T., & Rubega, M. (2009). Digital Portfolios New Hampshire Statewide Collaboration Grades K–12. Retrieved from https://collab.sakaizone.org/access/content/group/f736f783-f0e9-43eb-9f58-6e1a9e48f396/Presentations/sakaiboston093-090710095639-phpapp02.ppt

Bruff, D. (2010). Classroom response system bibliography. Retrieved http://cft.vanderbilt.edu/docs/classroom-response-system-clickers-bibliography/

Bruff, D. (2009). *Teaching with classroom response systems: Creating active learning environments*. San Francisco: Jossey-Bass.

Clark, L. (2004). Computerized adaptive testing: Effective measurement for all students. *T.H.E. Journal, 31*(10),14, 18, 20.

Cresswell, A. (2000). Self-monitoring in student writing: developing learner responsibility. *ELT Journal 54*(3), 235–244. Retrieved 3 August 2006 from http://eltj.oupjournals.org/cgi/content/abstract/54/3/235

Crouch, C. H., & Mazur, E. (2001). Peer instruction: Ten years of experience and results. *American Journal of Physics, 69*(9), 970–977.

Dornisch, M., & Sabatini McLoughlin, A. (2006). Limitations of web-based rubric resources: Addressing the challenges. *Practical Assessment, Research and Evaluation, 11*(3). Retrieved 5 August 2006 from http://pareonline.net/pdf/v11n3.pdf

Duncan, D. (2005). *Clickers in the classroom*. San Francisco: Pearson.

Gagne, R. M., Bridges, L. J., & Wagne, W. W. 1998. *Principles of instructional design*. Orlando, FL: Holt, Rinehart and Winston, Inc.

Hafner, K. (2004). In class, the audience weighs in. Retrieved from www4.uwm.edu/ltc/srs/faculty/docs/cnetarticle.pdf

Jennings, J., & Renter, D. (2006). Ten big effects of the No Child Left Behind Act on public schools. *The Phi Delta Kappan*, 88(2), 110–113.

KITE (2001a). Case 8119-1. Kite Case Library. Retrieved 22 August 2006 from http://kite.missouri.edu

Leland, E. (2008). A few good online survey tools. Retrieved from www.idealware.org/articles/fgt_online_surveys.php

Lin, X., Hmelo, C., Kinzer, C. K., & Secules, T. J. (1999). Designing technology to support reflection. *Educational Technology Research and Development, 47*(3), 43–62.

Lorenzo, G., & Ittelson, J. (2005). Demonstrating and assessing student learning with e-portfolios. Retrieved from http://net.educause.edu/ir/library/pdf/ELI3003.pdf

Miller, W. (1995). *Reading and writing remediation kit.* San Francisco: Jossey-Bass.

Paulson, L. F., Paulson P. R., & Meyer, C. (1991). What makes a portfolio a portfolio? *Educational Leadership, 48*(5), 60–63.

Penuel, W. R., Boscardin, C. K., Masyn, K., & Crawford, V. M. (2007). Teaching with student response systems in elementary and secondary education settings: A survey study. *Educational Technology, Research and Development*, 55(4).

Quellmalz, E. S., Timms, M. J., & Buckley, B. C. (in press). 21st century dynamic assessment. In J. Clarke-Midura, D. Robinson, M. Mayrath (Eds.), *Technology-based assessments for 21st Century Skills: Theoretical and practical implications from modern research.*

Razzaq, L., Feng, M., Nuzzo-Jones, G., Heffernan, N. T., Koedinger, K. R., Junker, B., Ritter, S., Knight, A., Aniszczyk, C., Choksey, S., Livak, T., Mercado, E., Turner, T. E., Upalekar. R, Walonoski, J. A., Macasek. M. A., & Rasmussen, K. P. (2005). The Assistment project: Blending assessment and assisting. In C. K. Looi, G. McCalla, B. Bredeweg, & J. Breuker (Eds.), *Proceedings of the 12th Artificial Intelligence in Education* (pp. 555–562). Amsterdam: ISO Press. Retrieved from http://nth.wpi.edu/pubs_and_grants/papers/2005/RAZZAQ-0555.pdf

Roschelle, J., Penuel, W., & Abrahamson, L. (2004). The networked classroom. *Educational Leadership, 61*(5), 50–54.

SRI International (2007). Calipers: Simulation-based assessments. Retrieved from http://calipers.sri.com/assessments.html

Thissen-Roe, A., Hunt, E., & Minstrell, J. (2004). The DIAGNOSER project: Combining assessment and learning. *Behavior Research Methods, Instruments, & Computers, 36*(2), 234–240.

Tombari, M., & Borich, G. (1999). *Authentic assessment in the classroom.* Upper Saddle River, NJ: Merrill.

Vandervelde, J. (2006).Rubric for electronic portfolio. Retrieved 25 August 2006 from www.uwstout.edu/soe/profdev/eportfoliorubric.html

Wainer, H., & Dornas, N. (2000). *Computerized Adaptive Testing: A primer.* Mahwah, NJ: Lawrence Erlbaum Associates.

Waters, J. (2009). E-portfolios come of age. *T.H.E. Journal.* Retrieved from http://thejournal.com/Articles/2009/11/09/ELearning.aspx?sc_lang=en&Page=1

Epilogue

Moving into the Future

The purpose of this book has been to demonstrate ways that technology can be used to engage and support meaningful learning. In each of the chapters, we briefly described how different environments or applications can be used to engage different types of learning outcomes. In many of those examples, we described specific software applications. If you do not have access to a particular item, don't despair! There are likely to be other, similar applications that can be used, and the proliferation of Web-based tools certainly increases availability. We have offered examples of how to use technologies to engage meaningful learning. Our purpose was not to show you *how* to use these technologies (as in step-by-step). That is impossible, as we do not know what kinds of hardware, software, students, teachers, administrators, and support materials you may or may not have in your school. Our goal is that you generalize the ideas that we present to your teaching and learning situations, rather than replicate the activity.

21st Century Teachers

We have focused throughout this book on meaningful learning and the knowledge, skills, and standards related to the students you are fostering. Each chapter listed potential NETS and 21st Century Skills that students might meet from the various learning activities described. You may be interested in ISTE's NETS for Teachers (http://iste.org) as well, especially if those standards are used as an evaluation tool for your teaching performance.

Perhaps one of the most exciting changes brought about by the emergence of technological innovations such as social networking and Web 2.0 applications is the ability for teachers to connect with and learn from other teachers. Teaching has historically been an isolated profession, with contained classrooms and little collaboration beyond that which might occur within one's school, for those fortunate enough to have like-minded colleagues. The explosion of excellent teachers' blogs, social networking sites, Twitter accounts, and wikis enables a nearly instantaneous exchange of ideas, as teachers can, for example, post a Twitter query and receive answers not just from the teacher across the hall, but from practitioners around the world. Subscribing to thoughtful blogs (e.g., http://coolcatteacher .blogspot.com/, http://weblogg-ed.com/, www.speedofcreativity.org/, http://davidwarlick .com/2cents/, http://nashworld.edublogs.org/, www.infosearcher.com/) or joining online communities (e.g., http://tappedin.org) can provide a window into what others are doing and give you new ideas. Commenting on blog postings and engaging in online community activities can result in meaningful dialogue, opening the door to new professional connections and growth.

In closing, we offer some final Things to Think About based on an article published two decades ago (D'Ignazio, 1992). It highlights the axiom, accredited to Jean-Baptiste Alphonse Karr and loosely translated, that "the more things change, the more they stay the same." The following thoughts and questions will, we hope, encourage you in critically thinking about whatever technologies are being touted as the "latest, greatest" and how you can truly maximize their potential to be powerful "learning-with" rather than merely "learning-from" tools.

Important New "Common Sense" Criteria You Might Want to Think About

Theory   Much of the technology currently being introduced into today's classrooms will be used to reinforce outmoded, ineffective methods for teaching and learning.

School-district technology planning committees should direct the acquisition and implementation of technologies for one overriding purpose: To support teachers in their efforts to adopt new teaching practices and new methods for managing their classrooms.

In a given classroom:

1. Are the teacher and students engaged, enthusiastic, inspired, or excited?

2. Are students constructing their own knowledge (authoring, piloting, navigating, retrieving, organizing) or simply consuming knowledge that was created by others?

3. Does the classroom working environment for teachers and students resemble a real-world workplace of the future?

Does technology:

4. Help the teacher and her students to do their lessons better, easier, or more quickly?

5. Encourage students to responsibly manage their learning?

6. Encourage the teacher to share teaching responsibilities with his or her students?

7. Encourage students and teachers to collaborate to construct knowledge, share knowledge, nurture each other's learning, solve problems and cope with unforeseen events and situations that arise?

8. Foster increased student manipulation of real-world materials or separate the students from these materials?

9. Increase constructive communication and cooperation among students? Among the students and the teacher?

10. Stimulate individual and group thinking, reflecting, weighing, testing, and experimentation with new ideas and unfamiliar concepts and information?

11. Offer multiple windows, doors, and pathways for learning based on students/individual cognitive style and strengths?

12. Help students and teachers adapt to constant change and offer them healthy change-management strategies?

13. Help teachers and students create a daily classroom culture that respects and rewards people for being decent, polite, and considerate toward each other?

14. Help teachers and students create a daily classroom culture that respects and rewards people for working together; a classroom where the excitement of exploration, mastery and communicating new knowledge is shared by all and makes each lesson a thrilling and moving experience?

15. Help improve a student's self-esteem? Does it help improve a teacher's self-esteem?

16. Help teachers and students experience their humanity in deeper and richer ways, or does it diminish, stifle, or mute their humanity?

17. Inspire teachers and students? Does it unleash their imaginations? Does it enrich teachers' and students' moral, ethical, and spiritual lives and spiritual nature?

No technology—present or future—can meet all of the criteria outlined above, at any given moment. However, it is important for us to establish these criteria and construct a practical yardstick at the classroom level to measure what kind of technology we can afford, what kind we want, what kind we need, and how best to implement it.

Reference

D'Ignazio, F. (1992, Sept.) "Are You Getting Your Money's Worth?" *Computing Teacher.*

Rubrics for Assessing Characteristics of Meaningful Learning

Assessing Active Learning, where learners explore and manipulate the components and parameters of technology-based environments and observe the results of their activities. If your learning activity or environment includes active learning, to what extent does the environment promote manipulation of real-world objects and observations based on these activities?

Learner Interaction with Real-World Objects

Little of the learner's time is spent engaged with tools and objects found outside school.	Learners are often engaged in activities involving tools and objects found outside school.

Observation and Reflection

Students rarely think about or record the results of actions taken during activities.	Students often stop and think about the activities in which they are engaged.	Students share frequent observations about their activity with peers and interested adults.

Learner Interactions

Students manipulated none of the variables or controls in environment.	Students manipulated some variables and controls in environment.	Students manipulated all or nearly all variables/controls in environment.

Tool Use

Students used no cognitive tools.	Students used some cognitive tools to support explorations/manipulations.	Students used nearly all cognitive tools effectively.

Assessing Constructive Learning, where learners articulate what they know and have learned and reflect on its meaning and importance in larger social and intellectual contexts. If your learning activity or environment requires constructive learning, to what extent does the environment cause learners to perceive puzzling dissonance and form mental models to explain incongruity?

Dissonance/Puzzling

Students engage in learning activities disparity because activities are required, rather than an intrinsic interest.	Learners frequently seem to be operating based on a sincere curiosity about the topic of study.	Learners are consistently striving to resolve between observed and what is known, operating on a sincere desire to know.

Constructing Mental Models and Making Meaning

Learners rarely create their own understandings of how things work.	Learners are often expected to make sense of new experiences and develop theories.	Learners routinely wrestle with new experiences, becoming experts at identifying and solving problems.

Assessing Intentional Learning, where learners determine their own goals and regulate and manage their activities. If your learning activity or environment requires intentional learning, to what extent does the environment cause learners to pursue important, well-articulated goals to which they are intrinsically committed? To what extent can learners explain their activity in terms of how the activities relate to the attainment of their goals?

Goal Directedness

Learners are often pursuing activities that have little to do with the attainment of specified goals.	Learners are generally engaged in activities that contribute to the attainment of specified goals.

Setting Own Goals

Learning goals are provided by educators.	Learners are sometimes involved in the establishment of learning goals.	Learners are routinely responsible for developing and expressing learning goals.

Regulating Own Learning

Learners' progress is monitored by others.	Learners are involved as partners in monitoring and reporting progress toward goals.	Learners are responsible for monitoring and reporting progress toward goals.

Learning How to Learn

Little emphasis is placed on metacognition. There are few opportunities to discuss the learning process with peers or educators.	The culture of the learning environment promotes frequent discussion of the processes and strategies (both successful and unsuccessful) involved in learning.

Articulation of Goals as Focus of Activity

Learners don't see the relationship between the activities in which they are engaged and specified learning goals.	Learners describe the activities in which they are engaged in terms that relate directly to the specified learning goals.

Technology Use in Support of Learning Goals

The use of technology seems unrelated to the specified learning goals.	The use of technology contributes to the attainment of specified learning goals.	The use of technology makes a powerful contribution to the attainment of specified learning goals.

Assessing Authentic Learning, where learners examine and attempt to solve complex, ill-structured, and real-world problems. If your learning activity or environment includes authentic problem solving, to what extent does the environment present learners with problems that are naturally complex and embedded in a real-world context? To what extent do the problems you present cause higher-order thinking?

Complexity

The tasks learners face have been designed for schools (i.e., separated into "subjects" and developed to simplify learning.)	The tasks learners face are embedded in theme-based units that cross disciplines and present issues in context.	Students accept challenges as they exist in real world, using language, math, science, and technologies to accomplish important tasks.

Higher-Order Thinking

A large percentage of what is expected is memorization. Students are rarely asked to evaluate, synthesize, or create.	Students are often asked to develop ideas and solutions, often in groups, and demonstrate the abilities to create and reason.	Learners routinely generate hypotheses, conduct investigations, assess results, and make predictions.

Recognizing Problems

Students are not expected to be problem finders, but are instead expected to be able to solve occasional well-structured problems presented to them.	Students occasionally face ill-structured challenges and are expected to refine their problem as well as solve it.	Students frequently face ill-structured challenges and develop proficiency in identifying and defining problems.

"Right Answers"

The "problems" presented to learners tend to have "right answers," "correct" solutions that the students are expected to eventually reach.	The problems presented are new to the learners, and generally involve complex solutions of varying quality, rather than "right answers."

Assessing Cooperative Learning, where learners collaborate with others and socially negotiate the meanings they have constructed. If your environment or activity includes cooperative learning, to what extent does the environment promote meaningful interaction among students and between students and experts outside of school? To what extent are learners developing skills related to social negotiation in learning to accept and share responsibility?

Interaction Among Learners

Little of the learners' time is spent gainfully engaged with other students.	Learners are often immersed in activities in which collaboration with peers results in success.

Interaction with People Outside of School

Little of the learners' time is spent gainfully engaged with experts outside of school.	Learners are often involved in activities in which there is significant collaboration with experts from outside of school.

Social Negotiation

Little evidence that learners work together to develop shared understanding of tasks or of solution strategies.	Learners are often observed in the process of coming to agreement on the nature of problems and on best courses of action.	Learners collaborate with ease. Negotiations become almost invisible, yet the ideas of all team members are valued.

Acceptance and Distribution of Roles and Responsibility

Roles and responsibilities are shifted infrequently; most capable learners accept more responsibility than the less capable.	Roles and responsibilities are shifted often, and such changes are accepted by both the most and least capable.	Students make their own decisions concerning roles and responsibilities, freely giving and accepting assistance as necessary.

Index